T0157989

Bend in the Road

Bend in the Road

*Reinventing Yourself after the
Death of a Loved One*

BARBARA A. ROBINSON

authorHOUSE®

AuthorHouse™
1663 Liberty Drive
Bloomington, IN 47403
www.authorhouse.com
Phone: 1 (800) 839-8640

Published by AuthorHouse 08/07/2015

ISBN: 978-1-5049-1852-7 (sc)
ISBN: 978-1-5049-2684-3 (hc)
ISBN: 978-1-5049-1851-0 (e)

Library of Congress Control Number: 2015909886

Print information available on the last page.

TABLE OF CONTENTS

DEDICATION

Bend in the Road is dedicated to everyone who has lost a spouse or a partner and didn't know how they would go on in life without him or her. Sometimes you may have felt that you didn't want to go on. You sometimes felt that if you could just go to sleep and not wake up, that would be the solution to your aloneness and feelings of emptiness. You may be feeling guilty about an argument you had, and you not only don't remember who started it, you don't remember what it was about. Nevertheless, you didn't get the chance to apologize before he or she died.

You may now see that what your partner complained about, not having enough money to pay the oil bill, the telephone bill was too high. You now understand when he said:

"Turn off the lights when you leave the room because the light bill is skyrocketing. Don't water the lawn everyday because the water bill is too high."

Now that you are left to take care of the bills you can understand why he complained so much, but it's too late, he's gone. Don't play the blame-game; blaming yourself for what you cannot change. Live your life as he or she would have wanted you to live it. Always look good, always smell good and even if you're having a bad day, smile anyway.

This book is especially dedicated to the memory of my late husband, Jerome Robinson, Sr. (Jerry). I wrote the following poem to celebrate his memory:

I'LL NEVER FORGET

I'll remember holding you, loving you and enjoying being your wife.
I'll remember how proud you were when we brought our children into
this life.
I'll remember the parties, the cabarets, our trips and even the arguments.
I'll remember how we said our life together was heaven sent.
I know I'll never forget you no matter how hard I try.
You will always be a part of me and I'll remember you as the years go by.
I know that I'll shed tears in moments when I think of how things used
to be.
But our private moments will always be part of my most precious memories.
I know that God will be with me as I walk through the long years ahead.
But walking without my soul mate is a thought I simply dread.
I'll remember the good times, when we laughed, cried and played.
I'll remember the old times when we loved and we forgave.
You'll always be in my heart although you have gone away.
I'll remember death is only temporary; we'll be together again someday.

PREFACE

*I don't know what tomorrow will bring, or if there will
be a tomorrow for me; therefore, I'll live today as if it
were the last."*

This is the hardest book I have ever written. It's filled with emotional pain. Writing it forced me to reflect on my memories of a love that was both beautiful and emotionally draining and one I will never experience again. It also forced me to reflect on my own mortality. This book is about my life after my husband's death. It's my testimony of how God changed me into a woman, who learned how to travel the road of life alone and teach others along the way. It's about a woman who dances to her own tune. I discuss the rocky road of life my husband and I traveled together, and how if given the chance, I'd do it all over again.

There are things in my past I wish I could change. Since I cannot change them, I will not dwell on them. I choose to live in the NOW of life.

I share with the reader how I dealt with suddenly living alone, without the love of my life by my side. I discuss my depression and how I got through that difficult time of my life, in an effort to inform the readers that whatever, they are going through, they are not alone in their suffering.

I discuss the next phase of my life, where it took me after my husband's death. Finally, this book contains lessons I've learned, in my lifetime. Some lessons are motivational statements I often use to get me through the day. Some are words of encouragement I received from my colleagues and friends. People often say that children believe in magic. That's true but I'm presenting these motivational statements to let the reader know that magic is inside of us all; it's called "confidence." If we have confidence in ourselves and faith that God does answer prayers, we are on the road to healing and peace.

The lessons contained in this book are by no means all I've learned. In fact, I learn something new every day. I have actually learned how much I do not know and how much I have to learn. Nevertheless, lessons included herein are for the reader to benefit from my journey. Some of the lessons are taken directly from the Bible and applied to my personal life. Some are lessons I have learned after stepping in potholes called "mistakes."

Some of the wisdom I've learned may not fit everyone. But some will fit someone. Each one of us has baggage, something we regret doing. We all make mistakes; that's why pencils have erasers on them because of mistakes made by the user. I hope you can learn something from mine and that this book will help you dance on after your loss and find your own steps in the world

INTRODUCTION

I'll never forget my forty-seven years with my husband. In this book, I discuss how he and I first met, the family we built together, his death, and my life afterward. Life wasn't always beautiful between us. We had good times and bad times, but when I stop and reflect on our years together, I realize that the good times outweigh the bad times and I thank God for our years together.

Our marriage was a series of todays that melted into years and then decades. It has now been more than a decade since Jerry passed away. I want to take you along with me to some of those todays we faced together and some that I have faced alone. Some were days filled with ordinary things and others were an extraordinary testament to what God put in our path. From those "todays," I grew personally and spiritually. I want to share this with those who are experiencing the loss of a loved one, so that maybe I can help them get back on their feet and make their own new dance steps.

Today is December 4, 2010; I have been thinking of Virginia, a childhood friend with whom I have not spoken in over thirty years. In 1984 my husband and I went to Detroit on business and while there, we visited Virginia and her husband. Virginia was a few years older than I and two grades above me in high school. She and her family lived eight houses up the street from us on Coolidge Avenue, in the East Wynnton section of Columbus, Georgia. Virginia had a younger sister, Zelda, who was a year older than I was and a grade above me in high school. Growing up, Virginia hung out with an older crowd of teenagers, who were more of her age group. Because we lived on the same street, Zelda and I sometimes visited each other as children. After Jerry and I returned to Baltimore from

Detroit, Virginia and I called each other a few times but eventually lost contact.

Today Virginia crossed my mind.

"Mama, when you think about someone you haven't seen in a long time, there's a reason God allowed that person to cross your mind at that moment. Maybe that person needs to hear from you. That person may need to hear a familiar voice, or may need to hear from someone who is calling just to say, 'Hello, I was thinking about you,'" my daughter Jericka, said to me.

I took her advice and called Virginia, who is now Dr. Jones. She told me Zelda had died four months earlier. I was saddened since Zelda lived not far from me in Washington D.C., we should have communicated more often over the years.

Virginia shared with me that she too had lost her husband three years prior. Perhaps that's why God allowed her to cross my mind. She needed to talk about her loss with someone like me, who knew both her husband and her sister, Zelda, and could understand how she was feeling.

"People often ask me why am I staying in this big ole house alone," she said. "I tell them I'm staying here because this is where my memories are. I had forty-three years with my husband and our memories are in every room of this house. I know his spirit is still here. Yesterday I ran out of computer paper while working on a project that I needed to complete that day. It was raining cats and dogs outside and I dreaded having to get dressed and go to the store in that weather to buy paper. I walked into the room that my husband used as an office and on his desk was an unopened packet of computer paper. I didn't remember placing it there and he has been gone three years. I smiled and whispered, 'Thanks Baby, you're still looking out for me'. So I'll never leave this house. His spirit is in every room and still looking out for me," she said.

Without her being aware of it, her words helped me make a decision about a dilemma I had been pondering over for several months. Her words inspired me to decide to continue living in the house I had shared with my husband for over twenty years, in a community where we had lived for over thirty years. I was inspired to give up my downtown apartment and move back into our house. I had leased the apartment for seven years, while trying to deal with memories. I'll talk more about this later in this book.

It's funny how life can change at the drop of a hat. One day you may be planning a trip with your loved one, and the next day you are wondering how you will get through the day alone. Death doesn't always warn us that it's coming. Sometimes it just slips up on us and changes our plans without any warning, without giving you time to say, "Goodbye." During those times, we can only rely on God's grace and mercy to get us through the difficult times of losing someone we love, especially someone as close as a husband, wife, child, or parent.

The only way I know how to express the goodness of God and convey to the world how He used me to spread the message of going from a grieving, depressed woman to a person of great joy and peace is to tell my story.

When one of my colleagues is grieving I often ask the question, "Are you settling or living, settling for the life you have because of fear of the unknown, or living the life you want, the life that brings you joy and satisfaction?" Then I say to them, "Don't dance through life so fast that you don't enjoy the music of living."

PRECIOUS MEMORIES

It is better to have loved and lost than to never have loved at all. To love and be loved is the ultimate blessing.

I call this chapter, "Precious Memories" because of how dear remembering moments in my life are to me and they become more precious the older I get. Memories of meeting my soul mate who became my lifetime partner, memories of giving birth to my children which are God's blessings, memories of following my dream of earning a college degree regardless of the obstacles and challenges I faced are all precious. The memory of how my husband and I faced life's challenges together, the times when we had little money and at times no money, yet we managed to provide for our family, are special in my garden of precious memories

I have been blessed to travel nationally and internationally and have seen things many people only read about. God had His reasons for allowing me to live to see the year 2015 and for that I am blessed. I have been fortunate to live to see my children, grandchildren, great-grandchildren and to watch them grow. I am blessed that they are healthy. God has been good to me. There have been times I know that I have not pleased Him, yet He blesses me anyhow. If I had a million tongues, I could not thank Him enough for what He has done and continues to do in my life. If I never get another blessing, He has already blessed me enough.

My husband, died in 2004 and the thought of not seeing him again brings back unimaginable pain.

Jerry was elated when we finally had a son; after four girls, which included a set of triplets. When our son, Jerome, Jr. was born, Jerry was working in a baby clothing store. We gave our son a nick name, "Butchie." Sometimes we shorten it to "Butch." When Butch was born, some of Jerry's friends made a sign which read: "Jerry has done it at last, he finally has a son," and hung it on the outside of the building next door to where he worked. They knew how much he wanted a son to carry on his name. He had talked about that often enough.

"I love my daughters," he said, "But when they get married they will take the name of their husbands. I want a son to carry on the Robinson name."

He was adamant about that. When our son was born I named him, "Barato Anton," using a play on my name "Barbara Ann." Two weeks later, I received a copy of his birth certificate in the mail. It was sent from the hospital for us to review the information to ensure it was accurate. When Jerry saw the birth certificate, he immediately asked me to change our son's name to "Jerome Robinson, Junior." I did and his birth certificate now reflects the scratched out name of "Barato Anton," and shows the name to which he now answers, "Jerome Robinson, Junior," without a middle name.

Jerry was my husband, my best friend, my soul mate, my mental and verbal sparring partner. He and I were as different as night and day, we often debated and argued about almost anything. If I said, "Up" he said, "Down." If I said, "Yes," he said, "No." I think sometimes we just waited to see how the other would feel about an issue or how we would react in a situation just so the other could react differently, or have a different opinion. We got a kick out of discovering how much we disagreed with each other. It brought spice into our relationship, 'cause after we argued, we made love. I know you are probably saying that our life was crazy, and you are right, but that was who we were.

Jerry had an outgoing personality and enjoyed being around people who liked to party. I, on the other hand, was a loner and sometimes enjoyed being around artsy people, or just being off to myself with a pen and pad, writing. Later in our married life when we finally could afford another home, I wanted to purchase a house near the ocean so I could hear the waves beating against the shore. That meant we would have to move out of Baltimore and away from Jerry's friends. It would have made me happy to move out of Baltimore and put some distance between his friends and us. I believed his friends were the reason for a lot of our disagreements. Many of them drank alcohol what I considered excessively, especially corn liquor, and when Jerry was with them, he drank too and stayed out all night gambling. Jerry was apprehensive about moving away from his friends. He said he would miss them; therefore, we didn't move out of Baltimore, we moved into the suburbs, and took vacations where we stayed at hotels on the ocean.

I sometimes accompanied him and his friends to parties. I also sometimes went with him to gambling games at the homes of his buddies. I didn't play cards and sitting, watching was boring; I would fall asleep on the sofa or in a chair while waiting for him. I did not enjoy those times; it was a way of me fitting in with the crowd, and connecting with my husband.

After his death, I didn't know what I would do with the rest of my life. I no longer had a companion. I had never lived alone. I went from living at home in Columbus, Georgia, with my mother, stepfather, a younger sister, and a younger brother to living with a roommate when I attended Morgan State College in Baltimore, Maryland, — it is now a university — to living with Jerry.

When I first arrived at Morgan State College in September 1957, a room had not been reserved for me in Harper House, the freshman women's dormitory. Therefore, I had to live off campus in what was called an, "approved home." An approved home is one that has been approved by the collage and the landlord or owner, provides rooms for rent to students at a rental fee less than that of living on campus in a dormitory. Some students chose to live off campus; they had less restrictions and more freedom. Some didn't have a choice; they could not afford to live on campus. The college was required to inspect the off-campus rooms before they were offered for rent to students. But that was not always the case. For example, in a room that would be occupied by more than one student, should have separate sleeping accommodations for each student. Students should not have been required to share a bed.

I met Jerry two weeks after I had been at Morgan while walking up Cold Spring Lane going to the bus stop. He too was walking to the bus stop, carrying several record albums under his arms. He was leaving campus after visiting his girlfriend, a senior at Morgan. I later learned that he was married and separated from his wife. He also had a one-year-old daughter. His first wife had taken the baby and walked out because of his lifestyle, the same rocky road he and I experienced during the early years of our marriage. The message I am trying to convey is that my husband did not start out being my dream man, God molded us both into the people we became.

"Are you going to the bus stop?" he asked.

"Yes," I said, all the time taking in how handsome he was. Those brilliant-white, even teeth brightened up his smile. He was about five-feet, eight-inches tall, slim built, fair-complexioned with freckles, a thin moustache that cradled beautiful sensuous lips. I was hooked when I first saw him.

"Do you live on campus?" he asked.

"No, I live on Gilmore Street. Are you a student at Morgan?"

"No, I was visiting a friend. Do you mind if I walk with you?"

The way he looked me directly in my eyes and smiled when he asked me that question, he knew what my answer would be.

"No, I don't mind," I blushed like a school kid.

I pretended I was interested in the albums he carried, but I was really trying to prolong our conversation, hoping he got the message that I thought he was cute.

"Are those jazz records?" I asked.

"Yes! I loaned them to a friend and I just got them back. Do you like jazz?"

"I love jazz! That's my favorite music."

I lied to impress him. I knew nothing about jazz. I was digging on the Platters, the Coasters, the Penguins, and so on. But if he liked jazz, that had just become my favorite music.

He handed the albums to me. They were albums by Dakota Staten and Gene Ammons' album *Angel Eyes*. As the years went by, that song became my favorite. It still is my favorite instrumental piece.

We stood at the bus stop, shivering. The chill of the September air caressed my face. I turned to face him pretending I was colder than I really was. I wanted to get another look at him.

"Damn, he's cute!" I whispered to myself.

I smiled.

"I hope he didn't hear me," I whispered.

We stood in the chilly air and talked until the bus came and stopped in front of us. I boarded first, put my money into the fare box and walked to the back of the bus. I looked for two empty seats that were together, so he could sit beside me. I spotted two in the back, rushed to them and sat down. After paying his fare, he looked around until he saw me. As he walked toward me, I tried not to show my excitement, but I couldn't stop grinning. I turned my head and looked out the window, trying to play down my obvious interest in him. But he knew. Years later, he still teased me about how I fell for him at first sight. He was right!

When he sat beside me, I turned to him and smiled. He smiled back. His body language let me know that he was interested in me too. At least he showed interest in continuing our conversation. That was a start, I thought.

We talked all the way downtown where we had to change buses. I was not ready for us to separate but we were going in different directions and had to take different busses. We exchanged telephone numbers. I gave him the telephone number at Mrs. Hawkins house, the approved home where I lived. He promised to call me the following day, and he did. When he called, we made a date to go to the movie the following weekend. The following Saturday he came to Mrs. Hawkins' house to get me and we went to the Royal Theater. Afterwards, we stopped to get something to eat at a little diner up the street from the Royal Theater; he then brought me back home. Before the month was over he and I were dating every weekend.

Margie, also a freshman, was my roommate at Mrs. Hawkins' house. Because Margie's home was New York and I was from Georgia and Alabama, Mrs. Hawkins thought I was a country hick. She often referred to me as a country girl who was away from home for the first time. She asked me about picking cotton and if I ever milked a cow.

Mrs. Hawkins appeared to be in her seventies and operated a beauty salon in the basement of her home. She was active in the NAACP and was a staunch Christian woman, who went to church every Sunday and made Margie and me go with her. Mrs. Hawkins reminded me of what Margie would probably look like when she was her age. Both Margie and Mrs. Hawkins were the same height, short and plump. They were the same complexion and they both walked knock-kneed. I called Margie a "suck-up," because she was always sucking up to Mrs. Hawkins. She would sit in the kitchen while Mrs. Hawkins was cooking and tell Mrs. Hawkins her personal business. Sometimes Margie sat in Mrs. Hawkins' hair salon and watched her at work with the customers and joined in the conversations with Mrs. Hawkins and the customers.

I never discussed my personal business with Mrs. Hawkins. I was ashamed to talk about my childhood. She took my reluctance to share my personal family business with her as being "stand-offish," as she often called me.

Mrs. Hawkins liked Margie but she didn't care much for me. Margie's close-knit family was involved in her education. I, on the other hand, was from a family where my mother was an alcoholic and had been arrested numerous times for public drunkenness.

My step father was in jail for embezzlement and for assaulting an army officer. My sister, Sandy, had dropped out of school in the eleventh grade because she was pregnant. She and I had the same mother but different fathers. She and our brother Al had the same father. When my step father went to jail, we lost our house, car, and furniture. Mother, Sandy, Al and I were homeless. I was eighteen years old, Sandy was sixteen years old and Al was one years old. The only things we had were our clothes. That was my second time being homeless. I was homeless at sixteen years old when my step father, put me out for defending my mother when he was beating her.

Mother's sister, Mae Lizzie and her husband Bob lived in a one bedroom house at 603 Third Avenue in downtown Columbus, Georgia. Mae Lizzie said she and Bob had room for Sandy, Al, and Mother to stay with them. They would have to sleep on a pallet — a sheet, a blanket and a pillow — on the linoleum-covered living room floor, until Mother found a place for us to stay. But Mae Lizzie said she didn't have room for me. She said I was old enough to take care of myself. I was sixteen years old.

Margie's family came to visit her, sent her money, and she went home to New York every other weekend. I never received money from my family. The only money I had was from the Picket and Hatchet College Fund that had awarded me a scholarship grant in Columbus Georgia, and money I earned working in the library on Morgan's campus.

Mrs. Hawkins' home was a boarding house where several people lived. Margie and I shared a room and a bed on the third floor. Mrs. Hawkins used one of her rooms on the second floor as a "prayer room."

She took me into the prayer room several times and prayed over me because I was dating Jerry. Margie told her that Jerry wasn't a college student. But I didn't tell Ms. Hawkins that Margie was dating a married man who drove a city bus. I didn't tell her that Margie rode the city bus every day just to be with the driver. When Margie told Ms. Hawkins about Jerry, Mrs. Hawkins felt he wasn't worthy of dating me. She felt he had too much street-experience. I didn't care. His lifestyle was exciting to me; besides, I was falling in love with him. His circle of friends and associates were all older than I. They were seniors at Morgan, soldiers from Fort Meade Army post, people with whom he gambled, and people with whom he hung out at the nightclubs. Coming from Georgia and Alabama, the bright lights of places like Baltimore's Pennsylvania Avenue were mesmerizing to me.

Mrs. Hawkins called Margie's parents and told them I was a bad influence on Margie. Her parents then threatened to stop sending her money if she continued to associate with me. She and I were friends until I moved out of Mrs. Hawkins' house. Mrs. Hawkins thought Margie was staying on campus to study in the library. She didn't know Margie was actually spending time with the bus driver in a rooming house.

Mrs. Hawkins gave Margie a key to the front door of her house but she wouldn't give me one. One day in November, 1957, when it was bitter cold, I got sick in class at Morgan and was sent to the infirmary where I stayed for two days with a chest cold. Since I didn't have family in Maryland, the college wouldn't send me to an off-campus living arrangement while I was sick. When I was well enough to be released from the infirmary, I went to

Mrs. Hawkins' house. When I arrived, no one was at home. It was cold and raining, I had taken two buses to reach her house and I had to wait outside on her steps — she didn't have a porch — until she arrived home — about an hour. When Mrs. Hawkins finally arrived, her only comment to me was, "You look like a wet rat."

I said nothing. I was shivering from being wet and cold. I walked into the house and went straight to my room, took off my wet clothes and got in bed. The next day I was still feeling ill. I called Jerry and he took me to a doctor. After we left the doctor's office, I went to Jerry's apartment and spent the night. I was beginning not to care what Mrs. Hawkins thought or said about me. I confided in Margie that I thought I was pregnant and she told Mrs. Hawkins. When I wasn't at home one evening, Mrs. Hawkins searched my room, found a doctor's prescription for medicine, called the doctor, and asked him what was the nature of my visit to him. The doctor refused to give her any information.

The doctor said to Mrs. Hawkins, "She came in with a young man, I assumed was her husband. She was wearing a wedding band."

"She was wearing a wedding band or a high school ring turned backwards?" asked Mrs. Hawkins. "I just want to know whether or not she is pregnant."

Still the doctor would not give her any information. When I returned for a second visit, the doctor told me what Mrs. Hawkins had said.

I was glad the doctor did not discuss my personal business with Mrs. Hawkins. She was right; I was wearing my high school ring turned backwards on my middle finger. Jerry and I had gone to the doctor to see if I was pregnant. I had started having morning sickness and I missed my period. I was afraid of being expelled from Morgan for being pregnant and not married if Mrs. Spellman, the dean of women, learned of my pregnancy.

"What you do with your life is your business," said the doctor. "But if you were to ask my advice, I would tell you to find another place to live. That woman is vicious. I can tell just by the things she said on the telephone and I've never met her. If I were you, I'd get the hell out of there, fast!"

After that I went to Mrs. Spellman and asked if she could find me another place to live.

I moved from Mrs. Hawkins house to Mrs. Hughes, who ran a boarding house on Druid Hill Avenue.

I lived in two "approved homes," and each time I shared a bed with a roommate. Mrs. Hawkins' house was 912 North Gilmore Street. The second house where I stayed was 1413 Druid Hill Avenue with Mrs. Hughes. At Mrs. Hawkins' house Margie and I shared a double bed. However, at Mrs. Hughes, Frances and I shared a single bed. At Mrs. Hughes house the room wasn't large enough for a double bed. The single bed was the size of a cot, just barely large enough for one person. There was no clothes closet in the room; we hung our clothes behind the door on nails in the wall.

Two men who lived in New Jersey and were in Baltimore working on a construction project, stayed in the other rooms. They would be leaving Baltimore to return to New Jersey when the project was completed. Yet, their room joined that of two teenaged female college students. The doors to the rooms didn't have locks, and, if I needed to use the bathroom in the middle of the night, or wanted to take a bath when I came home from classes, I had to go through the men's bedroom. There was no other access.

Before the completion of my first year of college, Mrs. Spellman called me into her office and instructed me to withdraw from Morgan. Margie said Mrs. Hawkins called Mrs. Spellman the same time she called her parents.

"Morgan girls are cultured girls and I can't have you embarrassing the image of Morgan by staying out all night. I heard about you. Either you move on campus or you will have to drop out of college."

"But I can't afford the tuition to live in a dorm. That's why I'm living off campus now," I lamented.

"I understand that and I made some calls. We are offering you the opportunity to complete this semester without having to pay tuition. If you return next semester, we will work with you to find additional financial aid but right now, you need to move on campus. If you continue to live off campus you are heading for a destructive lifestyle. You need guidance," said Mrs. Spellman."

I didn't know how right she was. But as most young people, we think we know everything and are indestructible.

I had told her about my life in Georgia when I lived with my mother and abusive step father and that he was in jail for embezzlement. My mother was then drinking every week, almost every day. Mrs. Spellman, like the teachers at my high school who cosigned for me to get to Morgan, saw the potential in me and was trying to help me succeed in life. I rebelled against their help.

Of course, Mrs. Spellman was right. But I didn't want to give up my newfound friends and the fun I was having every weekend. This was the first time in my life I could call my own shots on how and where I lived and I didn't want to give it up for the regiment of college dormitory rules. I was running around with an older crowd, drinking, going to all-night parties, taking dares to see who could drink the most alcohol, getting drunk and passing out, lying about my age to get in bars and nightclubs, and starting to cut classes. I look back on all of that now and ask myself the question, "Boy! Did I really call that fun?"

Mrs. Spellman wasn't about to allow me to bring disgrace on Morgan. When she gave me the ultimatum to either move back on campus or drop out of school, I chose to drop out of school. I figured that as soon Mrs. Spellman found out I was pregnant and not married I would be forced to drop out of school in a few months anyway. I was pregnant with our first daughter, Jericka. During those years — 1950s and early 1960s — if you were pregnant and not married, you had to resign from college. I was heartbroken when I had to make a choice about leaving college, especially when I learned I was pregnant. I wanted so badly to finish my college education. That had always been my dream, one day earning a bachelor's degree. However, I made a decision that regardless of how many years it took, if my life lasted, I would earn a college degree.

Moving back on campus meant that I would not be able to spend as much time with Jerry as I wanted. I didn't tell Mrs. Spellman that I was already pregnant. She, like Ms. Hawkins and Mrs. Hughes, didn't like Jerry. He wasn't a college student and they all thought I was throwing my life away by being with him. They called him a "loser."

The more people talked against Jerry, the more I was determined to be with him. I thought they were being unfair by labeling him a loser. He had a job, a nice apartment, wore nice clothes, was handsome, treated me nice, and when we went out, he covered all the expenses. I liked the way he paid attention to me. It didn't matter if the room was filled with other women; he never took his attention away from me. He acted as if I was the only woman in the room. Coming from a dysfunctional and violent family such as I did, I had low self-esteem and felt that no one wanted me. Jerry was a handsome man and because he paid attention to me, I felt like a beautiful woman.

Jerry and his first wife, Jean, were married for one year before he and I met. Jean thought they eventually would reconcile and move back together. After Jean left, Jerry moved into a third floor apartment at 2347 Eutaw Place. Other college students lived on the second floor in the same apartment building. That is where he met the senior he was dating. A preacher, his wife and their grown son lived on the first floor. Jerry and I lived together for a year before we got married.

One night after we had made love he said, "I'm going to marry you I don't care what anybody says."

The following week, September 24, 1958 with only two dimes in his pocket, Jerry and I rode the bus to Arlington, Virginia and were married by a Justice of the Peace. His divorce from Jean wasn't final; she had refused to sign the divorce papers. She still had hopes that they would get back together. That might have been the case until he and I met and fell in love. Five years later when their divorce was final, Jerry and I married again at the court house in Baltimore City.

Although we were married and had become parents, Jerry wasn't ready to settle down with a family, and quite frankly, neither was I. We were both wild. But in spite of what we might have done in our younger years, ours was a union that lasted forty-seven years until his death in August 2004.

Jerry and I were the parents of five children: four lived to become adults. Jericka was our first born. Born February 5, 1959, she is the oldest by eight months. On November 1, 1959, our triplets, Jeanene, Jeanese, and Jeanette, were born. Jeanette died seventeen days later. On April 8, 1963, our only son, Jerome, Jr. was born.

Jerry and I were blessed with five grandchildren whom he loved dearly. It saddens me sometimes when I remember that he never had the chance to meet our great-grandchildren. Jeanene married Tyrone and gave birth to Tyneisha and Lybrant. After two years of marriage, she and Tyrone divorced. A year later her third child, Joshua was born from another relationship. Butch is the father of a son, Jerome, III, — whom we call "Jay," and a daughter, Bianca. Jericka and Jeanese never had any children. Two years after Jerry's death Tyneisha gave us our first great-grandchild, Carlos. Five years later her second child, a daughter Aubrey was born and in 2013 Bianca gave birth to Brooklyn, our third great-grandchild.

When Jerry and I first married, we moved from 2347 Eutaw Place to a one bedroom furnished third-floor apartment at 217 East Lafayette Avenue. The living room was so small, only a daybed and a television could fit inside. That's where Jerry and I were living when Jericka was born. For months she slept in a car bed because we couldn't afford a crib for her. Jerry's cousin, Margaret, eventually gave us a crib that her son, Tyrone, who is now a pastor of his own church, and his sister Vanessa, had used.

After our triplets were born, we moved into a two-bedroom apartment at 26 South Exeter Street in Flag House Courts Projects. The projects brought more problems to our marriage. I discussed those problems in my first book, *And Still, I Cry*. In that book I talked about how every time the garbage chute got clogged up our apartment filled with smoke. I talked about the concrete floors and concrete walls, the mice and roaches, the families piled on top of each other in small apartments that resembled prisons cells. I talked about "Concrete City," and the 1968 riot.

My husband, our four children, and I lived in the projects for twelve years before we could afford to buy our own place. Together Jerry and I worked four jobs to earn enough money for a down payment on a house. I worked as a clerk in the District Court and a mail sorter at the post office. Jerry drove a cab on the weekends and worked at Acme Markets warehouse at night. When Acme went out of business he got a job at W.R. Grace Chemical Company. I wanted to move our children out of the projects and into the suburbs to give them a better chance at life than they would get living in an inner city project complex riddled with drugs and crime.

Jerry was apprehensive about purchasing a house and moving out of the projects. In the projects rent was adjusted according to your income. If we bought a home we would have a set mortgage to pay each month. Since he was hesitant about purchasing a house, I took the lead and contacted a real estate company headed by a woman who agreed to show me houses without my husband being with me. The majority of the realty companies I contacted were reluctant to show homes to women unless accompanied by their husbands. I guess they thought it would be a waste of their time. However, when I explained my situation to a female realtor, she understood. She came to the projects where we lived, picked me up in her car and drove me to see several properties until I found the house at 6705 Laurel Drive in Baltimore County.

After I found the house at 6705 Laurel Drive, I told Jerry what I had done. He made all kinds of excuses as to why we couldn't afford it, but I didn't accept any of them. We moved into the house in 1969 and stayed there until January 3, 1993, when we moved to our home at 4025 Essex Road where we lived when he died, which is only around the corner and two streets over from Laurel Drive.

I didn't let having children stop me from going to college. I always wanted a college degree and I was determined to get it. Dropping out of Morgan was the beginning of my road to a life of hard knocks and street life. Each semester I took three credits at Morgan State College. I didn't have enough money to go full time nor could I afford to take two semesters in a row. I worked, earned some money, went back for another semester, took more credits, worked again, accumulated more tuition money, then I would register for three more credits. That process continued for eighteen years, until I finally earned my bachelor's degree in 1975 from the University of Baltimore. Jerry, my friends, and members of my family doubted that I would ever graduate from college, but I knew I would, someday.

Flag Courts, as they were called by locals, were two blocks from choice neighborhoods, nice restaurants and rollicking night life in a section of East Baltimore called Little Italy. It was also three blocks from the night life of prostitutes, drugs, and strip joints on Baltimore Street that catered predominately to the white population. Pennsylvania Avenue in Baltimore was to black people what Baltimore Street was to white people. There was nothing desirable or inviting about Flag House Courts Projects, an enclave of warehouse-like apartment buildings were across the street from the project building in which we lived for twelve long, hard grueling years.

Innocence often had a short life span in the projects. Too many impressionable boys admired the fellows who stood on the corners with a wad of cash in the pockets of their jeans and sweat-pants. The honest working types stayed to themselves and tried to keep their children from that type of life. However, sometimes the most promising minds are no match for the peer pressure of a neighborhood ruled by its streets.

During my early years I was in the streets dancing to the tunes of the hood and listening to the music of the streets. God had other plans for me and for my husband. During the early years of my marriage I wasn't ready for God. I was too busy having what I thought was a "good time." But I was only fooling myself, I wasn't happy. I learned I wasn't living, I existed and although I wasn't ready for God, He was ready for me. He never took His hands off me.

GLORY DANCE

I don't know how long I have in this world, but as long as I am here, I might as well dance to the tune of my choosing.

Life's music is different for each person. Some people are artists, some sing, some write, some enjoy serving others, some enjoy ministering to others, some cook, some sew, some teach, some preach, some define themselves by what they wear. Each scenario is a form of dancing to the music of life. I call it their "glory dance."

Spring is symbolic of the beginning of life; flowers are just beginning to bloom; the grass is green again. In springtime, nature puts on a fresh look after winter has passed. Squirrels run back and forth from tree to tree, happy the cold weather has passed. Nature smiles as newly planted seeds come to life and push their way through the soil to meet the sunshine and rain. Plants that were normally kept outside in pots and vases were brought into the house during winter so they would not freeze and die from the cold weather. When the freshness of spring comes they are brought back outside.

So it is with new relationships and the reinventing of self into becoming a different person. When your loved one dies and you are left alone to face life without your companion, without your soul mate, without a shoulder to lean on, you have to redefine your purpose in life. Like new flowers blooming in the spring, it is time for you to bloom and become whoever God has ordained you to become in the next phase of your life.

When we are married or in a committed relationship, and one partner dies, it is devastating. Sometimes we don't know what steps to take to continue alone on our journey through life. We examine our lives, trying to determine what path to take. We ask ourselves questions, "Should I retire from life and go away to a secluded place and let life pass slowly by? Should I recoil into my own state of depression? Should I run from my shadow, start using alcohol or drugs to make the loneliness go away? Should I assume the life I have always lived during my married life, or should I reinvent myself and try a new career? Should I take a chance at a new life I have never before experienced or thought about, which may require that I be trained or re-trained, or should I continue dancing to my old tune?"

So often fear of growing old alone prevents us from making sound decisions about the rest of our existence. We get into relationships just to be able to say we have a man or a woman for a companion. We don't think things through and enjoy the new world that is before us and the chance to try something new. I am not saying to rejoice that your partner has died. I am saying since we cannot change the situation and crying will not bring back your loved one, it is now time to focus on yourself. You have to make good of a bad situation.

Couples who are happily married cringe at the thought of living the rest of their lives without their loved one by their side. They fear the unknown. They don't want to think of going to sleep alone, waking up in bed alone, and at the end of the day having no one with whom they can share their thoughts.

When we are in the midst of our married life, we don't put much thought into what it will be like to live alone, or maybe we do. We think about not having to come home at a certain time, not having to worry about preparing meals every day. But when the realization hits us, we are jolted into reality. We realize it's not a dream. We really are alone and lonely.

But we can't stop living. We can't drop out of life's stages of reality. Sometimes we have to rethink our lives and consider where we fit in. After your spouse is gone, consider what your role is now. God has a reason for leaving you here. Think about what would have happened if things had been different. Suppose God had taken you home to be with Him and left your spouse to live alone. Would your spouse have been able to carry on the responsibilities with which you are now faced? Would your family be in a better position? How different would life have been for everyone?

Life is a stage comprised of many scenes with many dances. Life plays many tunes. You choose the tune to which you want to dance. It's your choice to either live or merely survive. I choose to live. To God be the glory and I do the glory dance.

Maybe you never thought about what you would do or who you would become if you had the chance to start over. I never thought about it. But when the opportunity presented itself, I took a chance. Try something different, something new, challenge yourself. You don't know how much of a difference you can make in the world until you try.

Because my husband and I had been together for over forth-seven years, and because he died suddenly without warning, without a chance to say goodbye, people ask me how I cope with being a widow. I have talked with other women who recently became widows and I am amazed at how they have just given up and really don't want to do anything with their lives except feel sorry for themselves, reflect on how lonely they are and how much they miss their mate. They constantly dream about how their world used to be and they spend the major portion of their day crying.

I thought about those women and the questions people ask me about being alone. I pondered over what really made me not want to give up on life and made me want to keep dancing through life. There are many tips I used to help me become who I am. I call such tips "wisdom," something I acquired through the experience of living. Life throws us into many paths. There are different steps we must take to keep traveling on a positive road to success. At the end of this book are one-hundred and one lessons in life I learned from my own personal experiences, some I received from friends, colleagues and associates who have experienced the pain of losing a loved one. I can tell you what it feels like to lose a friend, a mother, father, grandparents, and even a newborn baby, but the grief of losing my husband doesn't compare to other losses. I offer my wisdom path to help others.

I once read an article in a community paper about several men who had lost their wives and formed a group that met once a month in the cemetery at the grave site of their wives. They sat in rocking chairs and reminisced about the life they had shared with their spouses. They shared memories with each other in an effort to bring each other comfort, to lessen their grief. I read the article and I understood how the men felt. I too thought about joining or forming such a group. Then I asked myself what purpose would it serve? How would such activities help me with my grieving? How could I find happiness and peace if I were to continue living in the past, allowing my past to define my present and my future? Such a group may work for others but not for me. I needed more involvement with life.

Before Jerry passed we operated several group homes as community-based residential facilities for people with developmental disabilities. These were people who once resided in mental institutions, nursing homes and some resided in their own homes with family members taking care of them; however, they now needed more professional medical care and SelfPride provided that care. SelfPride, Incorporated, was a nonprofit organization I started in 1990. Jerry was the site manager and provided the oversight of all our properties. Our son was the chief financial officer and managed all the accounting. I was the executive director and handled the overall operational responsibilities from human resources development, grant writing, training and all administrative duties.

Mr. Brooks owned and operated a residential and commercial cleaning company for over forty years. He and his wife, Mary, attended events hosted by SelfPride to raise funds for people with developmental disabilities. That's how Jerry and I met them. They also attended SelfPride's company Christmas parties. For almost twenty years Mr. Brooks and his company cleaned the homes owned by SelfPride, cleaned our office building every night, and also cleaned my personal residence. He attended Jerry's funeral and he died a few years after Jerry. By then, I had already been elected to a seat in the Maryland House of Delegates. When he died, I was the speaker at his funeral and I presented his wife with a citation from the Maryland General Assembly. "Keep Dancing," was the message I gave to Mary.

"Regardless of what you do, whenever you get a chance to dance, take it. It doesn't matter what your dance step or tune is, just dance!"

A year later, Ronald, their son, called and asked me to get in touch with his mother.

"She won't go out of the house. Sometimes she won't even eat all day. She just sits at the kitchen table and stares out the window. She's still grieving about Daddy. She cries all the time. You have done so well handling your husband's death. Can you help my mom?"

I called Mary and we talked for over an hour about her late husband, with her crying most of the time.

"I don't know what to do without him," she said. "I miss him so much. Sometimes I don't want to get out of bed. I just want to lay there and never wake up. I admire you for being strong enough to go on with your life. I wish I had that strength. It's been over a year since he has been gone and his clothes, tooth brush, toiletries, everything that belonged to him are still as he left them. I can't bear to change anything."

"Mary, I understand how you feel. I've been there. I wish I could tell you that things will change but I can't. Things don't get better, they just get different. We each must go through our pain in our own way. People think I'm strong and that I'm handling my life without pain and without tears. But the truth is, I still cry. I'll hear a song that reminds me of my husband. I'll see a person who resembles him or I'll see a couple enjoying being with each other and I'll start to feel lonely and overwhelmed with grief. Sometimes I wake up at night, roll over in bed, and the side where my husband used to sleep is cold, where it was once warm with heat from his body, and I cry. Sometimes I'll prepare a meal and as I sit eating alone, I cry. But after the crying is over, I start to think about what my schedule is for the following day. I try to keep busy and the busier I am the less time I have to grieve. I try new things, join new organizations. I am on the board of directors of twenty organizations, I'm writing another book. I can't stop, if I do, I'll stop living.

When do you think of him the most? When the house is quiet and your bed is empty? In the wee hours of the night and early in the morning? When you stretch your hand while yawning and unwinding from the previous night's restless sleep? No one is lying beside you in bed, and you remember, he's not coming home anymore. You're finally alone. You feel the cold crispness of the bed sheet and you realize that's what you're going to be faced with each night and each morning for the rest of your life. The cold reality begins to sink in. If you fill those lonely hours doing something to make your life complete, you won't have so much time to think about your emotional pain. If you don't have time to think so much, you may not hurt so much. You do what's necessary to keep going and pray for deliverance.

"As you know, in 2006 I ran for a seat in the Maryland General Assembly and I won. I knew nothing about politics or running a political campaign. I was the oldest person in a group of nine candidates running for one of three seats in the Maryland House of Delegates. Failure was not an option for me. I spent so much time campaigning, I didn't have time to grieve. I won because I out worked the other candidates. They all had jobs and by the time they got off work and started door-knocking, I was out for my second round. I started my days at seven in the morning. That's what I mean about trying something new; challenge your mind, Mary. Don't be afraid to try something you have never done before. You will be so consumed with succeeding, you won't have time to feel the aloneness.

Among other things, I am also considering teaching a course at one of the colleges. I worked with a college to organize two political organizations and I co-founded the Greater Baltimore Black Chamber of Commerce. I do things with my church. All those things keep me too busy to spend time having pity parties."

"Whew! Just listening to you makes me tired," she said.

We both laughed.

"At least I got a chuckle out of you."

We laughed again.

Mary asked me what prompted me to get into politics.

"Had you ever considered it when your husband was alive?"

"No! That's the strange part. A political career was never in my thoughts. But after Jerry died and I took a look at where my life had taken me I drew on my experience. Being a business owner in the health care industry for more than twenty years I had acquired knowledge of the needs of health care providers in Maryland. I knew of their needs for representation in Annapolis. As you know, my husband worked by my side while we expanded our business.

"As a member of the House of Delegates, I plan to concentrate on the needs of people who operate group homes, and provide in-home health care services. I have listened to seniors discuss their needs for laws to be changed and new legislation be introduced to help them age in their own homes and help improve the quality of their lives. Crafting legislation to focus on those issues leaves me little time to wallow in grief and self-pity. That's why I am going to call on you so you won't have time to have pity-parties either."

"Well, we'll see."

"I'm in the middle of my campaign for re-election. After the election is over, I'll call you and we'll get together for lunch and just talk."

"I guess I'll feel up to it. I don't get out much."

"I'm not taking 'no' for an answer. If you don't go, I'll sit on your doorsteps and sing as loud as I can, so your neighbors can hear me. You don't want to hear me sing. I can't carry a tune in a bucket. Your neighbors will call the police on you and me if they heard me sing."

We laughed.

"Okay! You sold me. We'll get together after the election. I know you're going to win."

"I'm giving it my best. I'll call you in a few weeks."

We ended the conversation and hung up the telephone.

Mary's feelings of apathy and depression were typical of the way we feel after the death of our spouse. I knew that whatever I decided to do with the rest of my life would require that I seek additional training or education, perhaps both. I planned to convey that message to Mary when we met for lunch. I planned to get her to help me start a nonprofit organization to help other women deal with the death of their spouse. I wanted to encourage them to reinvent themselves after their loss.

I understood Mary's feelings of loss and being alone, I too still feel the loss of my husband. Even being out of the country the pain is always there. In 2005 I traveled to Buenos Aires, Argentina with a group of travel writers. My flight included a two-hour layover and a change of planes in Florida. As I sat in Florida's airport waiting for my flight, my mind wandered back to a time when my husband traveled with me. It seemed that every man who walked past reminded me of him in some way. It was either the way they walked, the mannerism of the use of their hands when engaged in a conversation, or the clothes they were wearing. Anything and everything made me think about Jerry and miss him being with me. He was a great traveling companion. He and I both enjoyed what we called "people watching." My children called it being "nosey."

It didn't matter that our flight was sometimes an hour late, or that we arrived at the airport early, he and I enjoyed making up stories about the people we saw in the airport. We especially enjoyed the stories we invented about how people dressed what we considered strange.

I miss going on trips with him, discovering life together, seeing things for the first time again, through his eyes. He was like a kid discovering life. When we traveled, if an ocean was anywhere near our hotel, we always stayed in an ocean front room. I enjoyed sitting on the balcony listening to the waves. I remember times in the evening as I sat on the balcony looking out onto the ocean when all I could see was water and blackness. When we went on a cruise and sat on the balcony of our cabin, sometimes looking far off into the distance, I could see blinking lights from another cruise ship. I imagined the different people on the distant ship. I imagined someone on that ship, sitting on their balcony looking at the ship we were on. I could then fully understand the meaning of the statement, "Like two ships passing in the night.

I sat in the airport and remembered the fun times we spent together and I began to cry silently, so people sitting nearby couldn't hear me. The last time I went with the travel writers group, we had gone to Mexico and Jerry went with me. This time I was alone, and it hurt.

The overhead television in the airport waiting area where I sat was reporting that Johnnie Cochran, the attorney who defended O.J. Simpson in his murder trial, had just died. I couldn't concentrate much on the news. I was having my own pity party.

I stayed in Argentina two weeks. A month after I returned home, I went on a two week cruise to Spain, Italy, and France. I returned home, and two weeks later, I flew to Maui Hawaii to attend the Maui Writer's Conference and stayed for two weeks. As long as I was out of the country, everything was fine. I could cope with the aloneness, the emptiness of being without my husband and the coldness of sleeping alone. I just put it out of my mind and concentrated on enjoying myself in a place I'd never been and imagined that he would be waiting for me when I returned home.

HIS LAST GOODBYE

In order to see the rainbow, you must first endure some rain

April 9, 2004, Good Friday, the Friday before Easter Sunday, Jerry and I drove seven hours to visit his family and friends in his hometown of Greensboro, North Carolina. I didn't want to go to Greensboro for Easter that year. I wanted to stay in Baltimore and spend Easter with our children and grandchildren. I wanted to see our grandchildren dressed in their Easter outfits and all of us to go out to dinner Easter Sunday, as a family. Although I regret that we didn't get to spend Jerry's last Easter with our children and grandchildren, I'm glad we visited his family in Greensboro. It was the last time they saw him alive.

A&T College is located in Greensboro, North Carolina. College students, members of social clubs, friends searching for social activities, families of the football team and cheerleaders, all followed A&T's football team whenever they played out of town. Social clubs and some restaurants leased buses and sold tickets to trips in cities where the team was playing. Social club members and their patrons made the trips a three-day event, renting hotel rooms, planning parties at local hotels, and offering trips to shopping malls.

When A&T College played football games in Baltimore or Washington, DC, a social club from Greensboro, of which Charles, Jerry's brother, was president, Madeline and Ladison, Jerry's sister and younger brother, were members, leased four or five busses and sold tickets to the games that also included hotel reservations. They all stayed in hotel rooms, went to the games, returned to the hotel to party all night.

Each time A&T played Morgan in Baltimore, Jerry and I hosted a party at our house for club members and their guests. I did all the cooking and Jerry made sure the bar in our downstairs club basement was always stocked with top shelf liquor. If the game was played in Washington, DC, Jerry and I drove there, taking with us trays of food for the club members.

This time in April 2004 when Jerry insisted on going to Greensboro for Easter, although I was apprehensive about leaving our family, I didn't protest, I just went with him. My gut feelings told me to go.

We arrived in Greensboro about two o'clock, Good Friday afternoon and checked into the Four Seasons Hotel. After we unpacked our suitcases, we went to visit Roy Henry and his wife Nancy. Roy and Nancy were high school sweethearts. Roy and Jerry were best friends since high school. Roy and Nancy were the reason I enjoyed going to Greensboro. Roy had a sense of humor that made the trip worthwhile. He and Nancy had identical twin daughters, who were so much alike, I didn't know how their husbands could tell them apart.

Roy always had gallons of corn liquor waiting for Jerry to purchase and bring back to Baltimore. If the liquor wasn't at Roy's home, he and Jerry went to buy some from a local bootlegger, who brewed it in his backyard. Each time Jerry and I went to Greensboro, we always returned to Baltimore with corn liquor in the trunk of our car. Jerry had orders from his friends in Baltimore to bring back certain amounts — quarts, gallons, and half-gallons — of corn liquor. I'm glad we were never stopped by the state police or Highway Patrol, we would have been arrested for bootlegging or transporting illegal substances across state lines. During the trip to Greensboro, Jerry insisted that I help him drive; during the return trip to Baltimore, he wouldn't dare let me drive. He was afraid my driving might attract the attention of the police, who often hid in the shadows of the highway, waiting for speeding drivers. I was glad, because I hated to drive.

Jerry's friends in Baltimore called him, "Trunk Man!" Each time we attended an event, he and his buddies went outside and filled their cups with corn liquor from the trunk of his car.

Nancy pickled and canned fruits and vegetables. When we visited her, she had jars of pickled okra, pickled tomatoes, canned berries and much other delicious food boxed and ready for us to bring back to Baltimore. She also always had a hot home-cooked meal prepared and waiting for us when we reached Greensboro. Jerry, Roy, Nancy and I often sat for hours downstairs in their clubroom drinking and listening to Roy tell jokes. Sometimes during our visits Roy and Nancy hosted backyard cookouts and invited their friends, some of them were also Jerry's friends. They were people with whom he had gone to school, or people he knew while growing up in Greensboro. Some were friends whom I had met through Roy and Nancy.

It was strange that Jerry insisted on going to Greensboro for Easter that year. We had always spent Christmas, Thanksgiving and Easter with our Children and grandchildren. It was as if he knew this would be his last trip to his hometown — and it was his last. Easter Sunday April, 11, 2004, Jerry and I went to church with Madeline. After service, we went back to the hotel, changed clothes and went to Madeline's house for dinner. Jerry and I had stopped at his brother and sister-in-law, Charles' and his wife Liz's house but they were not at home. Jerry's younger brother Ladison, came to Madeline's house to visit with Jerry and me; however, Ladison's wife Gladys, who was from my hometown Columbus, Georgia, did not come.

Monday, April 12, Jerry and I prepared to leave Greensboro and return to Baltimore. We packed our suitcases, checked out of the hotel, loaded the suitcases into the car and went to Madeline's house to say our goodbyes. While we were there, Liz and Charles stopped by and Jerry got a chance to spend an hour with Charles.

What is usually a six-hour drive to Baltimore from Greensboro, turned into almost a nine-hour drive. It rained all the way back. We stopped several times at restaurants along the highway and purchased food. Jerry wasn't feeling well and the cold, hard rain wasn't making him feel any better. He didn't feel like getting out of the car to go into the restaurants to eat but he did so anyway. He looked so tired. I was worried about him but he assured me that he was alright.

When we returned to Baltimore, he had the worst cold. He stayed in bed for a week, never leaving the house. That was unusual for him. The following Monday he still seemed tired but he got out of bed and prepared to go to work just the same. "Work" meant going to the building we owned on Montgomery Street, in downtown Baltimore, three blocks from the Inner Harbor. We provided transportation for several senior citizen centers, for medical day programs, transporting people with developmental disabilities. Jerry liked to arrive to work before the van drivers got there, to ensure that they left on time for their run and that no one missed their run, otherwise he would have to be the driver. Jerry was the transportation supervisor. Our busses and vans were kept in the garage of our building. Some of the drivers' runs started at seven in the morning, Jerry would arrive by six-thirty, a half-hour before the drivers.

I was concerned about him this day. He was moving slowly, he looked tired and he had a terrible cough.

"Jerry, you don't look good. You sound tired. Why don't you stay at home today and rest?" I asked.

"I can't stay home. Jerome needs me," he said while sitting on the side of the bed putting on his shoes and socks.

It was unusual for Jerry to refer to our son as, "Jerome." All his life he called him either 'Butch" or "Butchie." So when he said "Jerome" I knew something was wrong.

"He may need you but what would he do if you weren't here? You need to get some rest."

"I don't know what he'd do if I wasn't here. But I am here and I'm not going to let him down."

When he coughed, there was a rattle sound in his chest, as if he had a bad cold. He put on his cap and walked out the door.

Jerry loved to drive the busses transporting senior citizens from centers and nursing homes to day programs and to other social events. He was well liked by all his riders. He got as much joy from transporting them as they did from being transported. When he was sick, they sent him get well cards. For holidays and his birthday, they baked cakes, pies, cookies and other desserts and sent them home to the both of us. They sent him friendly cards telling him how much they enjoyed his smile and friendly attitude. They came to his funeral in droves. But I am getting ahead of my story. We had Jerry with us a little while longer.

In May 2004, Jerry and I planned to drive to Chicago. I was going to attend a book conference and Jerry was going with me. We had planned to make a vacation of the trip. I loved to travel with Jerry, he was so much fun. Like me, he was adventurous and liked to experience and try new

26

things. When we traveled on either my speaking engagements or book-signing tours to cities and states where we had never been, we rented a car and went sightseeing in neighborhoods where tourists rarely visited. We wanted to see the "flavor" of the city. If I attended a meeting or conference during the day, he either played golf or went sightseeing without me. If he saw something he thought would interest me, we went back that evening when I had free time.

We often found neighborhood festivals and off-street shopping areas that we would not have known about if we had a tour guide. When we found new places to shop, such as antique shops and boutiques, Jerry didn't mind going with me. He shared my enthusiasm for unique finds.

On this trip to Chicago, we planned to take our time driving, stopping along the way to shop, sightsee, to spend the night at motels along the way, get up the next day, have breakfast, and start out again. We were looking forward to the trip; we weren't planning to drive our car. We rented a Mercedes sports van so that we had room to bring back items we would purchase during the trip.

"I'll go and lease the van. You pack the cooler with ice, sodas, and snacks to eat on the way. You make better snacks than I do. I'll stop at the store and get some chips and crackers," I said to Jerry.

I had already made reservations at the Convention Center Hyatt where the conference was being held. Butch drove me to the leasing office to get the van. I got the van, made sure it was filled with gas and returned home. When I arrived at home, Jerry wasn't there. Jericka met me at the door looking upset.

Jericka didn't live with us. She had a beautiful four bedroom, three-car garage home in Davidsonville, a community about thirty miles outside of Baltimore. However, she rarely stayed there. She spent the majority of her time at our house with her father and me. She was an FBI agent and her office was located nearer to our house than the forty minute drive to her house. She had claimed the back bedroom in our house as her room. She stayed at her house three days a week, the other four days she stayed at our house. She had helped me pack for the Chicago trip, and was there to see her father and me off.

When I saw the expression on her face, I felt anxious.

"Daddy is not here," she said.

My heart did a flop. My gut feelings told me that something was wrong.

"Not here? Where is he? He should be back by now. Did he call?"

I tried not to show my fear.

"He's in the hospital."

My heart did another flop. He hadn't appeared sick when I left to get the van. When Jericka said he was in the hospital, my first thought was that he had been in a car accident.

"He's what?"

"He's in the hospital. His legs were swollen and he was limping. I made him go to the doctor. He kept telling me that he was all right but I didn't believe him. You know how Daddy is. When he wants to go somewhere, he pretends everything is alright. But everything was not all right. I could tell he was in pain. He wouldn't go to the doctor until I started fussing at him. I told him to go just to make sure everything was alright. I didn't like the way his legs had swollen. And sure enough, the doctor told him to go directly from his office to the hospital."

I got scared. I didn't know what to do. The telephone rang. It was Doctor Lotlikar, our primary physician.

"Mrs. Robinson?"

"Yes, this is she."

"This is Doctor Lotlikar. I'm calling to give you a report on your husband. He told me you two were planning a trip today."

"Yes, doctor, we are going to Chicago. In fact, we should have been gone by now. What's the matter is he okay?"

"No, he's not okay. Your husband is a sick man. He had blood clots in both of his legs. I'm glad he came to see me when he did. If you two had gone on the trip you would have had to stop somewhere and admit him to a hospital. His condition is very serious. He will be in the hospital for about two or three weeks."

"Oh my God! He didn't look sick this morning and he never said he wasn't feeling well."

"He probably didn't want to worry you but he is a sick man."

"Thank you for calling, Doctor. What hospital is he in?"

"He's in Harbor Hospital."

I hung up the telephone, my hands were shaking. I called the hospital admitting office to find out what room Jerry was in. They must have already determined he would be there a while; the telephone in his room was already connected. I called his room and he answered. His voice sounded weak but I felt relieved and glad to hear that sound. I tried to sound cheerful and I pretended to scold him for not telling me he was sick.

"See, when you're not sick you pretend you are but when you really are sick you don't say anything."

"I know but we had planned this trip and I didn't want to disappoint you."

"Jerry, we can go to Chicago anytime. The main thing is that you get better. I'm going to cancel the trip."

"No! You go on. You've already paid for the hotel room and made contacts in Chicago. I want you to go."

"I don't feel right going and leaving you in the hospital. Suppose something happens to you while I'm gone?"

"If something does happen, what can you do? Even if you're here and something happens to me there's nothing you can do about it. I'm in the best place to be cared for. I'm in the hospital. I'm in God's hands. I'll be alright. If you don't go, I'm going to feel bad for making you change plans."

I reluctantly agreed to go to Chicago. Because we had planned to drive and stop at motels along the way, we were leaving three days before the start of the convention. Since I had that extra time, I decided to fly. I called the airport and made flight reservations. I took the leased van back and flew to Chicago.

While I was in Chicago I spoke to Jerry on the telephone every night. When I returned to Baltimore Butch met me at the airport and drove me home. We talked on the way.

"How's your father?"

"He's getting better but he needs rest."

"I know. That's the same thing I said, but you can't tell him anything. He's so stubborn."

When I returned home, Jerry was eager to talk with me about us, but not about him taking it easy and not about pushing himself unnecessarily.

"I want us to have a talk," he said. "I thought a lot about us while I was in the hospital. I love you and I know you love me. Neither one of us

29

is going anywhere so we should stop all the arguing with each other over petty things and spend the rest of our lives enjoying the time we have left. We don't know when it will be the last time."

I shrugged him off and told him we had a long time left so let's not start talking about dying. After his death, I wished a million times I had listened to him and let him finish that conversation. Perhaps he knew more than he was saying. A month later he was gone.

I thank God that we did go to Greensboro for Easter that year, four months later Jerry was dead. Jerry's old friends Roy and Nancy didn't come to Baltimore to attend Jerry's funeral. I wondered why. They were so close; it was disappointing that they didn't come. However, I decided not to call them to ask why. Nancy didn't even call me to give her condolences, but Roy did call for the both of them. I couldn't understand Nancy's silence, until six months later.

Friday, March 18, 2005, Madeline called me and asked if I knew Nancy was dead.

"What Nancy?" I asked.

Never in my wildest dreams did I think she meant Roy's wife.

"Our Nancy," said Madeline.

"What? You've got to be kidding! What happened?"

"I didn't think you knew. Call Roy and talk to him. He's in a bad way. You know how close he and Nancy were."

"I'm going to call him right now. Lord have mercy! Now I understand why I haven't heard from her. I didn't even know she was sick."

"Neither did I but she's gone. I'll talk to you later."

We both hung up the telephone.

I called Roy and asked him about Nancy. I could tell by the sound of his voice he had been crying. Roy told me that Nancy died Thursday, March 17, 2005, on their forty-eighth wedding anniversary. Roy said he thought she was going to die Wednesday but it was as if she held on to make it to their anniversary. He was grieving as much for Nancy as I was for Jerry.

I thought about all the heartache I wrote about in my first book. I tried to think about the times when Jerry made me laugh, when he made me angry and even the disappointments. But none of that meant anything to me after his death. I only remembered the good times we shared. The times when we first met, how we enjoyed spending time with each other, how we enjoyed the same things, the night life, the parties, the music, and just being together. I remembered the times when the four of us, Roy and Nancy, Jerry and I, enjoyed sitting up all night laughing, telling jokes and just enjoying each other's company. Death will never be able to claim those memories.

Jerry loved me unconditionally. I felt comfortable with him. I didn't have to worry that I could no longer fit into a size seven dress as I did when we first met. I didn't worry that I didn't look so cute in the morning when I first woke up.

After his death, I felt lost. Imagine me, as strong as I pretended to be, feeling lost. I feared being alone and being lonesome. My family is the support group that kept me sane during my time of grief. Then opportunities to expand my career that I had not thought about began to materialize. God showed me that I would never be alone as long as I focused on Him. Romans 8:28. and Psalm 35 are my salvation and the ticket to my happiness. When I'm stressed, I reflect on those passages from the Bible. Everything I need to travel down the road of life, God will provide. Through my faith in God, I am in a position to accomplish my goals.

I didn't want to be without someone waiting to greet me when I arrived home after a grueling day at work. But God put so many things into my life that I didn't have time to focus on being alone. God was putting a new ministry in front of me and I hadn't quite realized it. When God told me to run for a seat in the Maryland House of Delegates, I was confused, so I asked Him to guide me. His advice was that He would direct my path if I just let Him lead. I asked God to be my protector.

"If I am not doing what is pleasing to You, Dear Father, I don't want to do it," I prayed.

I'LL SEE YOU TOMORROW

"A man is not old until regrets take the place of his dreams," — John Barrymore, 1943

Don't put a question mark where God has put a period, was the message I got from Jerry's funeral. God doesn't make mistakes. We may not understand why He allows certain things to happen, but He does not put anymore on us than we can bear. My husband's untimely death has shown me that when you lose a loved one, it's the little things you'll miss, the things you took for granted in the relationship, such as always having company at home with you. Even if you're not in the same room just the comfort of knowing someone is close by, someone who cares for you, someone who makes you feel safe is something you can't put a price on.

I remember the comfortable feeling I had when it rained and Jerry was at home in bed with me. The loud claps of lightening flashed across the sky and lit up the night, the roar of thunder seemed to shake the entire house. On nights like that, I snuggled close to him in bed and felt safe. When the storm caused the electricity to go out throughout the house and threw everything into darkness, I felt safe when he was with me. To always know that I had a handsome, dashing escort when I went to social events was comforting and flattering. To know that he would fry the fish for dinner because he did a better job with fish than I did, is something I miss. But the real blessing is that these things happened at all and will provide me with fond memories forever. Memory is a mental garden where seeds are planted every day.

One day I was sitting at the computer in the office in our home, the television was on and my back was to it. Every so often I turned around and watched what was on. *Law and Order SVU* (Special Victims Unit) was playing. Jerry walked into the office and sat at the desk.

He took out a syringe and a small bottle of insulin for his sugar diabetes. He held up the syringe so I could see it.

"See, this is what I have to use for the rest of my life," he said.

"Uh huh!" I replied and continued working on the computer.

I now wish I had stopped and listened to him. Obviously he was trying to inform me about his physical condition. But I assumed he was once again exaggerating about the severity of his health.

To get attention he sometimes exaggerated his illness. If he had a splinter in his finger he would go to the hospital to have it removed. I thought that he would outlive me. That just shows you that God has the final say

One day he had a cold and while talking to one of his friends on the telephone, he said, "Man I had pneumonia. I almost went away from here."

I was annoyed at him for lying. I interrupted his conversation.

"Jerry, why do you exaggerate like that? One day you are going to really be sick but because you have told so many lies, I'm not going to take you seriously."

He just laughed and continued talking on the telephone.

One night he had a headache. The next day while talking to Jericka, he said, "I was dizzy last night. I reached for your mama so she could help me but I couldn't find her. I got up to go to the bathroom and fell three or four times."

I looked at him, laughed, and shook my head.

"Why don't you stop lying? You know you didn't fall. Had you fallen you would have called me. And why couldn't you find me in bed? I was lying beside you all night. You are exaggerating again!"

"Well, I almost fell."

"How did you almost fall."

"Well, I could have fallen."

Then he chuckled at the fact that I had caught him in a lie.

He exaggerated so much about being sick when he wasn't, I often told him, "You cry wolf so often, one day it's going to backfire on you."

He would laugh and shrug me off.

July 19, 2004, was one of those days when I thought he was, "crying wolf." He actually was sick but I didn't believe him. I thought he was exaggerating his illness. After he died I blamed myself for not paying more attention to the signs of his illness. Surely they must have been there, I thought. Perhaps I was too absorbed in my own life to notice that he was getting physically weaker.

This day I looked at him with a frown on my face. It was obvious that I was annoyed but he didn't say anything about my annoyed expression.

"What is it, Jerry?" I asked in an agitated voice.

I hadn't noticed how bloody the paper towel he was holding to his nose had become.

"My nose won't stop bleeding."

He had nosebleeds before and they always stopped. I again thought he was exaggerating when he said the bleeding wouldn't stop.

His voice, muffled by the paper towel, quivered as if he would break into tears at any moment. Then I realized that he was frightened and I noticed the blood now oozing onto his hand under the paper towel. At that point I got worried. I thought this time it's for real.

"Do you want me to take you to the hospital?" I asked.

He looked annoyed with me as if to say, "My nose is bleeding. The front of my shirt is bloody. The paper towel that I'm holding to my nose is soaked with my blood, and you ask me if I want you to drive me to the hospital! What do you think?"

But he just said, "Yes."

I reached for my pocketbook, got my car keys, saved the document I had been working on in the computer and walked with him into the garage. His car was blocking mine. He got behind the wheel of his car and moved it so that our vans and buses and some of our employees' cars would not be blocked. He parked his car against the wall of the garage and got into my car and we drove out of the garage.

"Which hospital do you want me to take you?"

"Take me to Saint Agnes. I'll show you the way."

His nose continued to bleed. I thought it was a simple nose bleed. I didn't know he was as sick as he was.

When we arrived in the Emergency Room at Saint Agnes Hospital, the triage nurse took one look at the bloody paper towel Jerry was holding to his nose, and immediately took him into another room to be examined. She didn't waste time letting him fill out papers as they usually did before the doctor saw a patient.

I sat in the waiting room. I thought they would give him some medicine to stop the bleeding and I would then drive him home. After I had waited for about forty-five minutes, I began to worry. His examination was taking longer than I anticipated. A few minutes later a nurse came from the area where they had taken Jerry and called my name.

"Is there a Mrs. Barbara Robinson out here?"

"Yes, that's me!"

The nurse stood in the doorway holding the door open to the examination room.

"Your husband is in there. He asked me to get you."

She pointed to a small private room. I entered the room and saw Jerry dressed in a hospital gown, lying in bed, holding a small metal tray under his chin. His nose was packed with cotton that had turned red with his blood. He removed the bloody cotton balls and inserted a fresh cotton ball into each nostril. It was obvious that his nose was still bleeding as much, if not more, than it was when we first arrived. A few minutes later, he again took the blood-soaked balls of cotton from his nostrils and replaced them with clean ones. The amount of blood that was coming from his nose alarmed me. However, I tried not to show my concern. I tried to make light of the situation. I would not look directly at him, I didn't want him to see the concerned expression on my face and the fear in my eyes.

"What is this? Are they going to keep you?" I asked.

"It looks like it. They don't know why my nose won't stop bleeding. I think they want to conduct some tests. They're concerned about my old ticker (heart). I might be going away from here, girl," he teased.

"Aw, you ain't going nowhere. You can't leave me. Besides, You're too ornery to go anywhere," I said jokingly.

We both laughed.

I sat in the chair beside his bed and waited for the doctor to give us Jerry's prognosis.

When thirty minutes passed and the nurse still had not returned to tell us anything, Jerry turned to me with a concerned expression.

"It doesn't make sense for you to sit here while they're running tests. Why don't you go home and when they're finished examining me, I'll call you and you can come back and get me. It will probably be another couple of hours or so before they're finished with me. In the meantime you can go on home and get yourself something to eat. Leave my clothes I'll need them to wear home."

I kissed him on his forehead, left the hospital and went home. I had been at home about two hours when Jerry called and said the hospital had admitted him. The doctors wanted to run more tests so they were going to keep him overnight. I honestly believed that he would be released the following day. But when the next day came and I went to the hospital to see him he said the doctor had examined his heart and didn't like the sound of it.

I really started to get worried, no, I got scared! When the second day came and he still had not been released from the hospital, my gut feelings told me this was something different from his other hospital stays. He had been in various hospitals several times during our forty-seven years together and each time somehow I knew he would be alright. But this time was different.

I visited him every day and each time I was in his hospital room I was reluctant to leave. My gut feeling kept telling me to stay at the hospital with him just a little while longer. Something kept telling me to enjoy my time with him. I usually arrived at the hospital around 5:30 p.m. and stayed until after seven. The television program "Jeopardy" came on at 7:00 p.m. and stayed on until 7:30 p.m. "Wheel of Fortune" came on at 7:30 p.m. and stayed on until 8:00 p.m. Jerry and I watched Jeopardy together each day. We both were cheering for Ken Jennings to be the first contestant to win a million dollars. I always stayed until the show was over and Wheel of Fortune came on.

When I went to visit Jerry on the fourth day and he wasn't in his room, I began to cry so hard that one of the doctors called a nurse to come and see about me. The nurse asked me if I wanted a sedative. I told her I did not. I was just worried about my husband. The nurse sat with me until I could compose myself. She held my hand the entire time while I cried. It was something about the way she consoled me that made me suspicious that she knew more about my husband's condition than she was telling me.

After I calmed down, the nurse informed me that the doctor wanted to talk to me about my husband's condition. A sick feeling went to the bottom of my stomach. The nurse called for the doctor to come to my husband's room; Jerry still had not returned to his room. When the doctor arrived, he walked into the room smiling, his hand extended for a handshake. That was a plus, I thought. I was sitting in the chair besides Jerry's bed. The doctor stood in front of me, then sat on the side of the bed facing me. He spoke in a gentle voice.

"I'm Doctor Anderson, one of the doctors treating your husband. He's a sick man."

That was the second time a doctor had referred to my husband as a "sick man." Dr. Lotlikar had said the same thing when we were planning to go to Chicago.

"What do you mean by 'a sick man' Doctor? Does that mean he won't get well?"

I was really anxious!

"Your husband needs a heart bypass operation right away. His heart is deteriorating rapidly but we have delayed the operation because his kidney was so weak. The doctor said Jerry would eventually have to use a dialyses machine for his kidney. They prolonged the heart surgery a few more days trying to strengthen his kidney but his blood pressure kept going up.

Although Jerry was seriously ill, he remained in good spirits. He joked that he might not make it. At least, at the time I thought he was joking now I'm not so sure. Perhaps he knew that this time he wouldn't be coming home.

One day he said what I thought was a joke.

"The Big Fella (Jesus), may be calling me home any day now. I don't know."

Then he smiled.

"You can't and leave me. Who would I have to argue with?" I said jokingly.

Then I laughed, trying to provide some humor and also trying to hold back my tears and not let my voice quiver and reveal how scared I was.

"I'd like nothing better than to come home and argue with you again, but this time, I don't know. But it just shows how much I care about you," he said.

"Yeah, yeah," I teased.

I looked in his eyes. His lips were smiling, but his eyes looked tired.

"You look tired. How do you feel? Are you hurting?"

"No, I'm not hurting but I am kind of tired."

"I'll go on home and let you rest. I think I'll tell the nurse that you don't need any more visitors tonight. You need to get some sleep."

"I'll be alright. You go home before it gets too late and call me when you get there. I Don't want you out at night alone. Somebody might try to grab you then I'll have to get out of this bed and protect you, and I don't want to have to get out of this bed and hurt nobody," he joked.

"Yeah, picture that!"

We both laughed, but his was a weak laugh. I kissed him on his forehead and left the room.

When five days passed and Jerry's health wasn't improving the doctors said they couldn't wait any longer, and had to operate on his heart right away. He was transferred to Union Memorial Hospital where there was a great team of heart specialists.

A week later, Jerry had heart surgery and the doctors said they were pleased with the outcome of the operation. After it was over he was taken to the intensive care unit to recover. The nurses put a clean gown on him and washed him up. I was allowed to visit him for a few minutes, but he wasn't aware that I was in the room. He was still sedated and unconscious. I cried when I saw all the tubes in his body and all the machines around his bed keeping him alive. He looked so helpless and I felt helpless. I couldn't do anything to help him. But he was alive and recovering, that was a blessing.

The following Sunday August 1, our entire family visited him in his room, all four of our children and all the grandchildren. We hadn't planned to meet there it just happened. Jerry appeared to be recovering well, he was joking with everyone, kidding with our daughter Jeanene pretending to scold her for taking the piece of apple pie from his dinner tray and eating it. But something was different about him, about the way he joked. He seemed to be trying to enjoy our conversation, but he wasn't as jovial as usual. It was something about the way he laughed that didn't sound right.

I had laughed at his jokes for forty-seven years. He had a great sense of humor. I loved to hear him laugh. The sound of his laughter was infectious. Hearing him laugh made people around him laugh too. Plus he still had his own beautiful teeth. He visited the dentist often. Although he was trying very hard to be his jovial self, he wasn't. He also didn't eat any of his food. It remained on his bed tray. He tried to cough but it appeared to hurt him. He looked at me, winked his eye and smiled. He used to do that in church when he stood with the other ushers.

"Are you flirting with me, Mister? I'm a married woman and my husband is a mean man. He don't play and he don't allow nobody to mess with his woman," I said jokingly.

He gave a faint laugh. Our grandchildren also laughed.

He weakly raised a fist and shook it at me, indicating he could still fight.

"I fooled your mamma," he said to the family not directing his remarks to any specific person.

I put my hands on my hips as if I were flirting with him.

"Fooled me how?" I asked.

"You thought I was going to kick the bucket when I went under the knife. But I fooled you. You can tell your boyfriend that he's out of luck. The old man is still kicking and if I catch him messin' with my woman, I'm gonna kick his ass (he pronounced the word 'ass' as 'ice')," — that was our private joke of him trying to imitate a southern drawl.

We all laughed.

"Pop Pop, you're still in the hospital you just had a heart operation, and you're talking about beating somebody up. Don't you think you should get well first?" teased our granddaughter, Bianca.

Jerry made a fist and shook it in the air.

"I still got strength. I can handle myself."

Then he flinched, reacting as if a pain hit him.

"That's it! That's enough for today. Your daddy needs his rest. We'll come back tomorrow," I said.

I started asking everyone to leave the room.

I was concerned about the way Jerry was acting, as if he were in pain. But he was enjoying our company and didn't want us to leave. He insisted we stay a few minutes longer. We all stayed in his room until visiting hours were over but we didn't leave. The on-duty nurse came into his room and saw us but she said nothing. She didn't tell us that it was time to leave. She just turned and walked back out of the room, pulling the door shut as she left. We stayed another forty-five minutes, then we all left, not wanting to push our luck with the on-duty nurse any longer. We each kissed Jerry on his forehead and said we would see him the following day.

As I replay that scene over and over in my mind, I wonder if the on-duty nurse allowed us to stay in Jerry's room longer than we were supposed to stay because she knew how grave his condition was.

Bianca was twelve-years-old and in a week she would be thirteen. She was staying with me while her "Pop Pop" was in the hospital. All our grandchildren called Jerry "Pop Pop" and called me "Ma Ma." They all knew that I didn't like to stay in our big house alone. When Jerry first went to the hospital and we learned he was being admitted, Bianca volunteered to stay with me until her "Pop Pop" came home. I was grateful for her company. Since it was during the summer months and school was out, she could be my constant companion.

The following day, Monday, August 2, 2004, Bianca went to the office with me. She and I had a daily ritual of leaving the office and going directly to the hospital to visit her Pop Pop. When she wasn't on the computer, surfing the Internet, Bianca would answer the telephone when the receptionist left her desk. She enjoyed playing the "grown-up."

The day was a dry, warm, summer evening. It was dusk dark when Bianca and I arrived at the hospital. We entered Jerry's room, he looked pale. He wasn't as cheerful as he had been the previous day when we visited him. When he saw Bianca and me he gave a faint smile but I could tell something was wrong. His dinner tray was still on his bed, untouched.

Daniel, SelfPride's bookkeeper, was sitting in a chair beside Jerry's bed. Daniel was from Kenya and spoke with a heavy accent. He and Jerry had become "buddies" as they called each other.

"Hey Buddy, How you doing?" they'd say when greeting each other.

The television was on and Jerry and Daniel were watching *Jeopardy!*. Ken Jennings was still on his winning streak, still the champion. Daniel and I started a conversation about how long Ken Jennings had been on the show.

"Jerry and I have been watching *Jeopardy*, the entire time he has been in the hospital. I sure wish I could tell Ken Jennings how much we enjoyed him. I hope he wins, we're pulling for him. You'd think Jerry and I were winning the way we cheer each night he wins."

"Me too! I watch it every night. I thought I'd watch it with my buddy tonight," said Daniel.

I looked at Jerry, but he frowned and put his hand on his chest as if he were in pain.

"Are you hurting?"

"No, I don't hurt. I just want to use the commode. I can't use that bed pan."

He pointed to a bed pan in the corner of the room.

The stitches had been removed and Jerry was talking of coming home and playing golf. He had challenged his doctor to a golf game when he was well enough to go to the golf course.

"I told Doc. Just as soon as he takes the stitches out and lets me go home I'm gonna whup him something terrible on the golf course," Jerry said.

We laughed.

"You're still challenging people and you can't even walk?" I teased.

"Yep! But I can still play with the best of 'em and beat most of 'em."

"That's my buddy, always in charge," said Daniel.

We laughed but Jerry gave a weak whimper. Daniel and I looked at each other but we said nothing. I think we each knew what the other was thinking about Jerry's weak attempt to pretend he wasn't in pain.

Jerry was an avid golfer. He had many trophies from winning golf tournaments. On Wednesdays when he was supposed to be working, we could never reach him on his pager. When he didn't answer, we always knew he was on the golf course. He had been playing golf since he was old enough to carry a golf bag. He said when he was growing up in Greensboro during the 1940s he would caddy for white golfers so he could get the chance to play on the nicer golf courses in Greensboro.

A male nurse entered the room to give Jerry his medicine. Jerry told the nurse that he wanted to use the commode. The nurse lifted the cover of the dinner tray to see Jerry's food still untouched.

Jerry frowned and held his stomach as if he was trying to belch.

"He said he wants to use the commode. He doesn't like using the bed pan," I said to the nurse.

"Okay, I'll get the portable commode, but first I need to give him an enema," the nurse said.

"I'm going to leave you so that you can use the commode in peace. I'll see you tomorrow." I said.

I looked at Jerry and smiled.

He smiled back.

The nurse pulled the curtain around Jerry's bed for privacy while he was given an enema. Daniel was still sitting in the chair.

"I'm going to stay a little while longer with my buddy. I miss seeing him every day since he's been here in the hospital," said Daniel.

Then Daniel laughed with that sound that always cracked us up when we heard him laugh at the office. It sounded almost like the sound the caricature Woody Woodpecker made.

"You're gonna be sorry if you stay in the room when he passes his bowels. After forty-seven years of being married to him and living with him, I ought to know," I teased.

Daniel laughed.

"Yeah, but I gotta stay with my buddy."

"Okay, but don't say you weren't warned. You're gonna be sorry."

I laughed, put my hand on Daniel's shoulder, walked over to Jerry's bed and kissed him on his cheek.

Bianca also kissed him.

"See you later Pop Pop."

"Okay baby, come back tomorrow with your grandmother."

"Yeah, see you later 'Pop Pop'," I teased.

"Okay 'Ma Ma' see you tomorrow," Jerry said teasingly.

Bianca and I walked out laughing at Daniel staying in the room while Jerry used the commode.

"He's gonna be sorry he stayed, huh Ma Ma?"

Bianca laughed.

"Absolutely, you know your grandfather when he uses the bathroom at home."

We laughed at the thought of Daniel staying.

Bianca and I rode the elevator down to the lobby. I had parked my car across the street from the hospital. While driving to the hospital, Bianca and I had passed a restaurant around the corner from the hospital. I promised we would stop there after we visited Jerry. They had signs in the window and on the door advertising fountain sodas and hand dipped ice cream.

"Can we go to that restaurant we saw and get some ice cream?" asked Bianca.

"You must be reading my mind. I was just thinking about a thick, rich, cold, vanilla milkshake."

"And I was just thinking about a big thick chocolate milkshake, uhmmm."

She licked her lips and rubbed her stomach.

Bianca and I went across the street from the hospital to a little restaurant that was reminiscent of the ice cream parlors of the 1950s and bought milk shakes. There were posters of old cars and movie stars on the walls. Booths lined the walls and a juke box was in each booth. Ice cream sodas were made from scratch the old fashion way with hand-dipped ice cream, and soda fountain cream sodas. Customers sat in booths and on stools at the counter, sipping fountain sodas. Old records from the 1970s played while a wooden ceiling fan hummed softly as it turned, but did little to cool the air. Bianca and I ordered milk shakes. They were thick and creamy just like the good old days.

I was thinking that when Jerry was released from the hospital and regained his strength, he and I would come back to this little restaurant and get some milk shakes and ice cream sodas. He'd love that. We teased him about his love for ice cream. He ate a bowl of ice cream almost every night. Jericka said that when he and I got old and were living in a senior citizen home, all Jerry needed was a bowl of ice cream and he would be happy.

Bianca and I sat quietly enjoying our milkshakes and listening to the music.

"This is the way I remember ice cream parlors when I was a little girl. It don't get no better than this.," I said to Bianca.

She smiled and continued drinking her milkshake.

Later that night about eight-thirty, I was at home talking on the telephone with Sandy, our neighbor who lived across the street in front of our house on Essex Road. She was informing me that she and her husband Charles were planning to visit Jerry the following day. I told her Bianca and I had visited him earlier that day and he looked pale. While talking to Sandy I heard a click on the telephone line indicating that a call was trying to come through to my telephone.

"Sandy, someone is trying to get through to me. I'll call you back."

Sandy hung up and I clicked over to accept the incoming call.

"Hello, this is Union Memorial Hospital trying to reach Mrs. Robinson," the voice on the other end of the telephone said.

I started grinning. I thought it was the hospital calling to tell me to bring clothes for Jerry to wear home because he was going to be discharged the following day. After his operation the hospital had given me some pamphlets about the type of operation Jerry had and the information on the pamphlets said that patients usually go home within a week after such an operation. The doctor had informed me that Jerry was recovering well, so I figured it was only a matter of time before he was released.

I said to the caller, "This is Mrs. Robinson."

"Mrs. Robinson, this is Doctor so and so (I never did get her name) from Union Memorial Hospital. Your husband just had a cardiac arrest. I tried to resuscitate him but he didn't respond."

I gasped, paused, then I responded.

"I'm sorry, what did you say?"

The doctor's voice changed. It appeared that she realized that she should not have blurted out what she said. I had trouble understanding what the doctor said. My mind did not comprehend her words. Her statements appeared to be completely foreign to anything I had ever heard. We seemed to be in two different conversations. I had no idea who this doctor was talking to and I certainly had no idea what she was talking about. I know I didn't hear her correctly so I asked her to repeat what she had just said.

I tried to be calm, but I could not. My heart was racing too fast and I seemed to have lost a sense of where I was or what I was doing.

"Excuse me, what did you say? I didn't understand you," I shouted to the voice on the telephone.

She would not answer my question. She realized I was not taking her statement calmly, she seemed to realize that she had made a grave mistake. Her voice became more concerned about me, and how I was reacting to the news of my husband.

"Mrs. Robinson, is there anyone there with you?"

The voice was too calm. My whole body got cold and I started to tremble. I wasn't calm anymore. I couldn't control my anxiety.

"What did you say? I didn't understand you! Please repeat what you said!"

I screamed into the telephone. The doctor would not repeat her words. Obviously she realized that she should not have been so blunt from the beginning, in such a nonchalant way, telling me that my husband had died. How could she lie to me like that? My husband couldn't be dead, I had just left him.

"Are you alone? You shouldn't be alone. We need you to come to the hospital but don't drive yourself. Is there a family member you can get to come with you?"

"What did you say? Please repeat what you said! You didn't say my husband is dead did you? What did you say?"

I was screaming so loud I scared Bianca. She had been in the back bedroom watching television. When she heard me screaming, she came running into my bedroom.

I screamed into the telephone but the voice on the other end remained calm and soft spoken, not responding to my questions or to my hysterical screams.

The voice repeated what she had previously said.

"Mrs. Robinson, we need you to come to the hospital, but don't come alone."

The more I shouted for her to repeat her statement the more she repeated instructions for me to come to the hospital and not come alone.

"You want me to come to the hospital and bring some clothes for my husband to wear home tomorrow, right?"

"Mrs. Robinson, please come to the hospital. We'll talk when you get here but please do not drive yourself."

The voice was too calm, too controlled and too unemotional. I could not get her to say anything about her previous statement.

"Why won't you answer me?" I screamed. "Why can't you answer my questions? What did you say when I first answered the telephone?"

I don't know what the rest of the conversation was like. I started screaming and couldn't stop. I threw the telephone down as if it were a hot iron burning my hand. Suddenly the world was unreal. It was as if I were in a motion picture watching actors going through the motion of receiving bad news. I jumped up and down. I turned around and around in my bedroom, in a daze. I didn't know what to do. I felt disoriented, as if I couldn't understand what was happening. It was as if I were in a dream, watching someone else react to terrible news. Everything was happening in slow motion, then it was spinning, then back to slow motion again. I then fell to my knees and prayed, not a silent prayer, I was screaming.

"Lord, please let this be a mistake! Please let the doctor on the telephone had said that I need to bring clothes to my husband so he can wear them home. Please don't take him from me! Please don't take him from his family! We need him. I promise I'll be a better wife if You let him come home I will stop arguing with him. I'll do anything you want me to do! Please don't take him!"

I begged and pleaded with God.

I don't remember much about that night after the telephone call. I know that Bianca must have called her father.

"Come quick, something is wrong with Ma Ma," I heard her say to someone on the telephone.

A few minutes later Butch and his son Jay, were at the front door. Butch used his key to unlock the front door and entered the house.

"What's wrong? What's the matter?" asked Butch.

I was still crying and pleading with God. But when I heard the fear in his voice, I tried to control my own fear, but I could not. I turned to face him; the expression on his face was one of fear. He thought something had happened to me.

"What's the matter Ma? Are you alright? What's wrong?" he shouted.

His voice was quivering with emotion. He didn't know what to think. All Bianca had said was "Something is wrong with Ma Ma." and he had rushed over.

I tried to control myself enough to explain to him what was wrong, but I couldn't catch my breath. My chest felt as if I had been running a long time and was winded. Finally I was able to calm myself enough to answer his questions.

"A doctor from the hospital called me. I think they made a mistake. I think she said your father is dead but that must be a mistake. I have to get to the hospital right away."

I picked up my pocketbook and started for the door, oblivious that I was not appropriately dressed.

"Ma, you need to put on some clothes," said Butch.

I looked down and noticed I was still wearing my nightgown. To this day I don't remember putting on clothes. I just know that whatever it was, Butch had to button it for me. I couldn't stop my hands from shaking.

Bianca was still crying.

"If it is true that Pop Pop has died, please don't call Jericka. She will lose her mind," Bianca said to her father.

She was using wisdom much beyond her twelve years. She knew how close Jericka was with her father.

"There's no way I cannot call Jericka and not tell her. She would never forgive me if I didn't let her know that something happened to Pop. But I'm not going to call her until we get to the hospital and find out what's what," said Butch.

He called his father "Pop," and the girls called him "Daddy."

Butch called Frances, Bianca's and Jay's mother, and asked her to come to my house and stay with Jay and Bianca while he and I went to the hospital.

Butch's car was parked in my driveway. As we walked toward the car I began to scream and couldn't stop. I felt as if the scream had been bottled inside of me and had to get outside of my body and explode into the universe. I wondered if the neighbors heard my screams in the quiet neighborhood where we lived. Butch didn't try to stop my screaming; he just put his arms around me to comfort me and let me scream until I couldn't anymore.

We then got in the car and began the drive to the hospital. During the ride I continued trying to make a deal with God. I tried to bargain with Him promising what I would do if He spared my husband.

God answered my prayers. He said "No!"

We get answers to our prayers but sometimes they are not the answers we want to accept. "No," was not the answer I wanted to accept. I interpreted the death of my husband as God saying, "No!"

All during the drive to the hospital I continue trying to convince myself that my husband would be alright. I tried to reassure Butch of that as well. But deep inside I knew it wasn't true, yet I continued to hope.

"Your father is fine. They made a mistake. He's fine. You'll see. When we get to the hospital he'll be alright. He's probably sitting waiting for us to bring him home. The doctor is going to tell me she didn't say he couldn't be resuscitated. She is going to say that I misunderstood her and she was telling me to bring some fresh clothes for him to wear home."

Butch drove in silence. He never said a word during the entire drive. Every few minutes he reached over and gently touched my hand as if to say, "It's okay Ma., I understand. Everything is going to be all right!

When we arrived at the hospital, two security guards were waiting for us at the front entrance. I knew within my heart that my beloved husband was gone, but I wouldn't let my mind accept it. In my heart I had understood what the doctor said when she called me at my home. I just didn't want to believe it. I didn't take any of Jerry's clothes with me to the hospital for him to wear home. I felt that he wouldn't be coming home anymore. Not this time.

Butch and I rode the elevator in silence to the floor where Jerry's room was located. During the long elevator ride I was silently praying that my husband was alive. That elevator ride to the third floor was the longest ride I had ever taken. When we got off the elevator and walked toward Jerry's room, three or four people dressed in white uniforms were standing outside his room waiting for us. I later learned they were two nurses and two doctors. One of them was the doctor who called me at home to tell me about my husband. As we approached them I searched their faces hoping to see a smile to let me know that my husband was all right. Instead I saw sadness in their eyes.

"It's not true is it? Please tell me my husband is alright," I pleaded with any one of them.

Finally one of the women spoke.

I'm Doctor Anderson, I'm sorry," she said softly.

The sound of sadness was in her voice. It was the same voice that had called me at home. The same voice that had instructed me not to drive myself to the hospital.

I screamed and ran into my husband's room. He was lying on his back, his eyes closed. He looked as if he were asleep. I gently rubbed his forehead and whispered "I love you." Then I kissed him. His forehead, felt hard and cold, not warm and soft as it had felt the last time I kissed him the previous day. One of the doctors instructed a nurse to take Butch and me into another room. I guess I was disturbing the other patients with my screams.

We were escorted to a waiting room that resembled a living room with a sofa, chairs, and end tables with lamps. When we entered the room, one of the nurses who was waiting for us outside Jerry's room entered with us. I could tell she had been crying. Her eyes were moist and red. She told me her name but I don't remember it. I just remember that she had kind eyes and a sad smile.

I sat on the couch in the room and the nurse with the sad eyes knelt beside me.

"I'm so sorry about the loss of your husband. I can't imagine the pain you must be feeling. He was a joy to have as a patient. He was always smiling and in good humor. Even when it was obvious that he was in pain, he still maintained his good nature."

I cried harder. She was right, he was a joy.

The nurse handed me a box of tissues and took some for herself.

"What happened? He was doing so well yesterday when I saw him. What changed?" I asked.

"I don't know. He was doing fine when I checked him. I helped him to the commode and left the room to give him privacy, and when I returned a few moments later, he had expired. It was so sudden."

Another doctor entered the room, a tall, slender, black woman, who spoke with an accent that sounded as if she was from Jamaica. She said her name but I don't remember it.

"I can't begin to tell you how sorry I am. Do you want us to perform an autopsy to determine the cause of your husband's death?"

"No!" I shouted. "Please don't cut him anymore. Regardless of the reason, an autopsy won't bring him back. Let him rest in peace. He has been through enough cutting with his heart surgery. Just please, let him rest. No more cutting."

The doctor gently put her hand on my shoulder, smiled and said, "I understand." And she left the room.

The day before her father's death, Jericka had gone to Florida to attend a work-related conference. She wasn't expected to return to Baltimore until two days later. She had spoken to her father by telephone earlier that day.

Butch walked in to the hospital lounge and used his cell phone to call Jericka at her hotel room in Florida. As soon as Jericka said, "Hello" Butch couldn't control his tears any longer. He began to cry uncontrollably. He had tried to be strong for me but as soon as he heard his sister's voice he lost his composure. I went to him and put my arms around him and we both cried.

The nurse tried to comfort us.

Distraught after hearing the news that her father had died, Jericka threw down the telephone and started screaming. Butch immediately called back to the hotel and asked to speak to the hotel manager. He was crying and trying to explain to the hotel manager that his sister needed assistance.

"Please go up to room 218 and check on my sister. I just gave her some bad news that our father just died, she screamed and hung up the telephone. I'm calling from a hospital here in Baltimore, Maryland. She shouldn't be alone right now. Please go and help her."

Later Jericka told us that the hotel manager and a security guard came to her room. As soon as they got off the elevator on her floor, they heard her screams. They knocked on her hotel room door and although they could hear her screaming and crying, she would not open the door. The hotel manager used her key to enter Jericka's room. When they entered, they saw the telephone on the floor where Jericka had thrown it after receiving the message from her brother. Jericka was turning around and around in circles in the middle of the floor, in a confused state, she was jumping up

50

and down screaming and crying, shouting, "Daddy! Daddy! No! No! Not my daddy."

The manager put her arms around Jericka and held her while she screamed, her body retching with sobs.

When Jericka was able to control her emotions, her head aching from her screaming, she called the FBI Headquarters in Washington, D.C. and informed them of her father's death. She told them that she needed to return to Baltimore right away. Under the circumstances, the FBI tried to be as accommodating as they could. They contacted the airport and booked her on an emergency flight leaving Florida that following morning.

As Butch and I left the hospital that night, we met Jeanene and Jeanese, my granddaughter Tyneisha, and Jeanese's husband Wendell, coming into the hospital. Butch had called them from his cell phone.

I was crying and Butch had his arm around my shoulder guiding me down the steps that led from the hospital grounds to the street below, where his car was parked. Tears blinded my vision.

"Is it true about Daddy? How is he?" asked Jeanene.

"He's gone," Butch responded.

"Oh, no!" said Tyneisha. "Can we still go and see him?"

"Yeah, they'll let you go up," said Butch.

They continued up the stone steps from the parking lot that led to the door of the hospital. Butch and I continued walking to the parking lot, got into his car and drove home in silence. I cried all the way home from the hospital. Nothing seemed real to me. When we arrived home, I called my neighbor, Sandy.

"Sandy, he's gone," I sobbed.

"Who is this?" she asked.

She sounded as if I woke her from a sound sleep. After all it was then twelve midnight. I hadn't realized the hour was so late.

"It's me, Barbara. That was the doctor who interrupted our telephone conversation earlier. She called to tell me that my husband is dead!"

Then I boo-hooed. I couldn't contain the torrent of tears.

"What?" she shouted in disbelief. "I'll be right over," and we hung up the telephone.

I needed to talk to someone, anyone who could understand the pain I was experiencing. I thought about my friend Regina; we had been friends for over forty years. When we lived on the fourth floor in the projects, Regina and her children lived on the second floor. I called her and told her that Jerry was dead. She started crying and said she would be right over. She lived on the other side of the city. She was too distraught to drive; therefore she called her friend, Judson, who drove her to my house. I don't remember going to bed that night. It seemed that the house was filled with people, who had come to support me. I thank God for each one of them.

Jeanene and Jeanese had already called Jerry's relatives in Greensboro, North Carolina. His parents were deceased.

I started to call my friend, Gloria. But I remembered that her husband was still alive and I didn't think that she would understand my grief.

I said to myself, who do I know who will understand? Then I thought about Leronia, a friend who lived not far from me and who had lost her husband a few years earlier. I called Leronia and she called Pastor Reid, the Senior Pastor of Bethel African, Methodist, Episcopal, (AME) Church where Jerry and I were members. Leronia was also a member of Bethel and Bethel's attorney.

Jerry was a member of Bethel's Usher Board. I served in several positions, some of them were before Dr. Reid became Bethel's Pastor. I had been a Trustee, a Steward, a Missionary, a member of the board of directors of the outreach center, a consultant, and teacher of the Women's Outreach Center. As a representative of the Missionary unit, I was sent to Africa to teach women how to become entrepreneurs.

Jericka joined Bethel's Dance Ministry. At one time all of my children were members of Bethel; however; Jerome moved to Pennsylvania, and Jeanene and Jeanese joined other churches. Jericka and Bianca remained at Bethel with Jerry and me. When Jeanese was at Bethel she was a member of the deaf ministry where she signed to deaf members. Her first husband was deaf and was also a member of Bethel. When they separated, she left Bethel and joined another church and Jeanene went with her.

After talking to Leronia and Pastor Reid, I tried to sleep but could not. I cried all night long. Sandy was a registered nurse and desperately tried to reach my doctor on his emergency telephone number to ask him to prescribe a sedative for me. When she finally contacted the doctor, she informed him what happened and that she was a registered nurse and would be responsible for administering medication for me to get some rest. The doctor called the pharmacist the following day and prescribed medicine over the telephone. Sandy went to the drugstore and got the sedative. Thank God for that sweet, soothing, restful sleep only to dream about my husband.

When I wasn't sleeping I was crying. I didn't have an appetite. I had no energy or desire to get out of bed. I later learned that my house was filled with visitors and they all said they would be glad when Jericka arrived. They thought that because she and I were so close, her presence would bring me out of my depression.

Later that day Jericka arrived from Florida and I was still in bed. I was too distraught and consumed with grief to get up. Sandy was still at my bedside. I was in a mental hell.

The Sunday before Jerry's death, Bianca and I had attended the morning nine o'clock service at Bethel. After the services were over and Pastor Reid had finished his sermon, he asked Bianca and me to come to the front of the Sanctuary. We slowly left our seats, holding hands as we walked up the aisle to face the pulpit, our backs to the congregation. Pastor Reid was standing in the pulpit behind the podium. He came down to the altar where he could touch Bianca and me as she and I hugged each other. We stood at the altar facing Pastor Reid. He said a prayer for Jerry's recovery and asked the congregation to pray for, "Brother Robinson's recovery and for his family.

"Sister Barbara, Brother Robinson will recover and soon we'll see him marching down the aisle with the other ushers and take his place right there."

He pointed to the place where Jerry always stood when Pastor Reid said, "The doors of the Church are open. Come, give me your hand and give God your heart." This indicated that people could then come and join the church.

But Pastor Reid was wrong. My husband wouldn't be coming back this time!

GOING HOME CELEBRATION

I would rather live my life as if there is a God and die and find out I was right, than to live my life as if there isn't a God and die and find out I was wrong.

"Be still and know that I am God," Psalm 46:10

I didn't know anything about planning a funeral. I didn't know what funeral home to call. I tried to sit down with the funeral director when he came to our house but each time we started talking about Jerry's funeral arrangements, I ran from the room crying. I thank God for Reverend Brenda Carter, one of the ministers from Bethel AME Church. She knew which funeral director to call. She assisted Jericka with the planning of the funeral arrangements and determining where my husband would be buried.

In hind sight, I should have contacted several funeral homes and compared their prices. I didn't think of a funeral as being a business with competitive prices. I never planned a funeral before. I wasn't even thinking about having to purchase a burial plot. When I learned the cost of the funeral, almost ten-thousand dollars, I decided to bury my husband in the Veteran's Cemetery. Because he was a veteran, it wouldn't cost anything to bury a husband and wife there. However, our children could not be buried there.

"When Gabriel blows his trumpet and we all rise, I don't want to have to travel all over Baltimore looking for my family. I want us all to be together," I said to Reverend Carter.

I talked with Jeanene and Jeanese they both wanted to be buried somewhere else with their families. Jeanene wanted to be buried with her children and Jeanese wanted to be buried with her husband. That was their choice. When I tried to ask Butch his preference of where he wanted to be buried, he didn't want to discuss the subject of my death. I respected that. I'm his mother and he didn't want to face the inevitability of his mother's death, especially when he hadn't yet buried his father.

Jericka wanted to be buried with her father and me. She was heartbroken when she learned that she couldn't be buried with us in the Veteran's Cemetery. Since she wasn't married and didn't have any children, if she wasn't buried with her father and me, she would be buried alone. I didn't want that for her. Therefore, I chose Woodlawn Cemetery, which was close to our home, where the three of us could be buried together. I drive pass Woodlawn Cemetery every day when I drive up Liberty Road. It's a beautiful place but expensive. It was necessary to purchase three lots just as if I were purchasing property to build a house.

I was blessed that I could afford the two plots for Jerry and me. Jericka chose to pay for her plot. But suppose I hadn't been in a financial position to afford the two plots? Purchasing a plot for my husband drove the funeral costs to almost ten-thousand dollars. Plus placing an advertisement in the local paper was over two-hundred dollars. We wanted the programs that were to be distributed at the funeral to be in color and that cost one-thousand dollars. Yet Social Security only pays two-hundred and fifty-five dollars for funeral expenses. That amount only paid for the obituary to be listed in the local news paper.

Jerry's funeral needed to be planned. Who would eulogize my husband? Pastor Reid would be away the week we chose for the funeral. The funeral had to be on a day when Jerry's relatives from out of state could get to Baltimore. A reception following the funeral had to be planned. There were many arrangements to make. I wasn't mentally in a state to take part in any of the details of the planning.

The wake was held at the Vaughn Green Funeral Home on Liberty Road. I went to the wake and sat and watched people coming and going, some I knew and others I didn't.

It's funny but funerals will bring people together who have not spoken to each other in years. My mother used to say to her family when we went to funerals, "I hope nobody in the family has to die before we meet again."

Friends and family members came to the funeral home to view my husband's body and to socialize and fellowship with friends they had not seen in a long time. People I hadn't seen in years showed up at the wake. Had it not been a somber occasion with me losing the love of my life, it would have been nice to see old friends. Friends and neighbors came to our house prior to the funeral and brought food and beverages. We had so much food we donated some to a women and children homeless shelter at a Lutheran Church. I really appreciated that some of the visitors brought toilet tissue, paper towels, napkins and paper plates. People don't realize how important those items are when you have as many visitors as we did.

After viewing Jerry's body in the chapel of the funeral home, some of the guests went into another room to fellowship where refreshments were served. Jerry was a friendly, out-going man, who had many friends, more than I had. After approximately twenty minutes of watching the parade of people, I couldn't take it anymore. It was like watching a social event without the guest of honor being present. Old friends greeting each other, glad to see each other, exchanging telephone numbers and catching up on old times.

"Butch, please take me home. I have had enough of this. It's like a party, friends and acquaintances socializing, laughing and talking with each other. I'm not in the mood for such festivities," I said.

I said my goodbyes to those gathered, promised to stay in touch, got my pocketbook and walked out the door to the car.

Butch drove me home. I took off the new outfit I had purchased for the wake, got in bed and I refused to see anyone the rest of the day.

In preparation for Jerry's funeral I pretended it was an upcoming event such as a party or a backyard barbecue he and I had hosted many times during the years we spent together. I wouldn't allow myself to focus on the grimness of a funeral. In my imagination I told myself that Jerry wasn't at home because he had gone to purchase the crabs and beer for the cookout as he had always done. No, this was going to be one of the Robinson's shing-dings!

I didn't want to wear a black outfit to the funeral, nor did I want a loud-colored outfit. I purchased a dark brown suit to wear to say goodbye to my soul mate.

It was a dilemma determining who would ride in the limousines provided by the funeral home. I couldn't afford to have limousines for all of Jerry's family members to ride in. Some got upset because they were not asked to ride in a limousine. No one from Jerry's family assisted with the funeral arrangements.

When the funeral procession left our home on the way to the church, we drove up Essex Road, and a neighbor I didn't know saluted the hearse that carried my husband's body. That neighbor also stood in the middle of the street and stopped traffic, allowing the funeral procession to pass, showing respect for Jerry and his loved ones. I didn't know the man. He was a slight built white man who appeared to be in his late seventies. His shoulders were stooped and his thinning hair was grey. I didn't know if he was someone whom Jerry had befriended or just someone being neighborly. Whatever the reason, I appreciated his kindness that day.

When the funeral procession arrived at the church, Victor Holliday, a family friend, was waiting outside. The limousine in which Jericka, Butch, Jeanene, Jeanese, Tyneisha and I were riding pulled to the curb. Victor opened the limousine door to assist. I swung my legs out the door in an attempt to stand, but my legs went rubbery. I held onto the door to keep from falling. Victor held my other arm to help me steady myself. After I exited the limousine I looked at the door of the church.

"I don't want to go in there," I said.

I was thinking that going inside was final. I would see my husband for the last time. I couldn't think that this was a forever goodbye. My knees were weak, Butch rushed to my side, grabbed my arm and put his arm around my waist, tears streaming down his cheeks.

"Thanks Victor. I got her," he said.

"It's going to be okay, Ma. I got you. Lean on me," Butch said to me.

We walked inside the church and to this day, I have no idea who was there. We walked in as a family with me leading the way and Butch holding me up and keeping me steady until we reached the casket. I looked upon the face of my handsome sleeping husband, whispered "I love you," and took a seat on the second row. I could use the back of the first row to lean on when I stood up. Jericka sat on the first row directly in front of me, guiding the stream of sympathy-bearing people who had come to pay their respects. Butch sat beside me, still embracing me. He and I were comforting each other.

Months later when we talked about the funeral or about someone I hadn't seen in a long time, Jericka acted surprised and said to me that person had attended the funeral or the wake.

I don't remember all the people who attended the funeral. I do know that I saw people I hadn't seen in over twenty years. Some of them were people whom I supervised when I was deputy administrator of the district court. I left the district court in 1980 when I was appointed deputy administrator of the Supreme Bench, where I worked until 1985 when I left and started my career as an entrepreneur. It was 2004 and Lonnie Furgerson, who was now the chief clerk, and a friend, allowed the employees who knew me when I worked there — from 1966 to 1980 — time off to attend Jerry's funeral.

I went back to the casket and looked at my handsome husband as he lay sleeping, surrounded by and covered with flowers. The casket was gold trimmed in dark wood. I was glad Jericka had picked that one. I gently rubbed Jerry's cheeks with my fingers and whispered to him.

"You look good Baby, and you certainly went out on top of your game."

I walked back to my seat, my son holding my arm to steady me. Then Jericka walked to her father's casket, tears streaming down her cheeks.

"I'm going to dance for my daddy one last time," she said.

She then began to do the crazy dance she did at home when she and her father joked around. She danced in front of her father's casket, tears streaming down her face. Her back was turned to the congregation. She faced her father's casket

"This is for you, Daddy," she said in a broken voice between sobs.

Jericka danced and we cried.

She didn't care if the church was packed with on-lookers who might not understand her erratic behaviors, but God knew, her father knew, she knew, and I knew, that was all that mattered.

At home when she and her father joked with each other, Jericka sometimes did a silly dance to make him laugh. Especially if Jerry was supposed to wake up at a certain time and he wanted to sleep a little later. Jericka would do her crazy dance, make a "whooping" noise and dive on top of the covers as her father lay covered up in bed. He would pull the bedcovers over his head and pretend to be angry with her because she woke him up with her noise and silly dance.

She made up dance steps, waved her hands in the air over her head imitating a gorilla, then she'd turn around and around, shouting and shaking her shoulders; she jumped up and down swiveling her hips making crazy faces, while she poked out her lips and rolled her eyes. Her routine and antics always made him laugh and lovingly called her "goofy."

He used to joke with her and pretend he didn't know her.

"Why don't you go home and worry your own father?" he would jokingly say to her.

"You are my father," she'd reply and hugged him around his neck and kissed him on his cheek.

He pretended to wipe off the kiss and she'd kiss him again.

"No, I'm not your father. I'm just someone who took you in when you were left on my doorsteps."

Jericka would put her hands on her hips and cock her head to the side.

"Yeah, then why does everyone say I look like you?"

"They say if you feed them long enough they'll look like you. That's why you look like me cause I fed you and your mama."

Then he would laugh.

"Leave me out of your lie," I teased.

"What about Jeanene and Jeanese? They look like you too," said Jericka.

"Yeah, well, I fed them too. I fed your mama and Butch but your mama fed Butch the longest that's why he looks more like her than me."

They laughed again.

"Well, it's time to get up and feed us again."

"Your child is crazy and she's from your side of the family," he teased.

She'd throw a pillow at him and he pretended to fuss while he went into the bathroom to take a shower and prepare for the day.

Her father sometimes called her "Little Bit," "Sporty," or "Slick." He also sometimes called me "Slick" as a nick name.

That was her daddy!

At the funeral Bianca and Joshua went into the pulpit and spoke about what their Pop Pop meant to them. I didn't know they had planned that as part of the program. I had been so depressed I didn't know what was planned. They had prepared words to say about their grandfather. I was so proud and moved by their show of love and respect.

Reverend Brenda Carter preached from the title "Endless Love." During her sermon she said, "God was the only one strong enough to take Jerry from Barbara."

I thought that was so apropos.

I told Reverend Carter that I wanted to say goodbye to my husband in my own way. I wanted his funeral to be like a going-away party, a gathering of his friends and family, instead of a time of weeping. I wanted people to celebrate his life rather than mourn his death. Death could not cheat us out of the forty-seven years we spent together. The earlier years of our life together were turbulent but we outgrew them, together.

When my husband and I gave our lives to God and joined a church, we became the people we are today, grandparents, Christians, respected members of various organizations in the church and the community. He and I had known heartache from each other and we learned the joy of forgiving, loving, and respecting each other.

I wanted people to remember the good times my husband and I shared instead of focusing on the bad. I knew there were friends of his in the congregation who probably remembered how Jerry and I used to argue about his drinking, gambling, staying out all night, selling corn liquor from the trunk of his car and other challenges to our marriage. Some of them had been with him when some of those situations happened. Some of them were his drinking and gambling buddies. But none of that past baggage meant anything to me anymore. Regardless of how difficult our life together was, Jerry always respected me as his wife and he demanded that his friends respect me too.

I could have gotten anyone to deliver the message at Jerry's funeral. I could have gotten a member of the Senior Usher Board, a member of our family, one of his friends, or a member of the Bethel congregation. They all knew him and loved him. But I chose to deliver my goodbye my way. I wanted to tell the gathering of friends what my husband meant to me.

After viewing my husband's body, people came to where my family and I were sitting to shake our hands and give words of sympathy. Jericka was the only person sitting on the front row directly in front of me. As people came to shake my hand, she told me who they were. I wasn't thinking clearly and couldn't see through my tears.

Reverend Carter called me to the pulpit.

"Come on Queen. Say your message to your husband as only you can."

I stood up and prepared to walk to the pulpit. My legs were unsteady and I was off-balanced. I stumbled, held onto the bench in front of me and felt someone rush to my side. I didn't know who it was. I just knew that someone was there to assist me.

Then I heard my son's voice.

"It's okay Ma, I got you."

Butch put one arm around my waist, held my hand with his other hand and walked me to the pulpit, propping me up to keep me from falling.

With a show of confidence, I squared my shoulders, threw back my head, put my chin up, and said, "I can do this!"

Butch helped me up the steps into the pulpit. It seemed like the walk to the podium was long but it was only a few steps away. When I reached the podium, I held on to it to keep me steady. I looked out into the sanctuary and saw that it was almost filled with people. I hadn't realized there were so many people present. I cleared my throat, whispered a silent prayer for courage, and paused a few moments to steady my voice.

As I stood in the pulpit, I thought about giving a speech as I had done many times before. I imagined Jerry standing in the back of the room with my books, waiting for me to begin my speech. He and I had played this scene over and over for many years. I pretended this was just another speaking engagement and book-signing event.

When I squared my shoulders and held my head high with a haughty gesture, I was playing the role of a grand dame, about to give her famous motivational speech. The handsome man lying before the altar in the beautiful flowered covered casket was not my husband. In fact, that was not a casket. It was an arrangement of flowers given to me as the guest speaker at this conference. Yes, I was playing this role well.

The ushers, my husband's buddies, were standing proud showing off their new suits, their hands behind their backs, chest stuck out, a proud look on their faces, knowing that the ladies in the congregation were whispering about how handsome they all looked.

Joe Walters, who was one of the ushers at Bethel and Jerry's friend, came to our house to choose a suit for Jerry to be buried in. Joe called me a couple of days before the funeral and asked if he could pick out the suit and tie for Jerry to wear for the last time. He said the Men's Senior Usher Board had asked him to do that.

"We want him to be buried in one of our uniforms so we all can be dressed alike for the last time," said Joe.

I agreed.

All the men of the usher board marched into the Sanctuary behind Jerry's casket, carrying his flowers. Some of them were pallbearers. They took their places lining up in front of the casket, saluting their fellow usher for the last time. They marched down the aisle toward the Sanctuary doing what we called the "Ushers' Dance." Jerry would have been proud of the way he was honored that day by his colleagues.

Jerry loved the Usher Board members. For many years, he and five of his buddies on the Senior Usher Board prepared breakfast each Sunday. Each one took turns preparing the breakfast. After the 8:00 a.m. service and before the 11:00 a.m. service began, they would sit in Jerry's car and eat. Some of them didn't cook so well and gave Jerry money to buy the food and he prepared it for them. On Sunday morning he got up at 5:00 a.m. to cook the food, put it into sealed plastic containers to keep warm and take it to church. He cooked fried chicken, fried frog legs, crab cakes, sausage and cheese, steak and eggs. They really ate well.

I teased him about how God was using him.

"They used to call you 'Trunk Man,' when you and your buddies drank corn liquor you had in the trunk of your car. Now God is still sending you to the trunk of your car to get food for your friends at church. God has a sense of humor."

We would laugh at how things had changed in our lives.

Then my thoughts turned from imagining that my husband was standing in the back of the room with my books, to him standing with his usher buddies, all dressed alike and being admired by the congregation.

I thought I saw him standing next to Joe Walters his main buddy. I thought I saw him look at me and wink his eye as he always did.

I whispered, "Are you flirting with me, Mister?" as I always did.

When I mentally returned to reality, I focused on the fact that my husband wasn't standing in the back of the room. I didn't let myself think that he would never be standing there again. I wouldn't focus on the thought of "Never." Maybe at a later date but not now. I wanted to savor the last moment of him before they closed the casket, the final curtain of a past life both beautiful and painful.

I stood silent a moment to compose myself.

"Take your time Queen," said Reverend Carter, who was sitting behind me in the pulpit in the pastor's chair, as I stood at the podium.

When I was composed and ready, I spoke to the people assembled. I told everyone that when I went to book-signings and speaking engagements, my husband went with me and was comfortable allowing me to take the bows, while he stood in the back of the room selling copies of my books. He knew my successes were also his.

"Thank all of you who have come today to celebrate my husband's going home party. Many of you would have delivered my last words to my husband had I asked you. Some of you offered to do just that and I thank you. But although you could have and would have done an excellent job, I wanted my message to be delivered in my own voice.

"Many of you have read my first book, *And Still, I Cry*, where I present my husband in a not so favorable light. Someone once asked him why did he allow me to write a book portraying him in a negative way? He answered, 'Because I want people to see who I used to be and with God's help see who I have become. I'm not the person I used to be and God is not through with me yet.'

"My husband could have written a book about me. He just chose not to. Our life together may not have been as some of you think it should have been, but it was ours. It doesn't matter what you thought about our life together. What does matter is what my husband and I thought about each other. A relationship that lasted forty-seven years speaks volumes.

"Yes, I'm speaking about the same person I wrote about in *And Still, I Cry*. At one book-signing a person said to him, 'Thank you for allowing your wife to write that book. It sure has been a blessing in my life.'"

Since my husband died in the hospital before he and I could say our final goodbye, I wrote those words as his final words to me. However, I wrote the following poem as my final words of goodbye to him. I know I'll see him again when my assignment on earth is complete, but in the meantime this was my farewell. This poem is called, "Love". I wrote it the day before the funeral. I read it at his funeral while standing in the pulpit, looking down at him lying in his casket. While I read the poem, the Senior Usher Board members stood at attention in front of the casket, facing it.

LOVE

"I know you cannot be with me through the long lonely nights.
I know you will not be there to lie beside me and awake by morning light.
I know that I will no longer have the pleasure that I truly do desire,
To feel your presence comfortable and warm, like embers from a fire.
I cannot sit and talk with you, the way we used to do.
Nor will I be able to enjoy the uniqueness that was you
I cannot hold you close to me, while time goes slowly by.
And every time I think of you I know I'll probably cry.
But I hope my friends will understand that it will take a while
To remember you without crying and instead just smile
I hope they remember that you and I were a team
And to forget about you right away is harder than it seems.
We shared so many memories that I think about each day.
And I know the love we shared is still here to stay.
Although you are gone from me, my love is as strong as the day we met.
And the bond we shared is something I will never forget.
Although you are gone, we will never be apart.
For as long as I breathe you will always be in my heart.
Our love for each other was rare, pure and true

I know I'll never love anyone, the way I still love you.
With you beside me I could walk the highest mountains
of life.
You put me on a pedestal and respected me as your wife.
With your love you elevated me to swim life's troubled sea
You encouraged me to be all that I was meant to be.
Some say you walked in my shadow but to us that was not
true.
You were proud of my accomplishments because they were
yours too.
So, my love, I will live my life like flowers blooming in the
spring.
Because you were my life, my world, my happiness, my
everything.
Through summer, fall and winter, my feelings of comfort
will never cease to be.
For you are now my guardian angel and I know you are
protecting me.
I won't say so long my love, I know you are waiting for me.
I'll join you in another lifetime somewhere across the sea
And so my love, til the sun and moon are only a dream
Til the oceans and rivers become a stream
Til the eye of the needle becomes the thread
Til the tail of a bird becomes its head
Til the day becomes night and the night becomes day
Til homeless people in all the shelters suddenly have a place
to stay
Til hate becomes love, love becomes hate, and the sky is no
longer blue
That is when I'll stop loving you."

As I finished the last line of the poem my voice quivered. I tried not
to cry but the tears began to fall. I stopped talking, bit my lip, and stood
quietly for a few moments, trying to regain my composure.

Reverend Carter whispered, "Take your time. It's going to be all right."

I couldn't stop my heart from beating rapidly. I couldn't stop my feelings from showing. I couldn't stop from feeling as if I were the loneliest person in the world. I couldn't stop the tears.

As I turned to leave the pulpit, Reverend Carter stood up and embraced me.

"You did an excellent job, Queen, as I knew you would. Your husband is smiling from heaven."

I squared my shoulders and tried to look brave and confident. I was relieved to see my son waiting for me at the top of the steps leading from the pulpit, waiting to escort me back to my seat. I walked toward his outstretched hand. He grabbed my hand and led me down the steps from the pulpit.

"Good job, Ma!" he whispered in my ear and hugged me.

As we walked toward my seat, my sister-in-law, Madeline, was standing in the row behind where I was sitting, smiling with teary eyes, Her arms opened, waiting to hug me. That's when I knew I had done a good job.

After the funeral the procession drove up Liberty Road to the Woodlawn Cemetery. Chuck, a family friend, drove my Mercedes transporting friends who were like family and wanted to ride with the family. People standing alongside the street saluted the procession as we drove by. A Baltimore City police motorcycle escort drove in front and guided the procession until we reached the county line. Then a team of Baltimore County motorcycle police officers picked up the lead and escorted us on to the cemetery.

When we arrived at the entrance of the cemetery, the procession drove inside, along the winding road to the site where my husband's body would rest. The police escort stopped at the entrance dismounted their motorcycles, stood beside them, and saluted the procession as we drove by. The procession drove past a flock of ducks swimming in a pond in the cemetery. As we drove by, I heard the ducks quacking, as if they were saying goodbye to my beloved. I didn't know the exact location of the grave site. We drove through the winding pathways of the cemetery until we reached a tent covered site with chairs and an open grave.

The procession stopped at the site, all the cars lined up behind the hearse and pallbearers took the casket to the grave in front of the tent.

Everyone got out of their cars and sat in the chairs until they were all filled. Others stood for the grave-site ceremony led by Reverend Brenda Carter.

Gloria, who had been a friend of mine for over forty years, and her son, Winston, stood in the distance on a hill overlooking the grave site, and watched. Winston was ten years younger than I. Gloria was ten years older than I. I wondered why she didn't join us under the tent. Why she didn't come to be with my other friends who were at my side for comfort. Following the funeral I didn't hear from Gloria until I called her two years later. Since she and I had been friends for so many years. I thought her behavior was strange.

A mound of dirt in front of the tent stood as a reminder of the finality of the event. The casket was on top of the grave, flowers were arranged over the casket, and around the open grave site.

Three Army National Guardsmen dressed in uniforms stood at attention. One held the American flag and another held a trumpet on which he blew "Taps." After he finished the tune, two of the guardsmen took the flag that draped the casket, and folded it in the traditional way. After the flag was folded, one of the young soldiers knelt before me, held the flag in both hands and presented it to me.

"Thank you Mrs. Robinson for allowing your husband to serve his country," said the young soldier as he handed me the flag.

Although I hadn't 'met my husband during his time in the army, I had shared his memories of his time served.

When the young soldier placed the flag in my hands, I laid it in my lap and I couldn't stop the flood of tears. My anguished sobs had my body retching with heartache and sorrow. Butch rushed to my side and held me as we both cried.

The casket was slowly lowered into the grave. I looked at the grave and saw my love being lowered into the ground. The mound of dirt lying on the side ready to be thrown over the heavy metal box, called a casket was a reminder of how final this event was. At that point I became aware of my own mortality. I was reminded that regardless of what happens, I would someday join my husband. My life's journey would end the exact same way, being lowered into the earth with dirt thrown over me.

I had tried to maintain my composure throughout the funeral. I had walked out of the church with my head held high. I thought about Jackie

Kennedy as she walked behind her husband's horse-driven Hearst and how the country talked about humility and she was a woman of substance. During the funeral and the journey to the cemetery, I tried to maintain that same type of control, but at the grave site, I could no longer hold back the grief. I cried out loud with anguish.

Lehman Strauss, author of *When Loved Ones Are Taken in Death,* writes, "We set out on the journey of life with high hopes. These hopes are often built upon plans we have made. We think in terms of our children's needs, their happiness, educational and future careers. We plan retirement with our mate in marriage. But one day we are suddenly stopped cold when the icy fingers of death snatch away one of our precious loved ones. Physicians, surgeons, nurses and friends, all have done what they could to save the life, but in the gracious and perfect providence of God, death has conquered. That life is now beyond recall. Nothing in this entire world can bring back those whom God has taken in death."

How well I understood those words that day as I watched my husband being lowered into the ground and knowing it would soon be filled with dirt. If we are going to live a kingdom life in this world we must define our role in it. I had no idea what my role would be now that I was walking the earth without my mate.

Two years later the young soldier who had knelt in front of me at the grave site and presented the American flag to me, who had thanked me for my husband's service in the army, was killed in Iraq. The truck in which he and three other soldiers were riding was bombed.

"Thank you young man for your words of comfort on my day of pain. May God welcome you home. When you get there, please shake my husband's hand and let him know you met me."

TRYING TO COPE

"Come to Me, all you who labor and are heavy laden and I will give you rest," Matthew 11:28

I am writing this paragraph today, August 25, 2004, two weeks after I buried my husband. He died at Union Memorial Hospital on August 2, 2004 and was buried in Woodlawn Cemetery on August 9, 2004. In the forty-seven years of us being together, this is the first time we have been separated this length of time. This is a strange feeling, being without him; he was a part of my life for so many years.

The first week following my husband's death I couldn't sleep at night. My doctor prescribed sleeping pills for me, but he would only give me a no-refill prescription. He knew, and so did I, that the pills only masked the pain, and that sooner or later, I would have to go through the sleepless nights without the pills as a crutch. I figured it was better that I do so sooner than later. So, I stopped taking the pills and sleep came to me little by little. It was two hours the first few nights, then three hours and then it progressively increased until I was finally able to sleep through the night.

Many people tried to separate us. They told him lies about me and told me things he supposedly had done. One thing I will say about my late husband, regardless of how rocky our marriage was at times, he didn't allow any of his so-called friends to speak negatively about me.

One night while he was in Sands Bar, which was directly across the street from the project building where we lived, Karl, one of his drinking buddies, called me a bitch and told Jerry he had seen me with another man. Jerry hit Karl in his mouth and knocked him on the floor.

"Don't you ever call my wife a bitch again!" shouted Jerry as he stood over Karl. "If I don't see my wife with another man, I don't want to know about it. Don't ever come to me telling me anything about my wife!"

The dazed, embarrassed, Karl got up, rubbing his chin and walked out of the bar.

That was the way Jerry was. Regardless of the marital problems he and I were having, he did not allow any outside force to separate us, not even members of his family.

The forty-seven years that Jerry and I spent together equate to over seventeen thousand days. If I focused on the one day that he died rather than focusing on the seventeen thousand days we shared, I would be doing our entire life together a disservice. We didn't allow anyone or anything in life to separate us and I will not allow death to cheat me out of the beautiful memories I savor of my life with a wonderful man. I will not cry because it's over, instead I will smile because it happened. Yes, my heart still aches and as long as I breathe, I will remember him but also as long as I breathe, he lives in my memories.

After Jerry's death I went into a state of shock. One day when Bianca spent the night at my house, my plans were to take her home after we had breakfast, then drive to my office on Montgomery Street. She and I had breakfast, we each took a shower, got dressed, I put on my makeup, and drove her home. I dropped her off at her father's house and waited until I saw her safely go inside. Then I went to the dry cleaners and got my clothes, went to the post office and mailed some letters, returned home, took off my clothes, got back in bed and watched television. I decided that I didn't want to go to the office that day. I didn't want to be around people. I wanted to lie in our bed and be alone with my memories. I could still feel Jerry's presence in our bedroom and I could still smell his cologne.

I wasn't ready to make changes in our house. I wanted things to remain as they were when Jerry was alive. I wasn't ready to give away all of his clothes, I gave some away. I cleaned out the dresser drawers and the chest in the bedroom. I threw away his under clothes. I didn't think anyone wanted them. I gave his shirts and sweaters and some of his suits to a men's homeless shelter. I gave his shoes to Adolphus, a man who worked for our company for over twelve years. But I couldn't give away his leather coat, his hats, and neckties. June 2010, I was finally able to emotionally let go of his hats and neck ties. I gave the hats to Buzzard, a family friend, and the neckties to Wendell, Jeanese's husband — my son-in-law.

I depended on my family and friends to help me through my journey of sorrow. It was hard for me to accept Jerry being gone forever, it gives such finality to his existence and to our relationship. I kept waiting for him to come through the door.

An electronic security system protects our home and whenever I am alone in the house I activate it. Each time someone enters the house through the front door the system chimes until it is deactivated by entering a number code. The system allows sixty seconds for the code to be entered, otherwise a signal will transmit to the security monitoring company indicating an intrusion. If an intruder attempts to break into the house, a signal is transmitted to the security company. The company will call my house to verify if everything is okay. If they are given our code number, the company will know that it was a false alarm. However, if someone at my house does not answer the telephone or answers the telephone and does not know the code number, the security company will call the local police, who will come to our house to see if everyone is safe.

Jerry always entered the front door, took off his coat, and put down whatever he was carrying before he deactivated the system. That meant the chimes rang a long time before being deactivated, and with every move he made the keys on his key chain rattled. I always knew when it was he who entered. I thought he allowed the chimes to ring too long. But that was Jerry.

After he died, I found myself listening for the chimes. I sat in our kitchen, looked through the sliding glass doors onto the backyard, at our swimming pool, and imagined I saw him walking around the patio, with the long-handled pool cleaner picking leaves out of the pool as he always did. At night I turned over in bed and listened for the sound of his soft breathing. I walked into our bedroom and imagined I smelled his cologne. I just could not imagine my life without my partner.

Jerry was always there for me. I prayed for God to help me deal with my grief. Every song on the radio reminded me of our life together. I believe that if God brings you to troubles and heartache, He will bring you through them. I had to rely on that belief to sustain me during my period of grieving. I received many words of comfort from my friends, the words, flowers, cards, baskets of fruits were all appreciated and needed, but they didn't take away the pain and emptiness in my heart.

I was hurting too much to be of any use to my family. I didn't want to get out of bed in the morning. I walked around the house all day wearing my nightgown and robe. I wouldn't comb my hair. I didn't even want to write anymore.

Jerry and I had an active social life. We were always attending parties, crab feasts, and back yard cookouts at the homes of his friends. But after his death I canceled all the engagements that he and I had planned to attend. I didn't want to be around people and have them feel sorry for me. I didn't want to hear the pity in their voices when they spoke of Jerry and me. I knew they were compassionate and actually felt my pain and shared my grief, but I was selfish, I wanted to feel the pain all alone.

I wasn't perfect but I rationalized that my imperfections were a result of Jerry's womanizing. I blamed him for the life I was leading but the truth was, I had choices. I chose to be in the streets, to go out every weekend and drink and smoke pot with my friends. I didn't have to commit infidelity, but I did. I called my behavior "payback." I was paying Jerry back for his unfaithfulness. I was getting revenge. But the truth is, revenge wasn't as sweet as I thought it would be. I compared every man I was with to Jerry and they all came up short. I wish I could take back the years I wasted looking for what I already had.

We all make mistakes when we are young and when the marriage is young. But one of the biggest mistakes couples make is not trying to work through their troubles together. My husband and I both made mistakes. We violated our wedding vows by being unfaithful to each other. That meant we brought other people into our relationship. But we still maintained a level of respect for each other. Although we both were unfaithful, we didn't let the other know it. We still tried to hide our infidelity. We suspected that each was unfaithful but we couldn't prove it. We didn't try to prove it. I don't think either one of us wanted to know for sure if the other was unfaithful. I'm glad we didn't try to prove it. Suspecting is one thing, knowing is another. As long as we didn't know for sure, we could continue to lie to ourselves, saying it didn't happen.

But when we realized that we really did love each other and that people who tried to break us up were envious of our relationship, we decided to stay together and not let anyone or anything come between us.

Jerry and I didn't rehash our past indiscretions. As the years rolled by we forgave each other without admitting any wrong-doing, and God forgave us both. One night Jerry and I decided we would confess to each other if we had been unfaithful. We were going to "come clean," and not keep any secrets from each other.

"You go first," he said.

"No, you go first," I said

"If you tell me what you did, I'll tell you what I did," he said.

"Jerry, you must think I'm a fool. I know as soon as I say that I have done something wrong, and I'm not saying that I have, but if I did, you would hold it over my head forever, and you still wouldn't admit that you have done anything wrong."

"Okay, so that means that you have been untrue to me?"

"No, that's not what I am saying. I'm saying if I did have something to tell, you would get angry and never let me forget it. Just like now, I haven't even said anything and you're getting upset."

"I'm not getting upset. Is there something you want to tell me?" he asked.

"Yes! I want to tell you that I love you and let's stop this madness. I don't have any secrets," I said.

"Neither do I. This was a bad idea."

We ended the conversation. I don't understand why partners in a relationship have a need to "confess." If they have been unfaithful and the other person in the relationship doesn't know, why tell? Confessing is only inflicting pain on the receiver of the message. What you don't know doesn't hurt. Many relationships are ruined because one partner has a need to "tell all." You will ruin someone else's life because you have a need to feel relieved of the burden of guilt? Let guilt be your punishment to never do it again but don't draw someone else into your web of pain.

When God forgives us for our transgressions, He doesn't keep a tickler file on our past.

He doesn't say, "My child, you asked me for forgiveness last week for the same thing you did this week. You are asking forgiveness again?"

If God can forgive an old sinner such as me, why couldn't I forgive my husband? It didn't matter what people said about us and our relationship. Our life was ours to share. We were a team. The only people we needed to please were ourselves and God. I don't care what the gossipers say. Everybody has baggage.

Most of us don't want to talk about death until the final moment arrives and we are forced to face our own mortality. We don't prepare our insurance papers and other legal documents for the inevitable. We leave our family members to handle our personal bills after we are gone. We often don't leave enough money to pay our funeral expenses, the mortgage, car, and other bills. After the death of a partner, we suddenly realize that we have become single. Often the surviving partner doesn't know how to manage those things because they were always managed by the deceased partner.

When my husband was in the hospital he tried to tell me where our insurance policies and other important papers were kept. I didn't want to listen to such talk. I didn't think I would need to know those things for many years to come. I thought he and I still had a lot of living to do. We had already planned trips out of the country we would take together, when he was well enough to travel. We planned to visit Australia, China, and Egypt. He hated to fly but traveling to those places was my dream and it became his.

Perhaps he knew he wasn't going to live much longer, and in his own way he tried to prepare me. Although I wouldn't listen, I thank God that our important papers were kept in a certain file. At least after his death, I knew the general location of where they were. I felt relieved when I found the insurance papers.

Jerry's creditors began calling me concerning debts they said he owed. I called a family attorney and asked if I was responsible for my deceased husband's credit card debts, car payments, and other personal debts he left behind. I didn't know if the bill collectors were legitimate or bogus. The attorney advised me that if Jerry's personal bills were in his name only and he hadn't left an estate, I was not obligated to pay his personal debts.

The letters I received from Jerry's creditors were addressed: "To the estate of Jerome Robinson, Sr." I contacted the creditors and informed them that my husband had died and didn't leave an estate.

One creditor asked if Jerry left a house.

"Yes, he did. But the house is not in his name only. It is in both of our names," I answered.

I thank God that the mortgage was in both our names. Had it been in Jerry's name only, I would have been forced to sell the house to pay his personal bills.

It was when I was alone with my memories late at night, after the funeral was over and all family members and friends had gone back to their own lives that the heartache was the most severe. That's when I really needed the telephone to ring. I wanted to talk to anyone about anything, I just wanted to hear a human's voice. But it didn't ring. It remained silent as if I had been forgotten. Friends had paid their respects. They had sympathized with my sorrow and shared my grief. I guess they felt there wasn't anything more they could do for me. They couldn't bring my husband back; therefore, it was time for them to move on, to go back to their reality. I understood their feelings, but understanding them didn't take away my loneliness.

Jerry always brought in the mail from our mailbox, which was on the side of the road at the end of our driveway approximately four car lengths away from our house. He was proud of that mailbox he made of wood and stood on a metal initial "R." Sometimes days passed and I never thought about the mail, I knew he would bring it in.

After my husband's death, I came to recognize the sound of the mail truck's motor as it drove up our street. I could tell when the mail man stopped at the house next door and when he stopped at our house. I looked forward to receiving mail every day. I lived for the letters and cards of sympathy. I even looked forward to receiving advertising flyers, grocery store pamphlets. I welcomed any form of communication from anyone. But after a while, the cards and letters stopped coming and the telephone rarely rang. As people went back to their regular routines, I was left to find a meaning in my life, something to keep me from feeling depressed and alone.

I thought about taking a drink of alcohol each day to get me through the day. We kept the bar in our club basement filled with top shelf liquor, so it was easy for me to have access to whatever I wanted. I started sipping mixed drinks, cocktails, rum and coke. After a couple of days of drinking alone, I thought about how I felt growing up in a household where my mother was an alcoholic. I remembered watching her dreams die as alcohol consumed her every wakening hour. I didn't want that for me. I had worked too hard throughout my career to watch my dreams die in a bottle of alcohol. I didn't want to become dependent on alcohol. I stopped sitting at home drinking and started going outside the house and getting involved with other activities such as attending social events and community organizations. In the beginning I felt uncomfortable attending alone. But slowly my confidence built up and I began to look forward to other activities. Sometimes I could talk either Jericka or Butch into going with me. Sometimes I went with friends. Other times I traveled alone.

Some of Jerry's habits annoyed me. He would pass gas in the morning when he first woke up. He sometimes belched after he had enjoyed a good meal and I had to frequently remind him to put his hand over his mouth. His breath did not smell so good when he turned over in bed to tell me, "good morning." When he came in the house after cleaning the yard or inspecting the houses we owned where people with developmental disabilities lived, he needed a shower, he brought the odors into the house with him. He would leave his dirty socks on the floor and he left the toilet seat up after he used it.

Those annoying habits are now memories I cherish. They were a part of him. Some of them showed how much I depended on him but failed to appreciate the role he played in our company and in the maintenance of our home. I don't feel his cold feet on me in bed in the winter anymore, but I wish I did. I don't have to feel his toenails scratching my leg in bed when he let them grow too long, but I miss that. He's not here to contradict everything I say so that he can say, "I told you so," but I wouldn't mind if he did.

Jerry knew me better than anyone. We shared intimate moments of what pleased each other sexually. He knew how loudly I snored at night because I had sleep apnea, but it didn't matter to him. He knew how I looked the first thing in the morning before I combed my hair and put on makeup and he still thought I was pretty. I had a fear of the dark and I didn't like going into our basement alone. No matter what time of night it was, even if he were asleep and I needed to go into the basement to the laundry room, I'd wake him up and without complaining he would get up and go with me.

I miss the thoughtful things he did for me such as waiting for me at the back door while I parked my car in our car port. I miss him calling me on the telephone at the office during the winter months to tell me not to stop and get anything to eat that he was going to cook. He either had fried fish, cooked potatoes and onions, or had hot soup waiting for me when I arrived home. He waited until I arrived home so we could eat together. If I told him I liked a certain thing such as chocolate Tandy Cakes, or he knew I liked to use a straw when I drank from a glass, if he saw those things, when he went shopping he bought them by the case. Two years after he died I was still using the case of straws he bought for me.

I miss the silly things he did to make me laugh, such as meeting me at the front door wearing only his brief undershorts and a cap turned backwards

I wish I had told him how much I appreciated the little thoughtful things he did for me such as: sending me flowers each Mother's Day, giving me a box of chocolates every Valentine's Day with a giant card signed "With love from your husband."

I wish I had said, "I love you," more often. I hope he knew how much I did love him.

I didn't eat breakfast in the morning as Jerry did. I had gotten accustomed to getting up in the morning after he left for the office and finding either a sausage, cheese and egg, or a bacon, cheese and egg sandwich waiting for me on the kitchen stove. Sometimes he made my lunch and packed it into plastic containers so it would stay fresh. There were times I didn't want the sandwich or I had something different in mind for lunch, but I never told him. I always took the sandwich and pretended I wanted it. I figured if I said I didn't want it, there may come a time when I did want it and he'd stop preparing them for me. So I just took the sandwiches and sometimes gave them away.

At Jerry's funeral, Faye, a woman who was a member of the Board of Trustees at Bethel, whispered in my ear, "I'm going to miss his breakfast sandwiches."

I had to pause to think about what she meant. Then it dawned on me, when I was a member of the Trustee Board, Jerry made a breakfast sandwich for me every Sunday morning. Sometimes I didn't want it and pretended that I forgot it and left it on the stove at home. Thinking he was doing me a favor, he would bring it upstairs to me in the church where we were counting money after service.

"You would forget your head if it wasn't attached to your body," he teased.

I smiled, took the sandwich, kissed him on his cheek and pretended to be grateful that he brought the sandwich to me. When he went back downstairs I gave the sandwich to Faye. Faye died in 2008.

I'm glad he was there to share so many memories with me. Good or bad they were our memories and no one can take them away. When I hear Yolanda Adams sing, "This Too Shall Pass," I know the message is for me.

One Sunday in church during morning services, Pastor Reid talked about letting go and leaving negative thoughts and old hurts behind. I felt he was talking to me. I felt that God was sending me a message.

Months after Jerry's death, he visited me in my dreams. It was as if it were our secret that he was still alive. The scenes in my dream were real to me I couldn't wait to get to bed each night so my husband and I could be together again. It was like being in another world, a world where only Jerry and I lived.

In my dreams I went through my regular routine of going to the office and conducting business, but at the end of the day, I returned home to where Jerry was waiting for me.

I found it amusing that everybody thought my husband was dead and only he and I knew the truth. I felt that I was living a secret life about which no one knew. This dream continued for almost three weeks. The dreams didn't come every night but they did come.

Then one night in my dream, Jerry and I attended an event together. We returned home and just as I was about to kiss him, he changed. His face became a mummified skeleton resembling death. At that point, I realized how final everything was. I realized that my life with Jerry was really over. The dreams never returned again. It was as if God knew I couldn't let go and he was giving me time to stand on my own.

WHEN MY HEART CRIED

"Peace I leave with you. My peace I give to you," John 14:27

In December 1988, sixteen years before my husband's death, I was working as a counselor in an Employee Assistant Program (EAP), on a contract STAR had with a federal agency. STAR was my for-profit company I founded five years before I founded SelfPride.

Diane, an employee at the agency had lost her husband, Brian, in an accident seven years prior to her meeting me. Brian was on his way home from work one dark rainy night, when he was hit by an oncoming train as he crossed the railroad tracks behind his house. He was taking a short cut home when his foot got wedged between the rails. He couldn't get free in time to get out of the path of the on-coming train. Diane was having difficulty coping with her husband's death. She visited me in my office twice a week for grief counseling.

Her co-workers and members of her family thought she was grieving too long. They thought she should have let the pain go and moved on with her life years ago. Diane wanted to stop grieving and she thought her friends and family were right, she had been grieving too long, but she couldn't stop crying whenever she talked about Brian. She couldn't stop feeling lonely at night when no one else was around. She couldn't stop comparing her life now to what it had been before her husband passed. She couldn't stop feeling envious of her friends whose husbands still came home from work each day. She was feeling guilty for still grieving.

One day when she came to my office, it was apparent she had been crying. Her nose was red, her eyes swollen and red from rubbing them. She walked into my office, and as soon as she sat down, she began to cry. I handed her some tissues and let her cry. When she was able to control herself she spoke.

"I feel so helpless. I can't stop crying. My husband has been dead seven years and I'm still crying over his death. It's not every day that I cry but it's every day that I miss him. Sometimes I get overwhelmed and I can't stop the tears. All my friends say I should get over it and they're right. But every once in a while, when I think about him, I cry. Does that make me weak?"

"No, it makes you human. Sure, you need to get on with your life and not allow your life to be consumed by your past. I know people tell you it's time to move on, and they mean well. But you are the only one who can determine the length of your grieving time. Don't dwell in the past. Don't stay focused on your hurt, you are the only person who can tell yourself when to move on."

Diane was clutching her purse in her lap, she opened it and pulled out a tattered, worn letter-size piece of paper. She had been nervously fiddling with the straps of her purse the entire time she sat in the chair, twisting them around and then untwisting them. She handed me the folded paper.

"Someone gave me this to help me cope with my grief. It has helped me somewhat, I don't think I cry as often as I did, but I do still cry. Maybe the message can help someone else," she said.

I reached for the paper. It was a letter someone had written to her to console her. I glanced at it quickly and put it in my desk drawer. I didn't want any distractions from our conversation. It was obvious that she needed my attention at that moment. She must have felt the need too.

"You don't have to read it right now. But maybe somebody else might need to read it sometime. I hope it's useful."

I smiled and we continued our conversation. I listened while she talked. When she visited my office the following week, she appeared to be more relaxed than she had been the last time we met. She walked to the sofa in my office, sat down, crossed her legs and smiled.

"Wow! You seem to be awfully happy. What's the occasion?"

"I went out with my sister last weekend and I really enjoyed myself. I took your advice and stopped comparing every man I meet to my late husband. I made up my mind that I'll just enjoy who God sends into my life."

"Great, that's a start! I read the letter you gave me and I can understand how the contents may have helped you. Thanks for sharing it with me. I'll keep it for future use," I said to her.

"I thought about what you said last week. I still miss Brian, but I no longer feel guilty about missing him. I know my family is only trying to help me and I appreciate their support, but I no longer feel that I owe them an explanation about why I still cry."

"Do you think you're still crying too often?" I asked.

"Maybe I am according to their reasoning. But as you said, I should be the one determining how long to grieve."

"Do you think your grief is interfering with the quality of your life?"

"You know, at first I did. I'm not going to lie. I thought I was still alone because I still missed my husband. But when I thought about my conversation with you, I'm content not dating right now. My sister thinks I should start going out more. Although I enjoyed being out this past weekend and I always enjoy going out with my sister, but I'm not going to make a definite promise that I'll go out every weekend. If I meet someone, it's okay but I'm not looking. I guess that was my problem too, missing Brian and trying to please my family. Right now I'm just concentrating on pleasing me."

"I'm so glad you're now at least beginning to live in the present."

"I feel better than I did a few weeks ago. I'm glad you're here to help people like me."

We talked until the hour was over and made an appointment to continue the following week.

Two years later STAR's contract with the federal agency was over. Therefore, I never saw Diane again. I often wondered how she progressed with the new counselor. I forgot about the letter she had given me. When STAR moved out of that office, I cleaned out the desk, packed everything relating to that contract in a box and stored the records and files in a file cabinet in my home office.

Twenty years later, while going through some papers, I came across the paper Diane had given me all those years ago. I felt as if God was sending a message to help me. It was 1988 when she gave the letter to me and 2008 when I found it again. When I read it, I felt as if it was written to me.

All my friends, colleagues, employees, neighbors, and church family knew that my husband had died. I had a need to be alone at times and hoped they understood that during the time I was alone, I was trying to determine what to do with the rest of my life. I knew I had to go on with my life but I didn't know how. I didn't know what to expect as I journeyed through life without my husband. I appreciated my friends being patient with me during my grieving period and trying to understand my pain and what I was feeling. With each passing day after Jerry's death I got closer to my recovery, my healing.

I realize that everyone don't deal with death the same way. I had used that same statement many times to people whom I counseled during their time of grieving. I used that same logic trying to help others but now, it was my turn to take my own advice. It was difficult to do. Being on the outside looking in, I could understand other's pain and could help direct them through it. But when I was in the same situation, I didn't know what to do, how to react to my loss.

Some of my friends and associates found it difficult to cope with me and the pain I was feeling. They didn't know what to say to comfort me. They were reluctant to engage in conversations about Jerry and did not want to upset me; they seemed to tip-toe around mentioning his name.

They tried to give me advice.

"He's in a better place and you must go on with your life," they said.

They were right, he is in a better place, I didn't need them to tell me that! Knowing that he's in a better place doesn't lessen my pain of missing him. When writing about my husband's death in this book it was difficult for me to say he had "died," or that he is "dead" or his "death." It was easier to say he "passed away," or say, when I "lost" my husband, or dealing with my "loss." The words "death, dead, dying," all seem so cold and harsh.

Some of my friends and colleagues had also lost a loved one and dealing with my pain may have made them remember their own lost. I needed my friends, and family to help me cope with my pain. That's the selfishness of grief. You don't think about the pain of others, you're too busy trying to cope with your own.

I had experienced the death of my mother, father, grandmother, grandfather, other relatives, and I have even lost a baby when she was seventeen days old. But the death of my husband, someone with whom I shared my dreams, my secrets, and my most intimate thoughts, was and is a grief like none other I have ever known. But since I had to go on with my life, I had to also learn to handle my grief.

After my husband's death, for months, sometimes I needed to cry, and at times, I still do. But I don't want people to tell me that crying won't help. It does help. My crying spells usually only last a little while. It may be a fleeting moment that I will remember my husband's smile or a statement he said to me, and I'll begin to cry. I sometimes walk past the dresser in the bedroom we shared and the scent of his cologne reminds me of our time together. When I drive by the cemetery where he is buried I often whisper to him.

"Hello, Baby. I miss you. I wish you were here. I hope you knew how much I loved you and always will,"

Sometimes while driving or even while riding in a car with someone else driving I'll turn on the car radio, hear a song that Jerry and I both enjoyed, and I'll cry. When I have crying spells, I don't need anyone to say anything. I may need someone to sit with me, hold my hand or hold me and let me cry the pain away for that moment. After the pain lessens, I'm okay again, until the next time.

One sunny morning in September right after Jerry died I was sitting at my kitchen table, looking out onto the backyard. My thoughts were of Jerry and I silently began sobbing. I thought I was alone in the house, but I felt a hand on my shoulder and it startled me. It was Bianca. She had walked into the kitchen and saw me sitting alone. I turned to look at her and she saw the tears streaming down my face. She put her arms around me and hugged me until I stopped crying. She never said a word. She just let me cry and she cried with me.

She was thirteen years old and it was as if she knew I needed to cry. I thank God she understood my needs. I marveled at how wise she was at such a young age. She seemed to understand that I would soon be finished with my crying spell.

When my crying ceased, I hugged her and said, "Thank you for understanding. Ma Ma will be okay."

During the weeks after Jerry's death, there were times when I needed to talk about him. I wanted someone — anyone — to be around and listen to me. I just needed to talk, no one needed to say anything, and I needed to reminisce about our life together. There is nothing anyone could have said to bring him back to me. God took him to heaven, but when I talked about the life we spent together, the memories forty-seven years made, I felt closer to him, as if he were present, as if he were still with me.

Two weeks following his death Eva, a colleague of mine, came to visit. She had never visited me before nor has she visited me since. I was glad to see her. She and I had collaborated on business contracts with the State where we provided training to people on welfare. Eva is someone with whom I have a professional relationship. We had only been in each other's company at business meetings. STAR was doing business with the company where she worked. She had learned of my husband's death, came to my home to pay her respects. It was one of those days when I needed to talk. She and I spent the entire visit — four hours — with me talking about Jerry. Although she had never met him, she didn't interrupt me. She just listened and laughed at the right times. I was grateful to her for that time. Talking meant a lot to me, it helped ease my pain. Later I sent her a letter, thanking her for helping me through that difficult day, by lending me her attention.

When the wound of grief was fresh, during conversations with friends, I sometimes repeated myself and told the same story about Jerry over and over again. I forgot I had said that particular thing to that particular person before. I just wanted to talk about my life with my husband. My memory was not up to par immediately after his death, but with time, it got a little better. I'm glad my friends didn't remind me that they had heard that story before. They reacted as if they were hearing it for the first time.

There were times when my friends or staff at the office caught me daydreaming, remembering the good times I shared with my husband. Bianca and Jericka caught me daydreaming all the time, while sitting in my kitchen looking out at the backyard. I may have been remembering the backyard cookouts and imagining Jerry standing at the grill, wearing shorts, tennis shoes without socks, a sleeveless tee-shirt and a baseball cap turned backwards, barbecuing spare ribs.

Sometimes as I sat at my desk in silence, staring into the distance, crying softly, my staff came into my office to talk and let me share my memories with them. Although they saw me crying, they stopped by anyway. I'm glad they did. Their kindness was what I needed at that moment.

There were times while thinking about Jerry, tears welled up in my eyes, Jericka would notice the tears and began cracking jokes, or she'd do her crazy dance, like she did for her father, and that made me laugh.

During the early days of my grieving, my friends noticed that my attention span was shorter than it had been before Jerry's death. During certain conversations, I tried to concentrate, but it was difficult. I tried to continue my daily routine at the office but would get depressed, leave and go home. I tried to finish writing my books with the same pride and confidence I did when my husband was alive, but I had lost interest in those things. I eventually improved, I just needed time to grieve, my way.

After I listened to conversations from some of my staff, I realized that by shutting out people close to me, I was being selfish. I was acting as if I was the only person affected by his death. My husband and I were together at the office every day, but after his death, I wanted to be alone and reflect on our life together. I wanted to shut out everything and everyone else and keep his memory personal. I would imagine him sitting in his favorite chair by my desk. And when the chair was empty, I pretended the reason he hadn't been there all day was because he was out driving one of our buses and he would walk into the office at any moment. I wasn't thinking about him having a wonderful personality, being a likable person, having a lot of friends who too were grieving over his death. It never crossed my mind that they too may be hurting and feeling the void his death left. I was selfishly concentrating on my own pain.

My pain was so deep I didn't think that anyone in the world had ever felt that horrendous feeling. My emotional pain was so great that it affected me physically. There were rocks rolling around in my stomach. I had a constant headache. I didn't have an appetite. I felt a tugging at my heart, and I had no desire to do anything. I just wanted to be left alone.

If I saw a friend at the supermarket, standing in line at the bank, or at the dry cleaners, I would corner that person and began to talk about my husband. I probably made them feel uncomfortable when I talked on and on. I knew I was being selfish but I couldn't help it. I just needed to talk. After a while the grief lessened. I was able to see my friends on the street, or see my staff at the office and smile about that portion of my life.

After the death of your loved one, you may start remembering little things that you should have done, or should have said. They may be things that you should not have done, or should not have said. But either way, it's too late to have regrets.

If I had one more day with my husband, I would change my attitude about unimportant things on which I placed importance. I would enjoy being his wife and knowing that he loved me. He married me. There may have been times when we argued about me being jealous of him flirting with other women, and maybe those accusations were true, but one thing was for sure, God was the only one who took him from me. It doesn't matter now how many times he flirted, how many times he had been unfaithful; he always came home to me. He never left me.

I focus on the good times we shared, and there were many. I focus on remembering that whenever he purchased tickets to a social event, like a cabaret, jazz show, crab feast, or any type of gala, we always went together. When the kids were little, we would get a babysitter and we both went out together on weekends.

So many times I wish I could take back the mean things I said to my husband and the mean things I did that were so unnecessary. If he cooked himself something to eat and left dirty dishes in the sink, I refused to wash them.

"They can sit there until they grow whiskers!" I said in an adamant voice.

Eventually he would wash them but it would have been so much easier if I just went on and washed the dishes. It may have been just one plate or one pot, it didn't matter. I was trying to "teach him a lesson."

I sometimes got annoyed when my husband watched me undress. He would lay on the bed, his hands behind his head, and watch me. But, oh what I would give to feel his arms around my waist just one more time!

"Stop looking at me as if I were a piece of meat!" I said in an agitated voice.

He'd turn his eyes to face the wall, but when I wasn't looking, his gaze would again take in my body. I would get angry and go into the bathroom to finish dressing. I was really annoyed at myself for having gained weight, and I took my anger out on him. I was embarrassed at the sight of my sagging breasts that were once full and pleasing to look at. I didn't want him to look at my protruding belly and the extra rolls around my waist. But when I think back over those moments and remember the pleasing look on his face when he looked at me, I now feel that he was looking at me with the look of love. Although we had been together for many years, he still found me attractive. I wish I had understood that before he was gone, the feeling of being loved for who I am died with him.

When we first married I weighed one-hundred and five pounds and wore a size nine dress. In some dresses I wore a size seven. I had a small waist and I loved to undress in front of my husband. The sight of my nakedness excited him. And now there we were, forty something years later and he still enjoyed watching me undress. Only I wasn't accepting it as his enjoyment, I didn't want him to gaze at my overweight body and compare my body to other women he knew or had known. It was my own jealousness and insecurity that kept us from enjoying our time together as much as we could have.

I wish I had let the past go. I wish I had forgotten about Jerry's past transgressions and past acts of infidelity and concentrated more on the present, the "now" time in our lives. He didn't let the past rob us of being who God meant us to be. I allowed the past to rob me of some beautiful memories. But I thank God that I didn't allow the past to rob me of all the precious memories, because I eventually learned to leave the past in the past. I learned to let go of unpleasant memories and to live in the now of life.

FACING A NEW TOMORROW

"And let us not be weary in well doing, for in due season we shall reap, if we faint not," Galatians 6:9:

Losing my husband wasn't the first time I had to reinvent myself because of a loss, but it was the worst. The manner in which I left employment with the Maryland Court system in 1985, after an eighteen year career, devastated me. Judge Porter, who was the Administrative Judge at that time said, "Either resign or I'll fire you."

I had done nothing wrong other than refuse to be treated as a second class citizen because of my race and gender. Jerry was my rock, my shoulder to lean on. When the judge ordered me to resign, I felt that my career was ruined. I was forty-seven years old and I thought I was too old to look for another job that paid the kind of salary I was earning working in the court system. I had worked in the judicial system in Maryland for over eighteen years.

Judge Porter didn't have the authority to fire me without the consent and approval of the judges who were members of the Personnel Committee, plus the majority of the votes of the twenty-three members of the Supreme Bench; therefore, he asked me to resign. He had tried to get a majority vote but failed; I had an impeccable track record working in the Maryland Court system and the majority of the judges did not agree with him. He wanted me gone because I didn't fit the norm of the way he thought employees should behave. I wasn't a "Yes" person. That was during the years when the court system wasn't kind to people of color, especially women. I was one of those people who "didn't know her place," as he said many times to other judges.

I would go home and share my anger and frustration with my husband, and we comforted each other. He was experiencing similar treatment at his place of employment but he could contact his union for help. We had no such union in the court system — I was an at-will employee. The fact that I did not have to go through those years alone helped me survive. I am thankful that God allowed my husband to live through those times so he could be a comfort for me during my ordeal.

I had defended Kelly, a secretary who worked in the medical records department under the director, Dr. Smith (not his real name). Dr. Smith was a friend of judge Porter — not his real name.

One weekend, Dr. Smith hosted a catered birthday party at his home. That Monday morning he brought the leftover food to his office for his clerical staff, who were all black women. Kelly, also a black woman, refused to accept the leftover food, and her refusal upset Dr. Smith. In a meeting that evening with the court administrator and me, Dr. Smith talked about how he was dissatisfied with Kelly. He said she was too "high and mighty" and because she wasn't receiving public assistance — on welfare — she didn't know her place.

It aggravated me that a white man would say such a thing about a black woman, that she didn't "know her place." It also angered me that he felt comfortable enough to say those things in my presence, as if I would think such remarks were acceptable. However, that was the way things were when I worked in the Baltimore City court system in the 1960s, 1970s and 1980s. I couldn't let his comments go unchallenged.

"You mean because she didn't want your leftover, cold, stale, food, she doesn't know her place? Where do you suggest her place is, Dr. Smith?"

I was heated and my feelings showed in the tone of my voice.

"All I'm saying is the other girls in my office were grateful for the food. What makes her so different?"

He was annoyed that I had the audacity to question him. He was accustomed to doing what he wanted to do in his department until I was elected deputy administrator. How dare I, a black woman, question a white man, especially one with his credentials?

90

"First of all, the people who work in your office are not 'girls.' They are women. Second, accepting your leftover food was their choice. Not accepting your leftover food was Kelly's choice. Quite frankly, I would not have accepted your leftover food either. For your information, like me, Kelly came from welfare to where she is today. She went back to school to learn secretarial skills. She wasn't acting 'high and mighty' she was being herself."

I excused myself and left the meeting. Needlessly to say, Dr. Smith didn't like me siding with one of his employees. He told Judge Porter about our conversation and Judge Porter confronted me. He said my comments were insulting to Dr. Smith and I should apologize.

I refused.

"Dr. Smith's comments about Kelly were insulting and disrespectful to me. It is he who owes Kelly an apology for saying those things about her. He also owes me an apology. It was insulting to me that he talked about Kelly to me."

Judge Porter didn't like what I said. He turned and walked away. His actions and attitude warned me that my career with the court system was in danger.

I fought for African American employees to get raises, — although we were not called "African American" at that time, we were "Colored." I had seen the black race go from being called "Negro," to "Colored," to "Black" and finally to "African American." There was a time when if you called a person of color "black" those were fighting words. However, after the riots of the 1960s, when the mantra was, "Black Power," the word "black" referring to a person of color was acceptable.

Judge Porter sent a message by his law clerk that I was to resign or I would be fired. I went to the office of a judge whom I thought would help me. When I asked him to intervene for me as one judge to another, he started talking about how good Judge Porter had been to him.

"He's not such a bad judge. I asked him for certain days of vacation and he approved them," he said.

I was fighting for my career and this judge talked about receiving vacation days.

Another judge told me not to mess up my career by trying to file charges of wrongful termination.

"These lawyers will have to appear before Judge Porter again after you're gone. I don't think you'll find anyone in Baltimore to take your case. If I were you, I'd resign and find something else to do with my life. You're a bright woman, use your skills in another profession."

It was clear that I would have to fight my battle alone. I decided to use that time to start the business I had always said I would start, someday. I took the last judge's advice and thought about what he said. I had worked in the court system for eighteen years; surely I learned something during those years. I thought about what I liked to do — write, design, and implement human resources training and development programs. I started thinking about how could I market those skills, and that's how STAR Associates, Inc., was born.

Thank God that my son was astute enough to manage the day-to-day operation of our family business. When I started STAR Associates, Incorporated in the basement of our home, twenty years prior to Jerry's death, I used an unemployment check and prayer as startup capital. Jerry kept the bills paid at home while I used my money to finance the business. Five years before he died, Jerry took an early retirement from his job in the chemical division at the W.R. Grace Company and started working full time in our family business.

The man Jerry had become was not the same person who started out years ago looking for happiness in a liquor bottle, night clubs and fast women. Joy came into our marriage when we both put our faith in God and realized how deeply we loved each other and how blessed we were to have a family such as we had.

We owned and operated three companies. STAR Associates, Incorporated, our for-profit company provided transportation, human resources training and development. SelfPride, Incorporated, our nonprofit company provided residential facilities for people with developmental disabilities and troubled youths. BeuMar, LLC was formed to handle my publishing and products associated with my writing and motivational speaking. All three companies were headquartered in our office building on Montgomery Street.

Jerry was the site manager for the eight residential facilities owned and operated by SelfPride, Incorporated. He also handled the management of the BeuMar Building. That meant he and I saw each other every day at the worksite.

Jerry would frequently walk into my office and take a seat in one of the leather-cushioned chairs that sat in front of my mahogany L-shaped desk. Sometimes he would sit there and I ignored him. After a few minutes he'd get up and leave. I could tell when he wanted to talk about something that I felt could wait until we got home. If something was on his mind — regardless if it was personal or about the family — he wanted to discuss it right then. He and I had many arguments at the office about conversations that I felt we should have discussed at home in private.

After his death I lost interest in the day-to-day operation of my companies. Butch also lost interest, but he kept the business going. He and his father were extremely close. Jerry was an integral part of the operation of the business and after his death it was as if a part of the business died with him.

Although we talked about how much we wanted to get out of the business of providing care to people with developmental disabilities and how much we had come to dislike it, Butch and I still held on, not willing to let go. He had a mortgage, a car note and two small children to support. We both were afraid to let go of the paychecks we received every two weeks. I loved providing a better life for our consumers but the surveyors from the Office of Health Care Quality (OHCQ), the agency that monitored the operations of health care providers and the agency that issued the license to operate, had their own personal agendas. Some applied their own interpretation of state and federal regulations. They also did not monitor all agencies equally and fairly.

After I won the election to the House of Delegates, I started looking into the way state agencies that allocate state funding operate. In an effort to discredit me OHCQ revoked SelfPride's license to operate community-based residential facilities. The Developmental Disabilities Administration (DDA), stopped SelfPride's funding and removed the consumers from SelfPride's homes. DDA alleged the residents in SelfPride's homes were in "imminent danger." SelfPride had been in operation for over eighteen years and all of a sudden people were in "imminent danger."

God said vengeance is His, He will repay. He also said He would make your enemies your footstool. He allowed Judge Porter to twice see the results of His work.

It was 1996 when I was inducted into the Maryland Women's Hall of Fame, the Maryland Commission for Women asked each inductee to submit names of individuals to whom we wanted to send invitations to attend the induction ceremony, held at the Governor's Mansion in Annapolis. Among the names I sent, was Judge Porter's. He didn't know who had invited him he just knew it was an invitation from the governor. It sure did my heart good when, at the induction ceremony by then Governor Parris Glendening, Judge Porter was in the audience watching me receive an award.

Years later, on Tuesday, December 4, 2007 in the Carl J. Murphy Fine Arts Center at Morgan State University, I attended the Inaugural Ceremony of Mayor Sheila Dixon, the forty-eighth mayor of Baltimore City. By that time, I was already a delegate and was invited in that capacity. Both Judge Porter and I were standing in line, waiting to be seated on stage with the other dignitaries to witness Mayor Dixon take the oath administered by the governor of Maryland, Martin O'Malley. Governor O'Malley was the forty-seventh mayor of Baltimore. Sheila, was at that time president of the Baltimore City Council. In 2006 when Mayor O'Malley entered the race to become governor of the State of Maryland, Sheila became the acting mayor of Baltimore until the election in September 2007. She was then elected mayor by the voters, becoming the first woman and the first African American woman in the 213 year history of Maryland government, to be elected mayor. She's also a personal friend of mine.

I turned to Judge Porter extended my hand for a handshake and with the biggest smile on my face I said, "Hello, Judge Porter. Remember me?"

"Yes, I do. How have you been?"

"I don't know if you remember me or not but I am now Delegate Robinson. I just want to say thank you for the push!"

He looked puzzled, as if to ask what I meant by, "push?"

I said nothing more.

I turned my back to Judge Porter and began talking to Ann, another state delegate standing in line with us. Ann had been engaging in a conversation with Judge Porter. It appeared they knew each other. I spoke to Ann in a voice loud enough for Judge Porter to hear me.

"I worked in the Maryland Court system over twenty-two years ago and I remember Judge Porter from those days."

Ann looked at Judge Porter and smiled.

He returned the smile.

"He must have been quite a supervisor if you remember him all these years," said Ann.

"No quite the contrary. As a matter of fact, he was the reason I left the court system, and you know what? That was the best move I ever made. I just thanked him for giving me the push to leave. Otherwise I would probably have spent years working in the court system, being miserable and waiting for retirement."

After I said that, I ended my conversation with Ann and walked on stage to my assigned seat.

God had allowed me to be blessed through Judge Porter. Although at the time I saw things differently. Rather than looking at my resignation as a blessing, at the time I thought it was devastating, but God had different plans for me. Leaving the court system was the best thing that could have happened to my career.

God has a way of making you move to the next step. Sometimes you may pray and ask God to remove a person from your life. Or you may be in a relationship and you pray that God stops you from being hurt by the relationship. The relationship may be an unhealthy one and you are not strong enough to break the bonds. God may have other plans for you. He may want to elevate you to a higher level in life but He can't do that until He moves an obstacle from your life. The obstacle that is keeping you from receiving your blessing may be the relationship or the other person in the relationship.

Therefore, since you are not mentally or emotionally strong enough to move from your residence or to walk away from the relationship, God will let the other person in the relationship push you away. That person may do something that makes it impossible for you to stay in the relationship.

That's what is meant by "a set up for a comeback" God sets you up for a comeback. You will come back stronger than you were before. But first

God has to get your attention. He has to get you in position to receive your blessing.

If my husband had lived, I would not be in politics. A political career was the farthest thing from my mind. I probably would have written several more books and Jerry would have traveled with me on speaking engagements and book-signing tours. But a political career? Never!

We don't have the courage to let go. We live in the past while still trying to embrace the future. We don't live in the now of life. We don't realize if we constantly live in the past we are living under conditions of the past. We don't realize that the future will soon become the "now" of life.

God in His infinite wisdom knew that my husband's season and assignment were over. I didn't realize it because I wanted to hold on to what I knew, what made me feel good, and that was Jerry's love for me. But God knew it was time for me to leave the court system. That assignment was over and He used Judge Porter to move me. He knew that the health care industry was over for me and he used DDA and the legal system to move me. My life as a wife was at an end because God had other issues for me to tackle. He used the death of my husband to move me. It was God's way of setting me up for a comeback. He was letting me know that it was time for me to move on.

GROCERY STORE ANGEL

God uses different methods to send us blessings.

Death does not show partiality, nor does it discriminate. Death comes when it wants to come and it comes in different ways. Memorial Day 2005 was the most difficult time for me. This was the first Memorial Day. This was the first Memorial Day without my husband and the first time we were not planning a Memorial Day backyard cookout.

I didn't want to go grocery shopping that day. Jerry and I had always shopped together. Sometimes he went to the mall with me to shop for clothes. He didn't like shopping with me but he went anyway, just because I wanted him to go. He'd get tired, sit on a bench in the mall, and wait for me while I went to different stores shopping. Sometimes I saw something I wanted in one store, I wouldn't purchase it right away, instead I went to several other stores to see if I could find something I liked better or to compare prices. But the majority of the times I returned to the first store to purchase the first item I saw. That boggled Jerry's mind.

"All I have to do is walk into a store, see what I want, buy it and leave. It's that simple. I don't understand why women go to so many stores and return to the first store and buy something they saw when they first started shopping," he said.

I laughed. I understood exactly what he meant.

"It takes us women longer to make up our mind. We must be sure we have found the right item and the best price," I said.

"Women!" he'd say and throw up his hands in exaggerated exasperation

I didn't realize how much I really depended on him in so many small ways. Even if he didn't go grocery shopping with me he waited for me at home to help bring the groceries into the house. I called him from my car phone as I pulled into our driveway to tell him to come and help me with the groceries. He met me at the back door, took the groceries from the car and into the house.

After his death, I had to get into the habit of shopping alone. It was difficult to drive my car into our driveway and he not be there waiting for me. Many times I sat in my car and cried, not wanting to go into the empty house.

It had been eight months since Jerry's death and I still couldn't get into the habit of shopping for one person. I only wanted to purchase a few items and leave. Shopping for one person took more time than shopping for two people. I didn't know if I should buy a gallon or a half-gallon of milk. I hadn't realized that not much food is packaged for single servings. It was difficult to find a loaf of bread that didn't spoil in my bread box because I did not use it in time. I couldn't use a whole loaf, it was too much. But it seemed that no one thought about single packaging food for one person such as widows, widowers, and people living alone.

The day was the Saturday before Memorial Day in 2005. Memorial Day was Monday May 30, 2005. Most people celebrated the holiday Sunday because they would not have to go to work Monday. If Jerry had been alive, we would have celebrated Sunday after church, so that his friends from the usher board could stop by and eat steamed crabs with him. He would have bought a bushel of steamed crabs, sat in the backyard, had baby-back spare ribs cooked on the grill, using hickory smoked charcoal. Our grandchildren would have gone swimming in our backyard pool.

Before I left to go grocery shopping I was remembering how it once was when we planned Memorial Day activities. Memories started flooding my mind. I stood in the kitchen looking through the patio door, out over the backyard and the pool and imagined him standing over the grill turning the sizzling ribs over white coals, while the smoke from the burning charcoals permeated the air, circulating around the neighborhood alerting the neighbors that the Robinson's were cooking out.

Jericka walked into the kitchen and saw me standing quietly looking out the sliding glass door. She pushed back the sliding door and exposed the screen patio door which let in the cool breeze. Although it was the month of May, the weather was breezy. She must have also been thinking of her father and knew I too was thinking about how we would be celebrating this holiday if he were alive.

"To celebrate the holidays, Daddy would have bought a bushel of steamed crabs," she said. "He and his friends would be sitting at that table over there eating them and drinking beer."

She pointed to an outdoor wooden table by the pool.

"Yeah, and the picnic tables and chairs with the umbrellas would be arranged on the deck around the pool," I said.

Although we had an in-ground heated pool, even when the weather was too chilly for the kids to go swimming, they went anyway. They liked to get in the water and play. Their "Pop Pop" loved to sit and watch them playing in the pool. Sometimes he got into the water with them. He would splash water all over the place pretending to swim and hadn't moved an inch. He couldn't swim but let him tell it he was the best.

I hugged Jericka and got my pocketbook and car keys.

"I'm going to the store. I'll be right back."

"You want me to go with you?"

"No, I'm not going to buy much. I'm just going up to Giant's. We're not expecting a lot of people like we did in days gone by."

I tried to add humor to make the time seem happier than it was without Jerry. I wasn't particularly interested in grocery shopping. My heart wasn't in having a cookout, but I didn't want to disappoint my grandchildren. It was a family tradition to have a backyard cookout on Memorial Day, Fourth of July and Labor Day. I hadn't made a list of the menu as we always did. I was just playing by ear. The pain of losing Jerry was still raw, and that particular grocery store held many memories. It was the closest store to our house and the store where Jerry and I frequented most often.

I went to the giant's grocery store, grabbed a shopping cart, and walked up one aisle and down the other. I looked at the ice cream, the Klondike Bars, Jerry always bought those. They were his favorite. When he and I shopped together I would walk down one aisle getting food and he would disappear down another, getting goodies for our grandchildren. At least that was the excuse he always used, but the truth was, the goodies were as much for him as they were for our grandchildren. He was a big kid at heart. That's why our grandchildren were so crazy about their, "Pop Pop" he could relate to them on their level.

Jerry would purchase the crates of baby-back ribs from the slaughter house. He went to his favorite place in Anne Arundel County to get the crabs, but everything else, including the ice, was bought at the Giants grocery store near our house. Regardless of what else we purchased, he always put steaks into the grocery cart. He loved steaks on the grill. Even if we weren't having a cookout, he put two steaks on the grill for him and me.

We would have my homemade "tater" salad. I always teased him about that.

"You buy 'potato' salad from the store. I make 'tater' salad. Don't be calling my taters 'po'."

He would laugh.

We cooked beans on the grill to get the smoky charcoal flavor in them. I made slaw, and always fresh collard greens, seasoned with smoked neck bones, smoked turkey tails, and I sometimes made Mexican corn bread. I would bake several sweet potato pies and cakes for dessert. Jerry often said, since my mother died, I made the best pies he had ever tasted. I didn't mind being second best to my mother.

We didn't have to have a reason for a backyard cookout. It could have been the Fourth of July, one of the grandchildren's birthday, Memorial Day, Labor Day, Jerry's birthday, my birthday, Mother's Day, Father's Day, Christmas when snow was on the ground, it could be raining, or just because it was a beautiful day. I sometimes stood in the rain holding an umbrella in one hand and turning ribs on the grill with the other. Or I may have been wearing snow boots and a heavy coat turning ribs in the snow.

One Christmas when we lived on Laurel Drive, it was snowing and we decided we wanted barbecue spareribs. Jerry made the fire in the backyard grill. I was standing outside when our next door neighbor, Helen, saw me and came outside holding a camera.

"Barbara, I didn't believe my eyes. I had to come out and see for myself. To make sure my eyes weren't deceiving me. I just had to take a picture of this. No one will believe me if I told them my neighbor was outside in snow knee-deep, cooking ribs on a grill."

We both laughed.

"Yep, it's me! We decided we wanted ribs. I told Jerry if he made the fire in the grill, I would cook the ribs, so here we are."

"They do smell good and they look good too."

"They're going to taste good too."

We laughed again while she continued taking pictures of me with her video camera.

I knew she wanted some of the ribs. Jerry asked me if I was going to send her some.

"No! She thinks I'm crazy for being out in the snow barbecuing. Why should I send her any?"

But as I thought about it, she was a good neighbor and I did look strange out in that weather, especially after a snow blizzard. So I sent her some ribs by one of my children. She called me and said how good they were.

"The only thing wrong with them was there wasn't enough."

"I laughed but I didn't take the hint that she wanted more. I just skipped all over that. I wasn't about to send more.

In the meat section at Giant's, I searched for a small steak for me. A woman dressed as if she had just come from church, still wearing what I call her, "Church hat," walked over and stood beside me. I watched as she picked up a large package of T-bone steaks, looked at them, held them a moment, then dropped them into her cart. She hesitated a moment longer, took them out of her cart and put them back into the meat case. She turned to go and once again reached for the pack of steaks. She saw me watching her and smiled.

"My husband loves steaks on the grill but at these prices, I don't know if I should spend that much money for them, He can eat ribs and hamburgers with the rest of the family," she said and started to walk away without the steaks.

I swallowed, trying to hold back my emotions, my throat felt as if knots were in it. I fought back my tears. As she walked away, I touched her arm to get her attention. She stopped and turned to face me. She looked puzzled as if to say, "I don't know you. Why are you touching me?"

But she said nothing. I spoke.

"You are blessed to have your husband still with you. My husband died eight months ago. I would give anything to eat steaks with him again."

I picked up the package of steaks she had put down and handed them to her. As I spoke I fought to control the tremble in my voice and I kept blinking my eyes to hold back the tears.

"Buy him the steaks and cherish every moment you spend eating them with him. Tomorrow is not promised to us. Don't have regrets over moments gone, moments you could have enjoyed."

She shook her head and I saw tears in her eyes when she placed the steaks into her grocery cart. Without saying a word, she hugged me and wheeled her cart away. I turned and pushed my cart across the length of the store to the dairy products section. There I stood, trying to decide which size carton of milk I should buy. I finally decided not to buy the milk, knowing it would spoil before I used it all. Then I moved on to the ice cream section. My eyes were misty. I couldn't decide about the ice cream either. My heart was heavy so I walked away without any.

I started walking toward the cashier and, I saw the lady with the steaks coming towards me. On her face was the brightest smile. She walked toward me her eyes holding mine, I could swear a soft halo circled her head. She came closer, I noticed the item she held in her hands and tears began falling down my cheeks.

"I saw you standing at the ice cream section. But I didn't see you get anything. I decided to help you decide."

She placed a large package of Vanilla Klondike Bars with nuts, into my cart.

"When you go through the line, they will know these are paid for."

She leaned over and placed a gentle kiss on my cheek, smiled and walked away. I wanted to tell her what she had done, what the Klondike Bars meant, but still unable to speak, I watched her walk away, tears clouded my vision and rolled down my cheeks. Those were the kind Jerry would have purchased, how did she know, I wondered?

I put the thought out of my mind, paid for the groceries, carried them to my car and drove home. I was feeling sad when I arrived home and realized I hadn't bought enough items for the cookout. I went downstairs in the basement to look in our big freezer to see what was there before I went back to the store. I opened the freezer and a packet of steaks fell out of the freezer. I caught them before they fell on the floor. On the freezer bag were the words written in my handwriting "May 29, 2003, steaks from Bullock's."

That was a year prior when Jerry and I went to Bullock's to have dinner and purchased a half of a cow. Bulloch was a place in Westminster, Maryland that raised cows, and packaged the meat for freezing; they also had a bakery and a restaurant. I held the packet in my hands, thought about the woman in the grocery store, I walked back upstairs to my kitchen, sat in a kitchen chair and cried.

I whispered to my husband.

"Oh, you haven't forgotten me, have you, Baby? I know you are with me today. You want me to have our family cookout as usual."

The woman was Jerry's angel and the steaks were to let me know he was there with us at our annual backyard cookout.

The ribs didn't come out right, neither did the barbecued beans. I had tried a different recipe than I was accustomed to using. Big mistake! I got the recipe from a show on television but I should have cooked everything my traditional way.

My children told me, "Don't make changes to recipes when it's not necessary. Like you always say, 'If it ain't broke, don't fix it.' Stop experimenting with our food, trying something new. Stick with tradition!"

I was trying to deviate from tradition, hoping to find peace in dealing with my grief by trying something new. But it didn't work. I sat in the kitchen and talked with my son about the backyard cookout. When I thought about Jerry not being here to handle the grill anymore, I couldn't stop crying. After the tears, I felt better. I had to tell myself that it's okay to cry sometimes and then move on.

One day I was feeling down, thinking about my life and how different it is today. Forty-seven years being with someone spoils you for being alone. I thought about how fine he was, how he liked to wear jewelry, a ring on his pinkie finger, a diamond ring on his wedding finger, a gold watch on his left wrist, gold bracelets on his right wrist, and gold chains around his neck. No fake, all real gold and diamonds, either he purchased them from the jewelry store or I gave them to him as gifts for Christmas or for his birthday. He always smelled good, and he wore expensive cologne. I know, since I bought it for him. He went to the dentist regularly and had his teeth cleaned. He still had all his teeth and the gold crown on one tooth on the left side of his mouth was always shining. He wore beautiful clothes, and his shoes always matched his pants. He was five-feet-eight-inches of love and weighed one-hundred and seventy-five pounds. He didn't exercise often but he was still in good physical condition. He didn't have a potbelly like most of his friends did. Maybe it was because he played golf every chance he got.

Anyway as I started to say, I was feeling sad while thinking about him when Jericka came home from work and told me about her day.

"Guess what? Remember Mandy, the white woman I told you about who didn't like me and after I was promoted and became her supervisor she submitted her resignation?"

"Yes, I remember you telling me about her."

"Well, she walked into my office today and asked if she could withdraw her resignation for July 30 and make it for August 30. I told her I didn't have any problems with that. After all I wasn't asking her to resign, that was her idea. Then she started telling me about her father."

"Her father, what about her father? I thought she didn't like you, now she's telling you about her personal problems?"

"That's what was so strange! She started tearing up when she talked about her father. She said he's seventy years old, completely bedridden, and wears adult diapers. Her mother has to take care of him. Mandy has a sister who lives a few blocks from their parents but she doesn't help her mother take care of their father. Mandy also has a brother but he lives out of state. Mandy is the only person around to help her mother. Mandy says her mother never asks her for anything so when she asked Mandy to help with her father for a week, Mandy felt her mother was tired and needed a break. Mandy says they have an aide who comes to assist her mother, but the bulk of the care rests directly with her mother."

"What happened to her father?"

"She said two years ago he had blood clots in his leg. He went to several doctors including specialists and they couldn't find anything wrong. After several painful months finally a doctor discovered that his leg was literally rotting. They had to amputate his leg up to his knee. Following that he learned that he had sugar diabetes and he had to inject himself with insulin every day, then he had to go on a dialyses machine.

"Her mother had to take him for treatments three times a week, then his heart started failing, he had a stroke on his left side and now it's like he has just given up. He can feed himself but he won't. Mandy's mother has to do everything for him even change his diapers. He'll only eat when she feeds him. Mandy says it's depressing going to visit them. She said her father used to be an outgoing person, he and her mother enjoyed an active social life and they were always together.

"'I just can't bear seeing him waste away. I know I shouldn't say this, but I feel he would be better off dead. At least he won't be suffering like he is now. And my mother seems to have aged ten years within the past year. She just looks so tired all the time,'" Mandy said.

Mandy wiped tears from her eyes.

"I told her to go home and help her parents! I said to her 'After all, you know how I feel about family! To me family comes first!'"

I looked at my daughter and tried hard to fight back the tears.

"Who does that sound like?" I asked Jericka.

Jericka's eyes got misty.

"It sounds like Daddy," she said. "When Mandy talked about her father, I thought about Daddy. I told her what you said about being glad that Daddy went out on top of his game. She said you're right. It's hard for her to watch her father just a shell of the man he used to be."

I thought about my handsome husband and how I missed him. But I also thought about his failing health. He too had blood clots in his legs. His legs had swollen so badly he could no longer wear his shoes. He had to wear sandals and he hated that. He had started giving himself injections of insulin in his thigh and after his heart operation the doctors told him he would have to go on a dialyses machine. I thought about him lying in bed, wearing diapers, not being able to take care of himself. He wouldn't have wanted to live like that. I miss him, God knows I do. It's so lonely being without him. But I am also glad that he went out the way he lived, with dignity.

A WALK OF FAITH

"But without faith it is impossible to please Him, for he that commeth to God must believe that He is, and that He is a rewarder of them that diligently seek Him." Hebrews 11:6 —

Smile even though you don't feel like smiling. Get happy first then God will turn things around for you. When we live a stressful life, we open up our immune system and that which makes us susceptible to disease. Learn how to get back your joy. According to Proverbs 17:22, your prayers will be answered if you change your attitude.

Faith in God is the only thing that kept me going after my husband died. Depression resulting from grief seemed to mentally weigh me down. Faith in God's promises and faith in my support group — my family — gave me hope that I would bounce back and become the confident person I had been prior to my husband's death. Some people have trouble believing in something unseen and placing faith in intangible things. But can you explain life? What makes a baby form in the human body as a small seed and grow to become a man or a woman? What makes huge trees grow from a small seed and what commands that all life end in death?

It would be great if God allowed married men and women or people in committed relationships, to live without their partner for a few months so they would appreciate them. "You never miss your water until your well runs dry," is a true statement.

God uses us even when we don't realize it. I wanted to write a book about romance, but God had other plans for me. He wanted me to write a book of poems and motivational quotes. I don't know where my book *Mind Bungee Jumping,* came from. I was sitting in the Arena Playhouse Theater with other authors at a reading and book-signing event where I realized that every author there was a poet, except me. I told the master of ceremonies to call me last. I sat in the back of the auditorium and wrote a poem called, "Live Your Dream."

When it was my turn to go on stage and read from my work, I read passages from my books. When I finished, I concluded with my new poem. After I read it, people in the audience wanted copies. However, I wouldn't sell it, hand written on a piece of yellow paper with scratch-outs. I went home, and for over six months, poems continued to pour from my mind. Everything from the sound of my husband sleeping, to my grandson doing his homework on Black History, presented a poem in my mind. It was as if a floodgate was suddenly opened in my head and poems came gushing out. When I finished, I had written fifty-four original poems. Jerry was my motivator. I finished my book, *Mind Bungee Jumping,* a few weeks before he died; however, it remained unpublished for more than five years. I didn't realize it until after his death that his presence was in every word and every line of every poem.

Jerry would be in bed sleeping while I sat in my favorite chair, worked on my book manuscript, and wrote poems longhand on a legal pad. The television would be blaring, the bright ceiling lights and the table lamp lights were on shining brightly, but he never complained. There was an office joining our bedroom where I could use the computer, but I wanted to be near Jerry. Listening to his soft breathing was a comforting sound.

I thought new furniture and a fresh environment would help me with grieving, and to an extent, it did. I rearranged the furniture in some rooms and replaced the furniture in others. The first thing to go was our bedroom set. I donated it to a non-profit organization so it could be sold to help people with disabilities and troubled youths. I gave away the chair I sat in while writing poems and manuscripts for my books. Although I replaced the chair with a more expensive one but rather than being inspired to write while sitting in the new chair as I had been while sitting in the old chair, I fall asleep. I learned that it wasn't sitting in the chair that inspired me to write, it was being near my husband, feeling his presence and listening to him breathe, that gave me a comfortable feeling from which I gained inspiration. The portable writing table I used regularly while lying in bed beside him has not been used since his death.

I had new carpet installed throughout the house and new ceiling fans installed in all the rooms and donated hundreds of books to Goodwill Industries. I replaced our kitchen set with a different type. I was trying to reinvent myself by starting over as much as I could, beginning with my surroundings.

I didn't realize how much along the road to healing I was, until I talked to Anna, a friend with whom I went to high school, who lost her husband eighteen months prior to me losing mine. I had been a widow for eight months but I found myself comforting her.

She lived in another city and one of our childhood friends called me to tell me to get in touch with Anna because she was really taking the death of her husband hard. I called her on the telephone.

"I met my husband my first year at college. I walked across campus and walked right into him. We became inseparable, we dated that first year but I knew he was the one. I knew we would be married. We were married for forty-seven years. He was my life," she said.

"That's the same way I met my husband and we were married for forty-six years but we were together for forty-seven. So I understand your pain," I said.

"Only people who have experienced this kind of pain can understand."

She was right.

Different people handle pain in different ways, some cry, some fight, some overeat, some result in other violent behaviors, some become alcoholics, some become drug users, some retaliate, some use a combination of behaviors.

"When you smile, the world smiles with you, but when you cry, you cry alone." is a true statement. Try it if you don't believe me. If you walk down the street and smile at strangers, ninety-five percent of them will smile back at you, even though they don't know you. But if you walk down that same street crying, I'll bet you not one person you meet will start crying with you. Now if you stop and tell them a sad tale of why you're crying, some sensitive, emotional person may feel sorry for you and shed tears. But that's only after you have explained your reason for crying. If you smile at people whom you don't know, you don't have to tell them the reason for your smile. Just the fact that you smiled will often be reason enough for them to return your smile.

I could use the excuse, "If I hadn't been born into a family in which I was born, I could have been a writer, an actress, a singer, or anything else I wanted to become." But I could have done other things. I allowed myself to get caught up in drugs; to have children before I was matured enough to understand the responsibilities and the importance of parenting; before I had seen the world, and before I was old enough to be a nurturing mother. I could have stayed in college instead I chose to be with the "in-crowd."

Marriage isn't easy. It takes work, a lot of compromises, and a lot of give and take. Sometimes you may have to give more than you take. You may have to give more than the other person in the relationship is giving. Don't give up on your relationship because he or she wasn't what you expected. A lot of times our expectations are too high.

My husband and I would get up at five o'clock Sunday morning, dress for church so that we could arrive for six o'clock morning Bible class, before the eight o'clock Sunday morning services began. One Sunday morning as we dressed for church, I watched him, put on his tie and I smiled.

He looked at me and returned my smile.

"What're you thinking about?" he asked.

I stopped putting on my stockings, and looked at him. I glanced at the clock on the night table beside our bed, looked back at him and smiled again.

"I was just thinking. We sure have changed. There was a time when we would be just getting home this time of morning, after being out drinking all night. We would be trying to beat each other home. But now, here we are getting dressed together, preparing to go to the same place, for the same purpose, to serve God, and we're both happier."

He nodded his head in agreement and laughed.

"You know, you must be reading my mind. I was thinking the same thing."

We both smiled hugged each other and continued dressing.

When people ask me what made my husband and I stay together as long as we did, given the turbulent life we led being married. I tell them, I don't know of any couple that has stayed together that hasn't had to overcome some obstacles. Some allow those obstacles to drive them apart rather than pulling them together. There was no blueprint or formula that my husband and I used to save our marriage. When things were not going right in our marriage, I did not sit at home feeling sorry for myself, eating and getting fat. No, I found other things to do, things that interested me. Sometimes I found other people to do those interesting things with me. Don't sit around the house alone throwing a "pity party." If you do, you will often find that you are the only one at the party.

Many marriages fail because one or both parties committed adultery, or because of money issues. Some marriages fail during the older years, because if one party inflicts pain on the other through infidelity, "playing around," they call it — depending on the number of years invested into the relationship, they aren't willing to forgive.

Many marriages fail during the early years of marriage, because the individuals in the relationship aren't ready for someone else to always be in their physical space. It takes more than a notion to share your living space with someone else. When you wake up in the morning, he or she is there. When you go to bed at night, that person is still there. You have to get accustomed to sharing the bathroom with someone and get accustomed to their personal hygiene habits that you didn't know about. You really don't get to know a person until you live with them.

LIFE BEYOND SIXTY

"A man is not old until regrets take the place of his dreams," — John Barrymore, 1943

If someone tells you that you are too old, tell them, "the older the wine the greater the kick."

You determine what's too old. Growing old is nothing more than a bad habit that a busy person has no time to form. Remember you only go around once in life and this is not a practice run. Don't worry about what people say about you, follow your dream.

I'm not looking for another love. Truthfully, I don't think there is another man who can take the place of my late husband. He often said that he knew me better than I knew myself. I denied it, but he was right. He spent many years getting to know me. I, on the other hand, just lived my life without any thoughts of getting to know myself. Some days I felt differently about the same thing. Jerry and I had gone through tough times together and survived. Our younger years were wild ones as most young people's are. However, we eventually settled down and became the people whom God meant us to be.

Society often implies that people over sixty don't have sex drives. There is a myth that they are not interested in sex. The thought of people, especially women over sixty, engaging in sexual activity is repulsive to some people. How dare they think feelings die because the skin becomes wrinkled and the eyes dim. That does not mean the mind has become dim. In the year 2030, maybe the world will understand that sex is forever. As long as you live you will have sexual urges.

Each person is unique and different. What satisfies one person does not necessarily satisfy another. Notwithstanding, there are people in their thirties and forties who don't want to engage in sex, for whatever reason. All I am saying, is just because you find yourself over the age of sixty does not mean that you suddenly don't think about sex.

When a woman loses her partner, her lover, her spouse, who has been with her since they were young and desirable, she finds that attracting a sexual partner can be extremely difficult in her golden years. Men don't find her body as desirable as when she was young. It's the younger women, who get the attention. Men in their sixties are attractive to younger women but women in their sixties are not necessarily attractive to younger men. Younger women think an older man is sexy, distinguished looking, dashing, and suave. Younger men think of older women as a mother figure, or a financial source. In recent years, people began to refer to women who were attracted to younger men as cougars.

One of my cars is a green convertible Mercedes-Benz. Sometimes Jerry and I rode to church together in either his car or in mine, and sometimes we used separate cars, depending on what we had to do after service. One Sunday we went to church in my car with me driving; however, when we left church Jerry wanted to drive home. He got behind the wheel and put the top down. I got in on the passenger side. There were several young people who appeared to be in their late teens standing on the sidewalk by my car. They had not attended church; they appeared to be hanging on the corner, smoking cigarettes. They watched Jerry put the top down, and made comments about how cool the car was. One young man whistled and said to the crowd:

"Damn! You see that M...F...go down? (referring to the convertible top). Man, that's a slick M...F...!" (They actually said the word).

Jerry grinned and pulled away from the curb. As we drove away, someone in the crowd shouted to us, referring to Jerry.

"Watch out Killer! Don't hurt nobody with your bad self. You're looking good!"

Jerry grinned, waved and profiled — leaning to the right and driving with his left hand.

The following Sunday when we left church, I drove home. I got behind the wheel and put the top down. Jerry sat on the passenger side. The same crowd of young people was standing on the same corner as they had been the previous Sunday. We drove past and someone in the crowd shouted.

"Look out, Grandma. I see you!"

Jerry was "Killer" I was "Grandma." Was that double standards? Yes! But that is the way of society.

When an older man attracts a younger woman and marries her, he is congratulated for his, "trophy wife." He shows her off to his friends and family as if to say, "I still got it. I can still attract a young good-looking woman."

But if an older woman is with a younger man, he must be after her money.

They'd say of her, "She's robbing the cradle. Why would she make a fool of herself being with that young stud?"

But the truth is, older men often cannot satisfy the older woman. His penis does not respond as it once did and the thought of an implant is repulsive to some women. Taking Viagra may work for some men, but if they have high blood pressure, diabetes or other illnesses, they may not be physically able to take Viagra. It may conflict with the medication they are already taking for other illnesses.

The thought of death is often looming in the minds of people over sixty. They are closer to their twilight years than they were in their thirties and forties. But even death should not be such a dreaded thought. It's inevitable. It is a trip we all must someday take. It's how we think about death that determines how happy we are in later life.

After Jerry died, I had to rediscover myself and reinvent the new me. So much of my life was wrapped up in "us," it was difficult defining life as "me" or "I."

In many motivational seminars that I have facilitated or, in motivational speeches that I have delivered, I have often said, "If you lose a loved one in the senior years of your life, I hope you still dance. Dancing means to do what you always wanted to do but never had the chance or took the time. It means not sitting around waiting to die. It means getting up, having the gusto to try something new even if someone tells you that you are too old.

Dancing to your own tune means doing what you want to do rather than what someone else expects of you. Life is too short to go to your grave with regrets."

I facilitated a seminar on motivational techniques at the University of Baltimore. After the seminar was over and participants were leaving the room, a woman walked to where I was standing at the podium, putting my papers into my briefcase.

"I enjoyed your seminar and I agree in principle with what you said, but I think it's too late for me to follow my dream," she said.

I stopped what I was doing, looked at her and asked,.

"What is your dream?"

"I've always wanted to become an attorney. But I'll have to take more undergraduate courses, go to law school, and I'll have to work as a law clerk. It will take ten years for me to finish and by then I'll be sixty-five years old. That's too old! I've already buried two husbands."

She was preaching to the choir. She was talking to the wrong person about being too old.

I was sixty-six years old when my husband died, but I didn't feel I was over the hill. Two years later I started a career in politics, something I had never thought about. However, when the opportunity presented itself, I jumped into the political race, competing with people half my age and who had more experience and political connections than I had.

Me, the person who, at age sixty-six without any political experience, political support, or political endorsements, went up against naysayers, challenged younger people, and won the election.

I always said, "It ain't over til the fat lady sings and this fat lady can't sing!"

I stopped what I was doing, put my hands on my hips and looked directly into her eyes.

"Let me see if I understand what you're saying. If you go back to school now to become a lawyer, it will take ten years and in ten years you'll be sixty-five. Well, let me ask you a question, how old will you be in ten years if you don't go back to school?"

When I asked that question, her face lit up, as if she had just discovered the missing piece of a puzzle.

I continued.

"It seems to me that if you're going to be sixty-five in ten years anyway, whether or not you go back to school, doesn't it make sense getting to be sixty-five being who you want to be?"

She laughed and hugged me.

"You know what? You're right. I'm gonna go for it, what the hell! I never thought about it that way."

"That's because you never met a fighter like me!" I said.

We both laughed.

"You never know until you try. It would be sad to get to the end of your life with regrets of not knowing if you could have completed law school. That's one thing I don't want to do, is to have regrets about something I wanted to accomplish but didn't have the guts to try. I made myself a 'bucket list' of things to do before I 'kick the bucket.' And you know what? I've accomplished most of them. I'm on a roll, kid."

We laughed again. This time the laughter was loud and hearty.

"Like I said before, what the hell!" she said.

She held out her hands and said, "Can I hug you?"

"Of course!" I said. "I'd be disappointed if you didn't. I'm a hugger."

"Me too," she said with a laugh.

She thanked me and walked away. Maybe she will or maybe she won't go back to school but what's important was for her to realize that age is an excuse and not a reason for letting your dreams die.

My assignment or my season for being with my husband was over. My problem was that I wasn't ready to let go and move on to the next stage of my life. I tried to hold on to my "wants" on my time. However, God's time is different than mine. We sometimes want to stay in a place where we feel comfortable. We don't want to turn loose our security blanket, whatever it is. Mine was my husband. I was secure in his love for me. I knew I could depend on him, and that whatever I did he was with me, we were a team.

Your security blanket may be plans for your future, a comfortable mortgage, or enough insurance so that you can take care of yourself financially in your senior years. It's wise to put those types of security plans in place, but don't get so comfortable or complacent that you just do nothing but wait to die. Sometimes we don't want to rock the boat. In order to live a full life, you have to sometimes take risks, that's called "dancing."

You ever walk into a place when someone addresses you as their elder and to you they look older than you? Or someone addresses you as, "Ma'am" and you say to yourself,

"I thought we were about the same age! Why is she referring to me as 'Ma'am?'"

That's because they are trying to hold on to the feeling of being young. They are not ready to let that part of their life go. It's a blessing living to get old. Doesn't getting old mean living longer? Living long enough to be called "senior," is a blessing many people don't receive. Look at the people you know who died young, in their twenties, thirties and even in their teens. Look at the children who never lived to enjoy life. God had other assignments for them and called them home early.

For whatever reason, God left you on earth to live a long life. That means your work on earth is not finished. Why then do you prefer to sit out the rest of your life when you still have work to do? To have lived to be over sixty is a blessing that only a few people get to enjoy. If you are still active, and in another career with no thoughts of stopping or retiring, you are doubly blessed and highly favored!

Accept who God made you to be. Accept yourself for who you are with all your short comings. Don't envy anyone for what you think you don't have. What's for you is for you. God made us all according to His plan. As bad as you think your situation is, there is always someone who wishes they were in your shoes. Look at the positive things you have done in life. No matter how small or how insignificant others may say your accomplishments are, be proud of what you have achieved. Your accomplishments, your talents, the hurdles and obstacles that you have overcome, are all blessings. Use them to bless others.

Develop your own skills, develop your own mind and develop your own plan for success. Develop the talents that God gave you. Who you are is a gift from God, what you become is your gift to God. Develop His gifts to say you are thankful for His blessings. If it means going back to school, taking courses, attending seminars, do so. You are never too old to learn.

I know it's hard when you lose your partner, your soul mate, but lean on God, have confidence in yourself and move on. When my husband passed, I realized that being his wife made me strong. He had given me personal space to pursue my dreams and achieve my goals. When I decided to continue my education, I didn't worry about how he felt about it. At first he tried to convince me that I didn't need a college education, but later I learned that he was afraid he would lose me because he hadn't graduated from high school. I discuss this in my book *And Still, I Cry*. When I decided to write books, I didn't ask his permission. When I decided to become an entrepreneur and start a business, I did so.

When Jerry realized that regardless of what he said, thought, or did, I was going on with my life and accomplish the goals I set for myself, his behavior and attitude changed. He eventually became proud of my accomplishments. His feelings of insecurity and jealousy turned to pride because I included him in my plans. Regardless of how much a person loves you or how insecure they may feel about you pursuing your dream, at the end of the day, you are the only person who will die for you; therefore, you should be the only person deciding how you will live. If you do not follow your dream, it is you who will die with regrets.

Jerry traveled with me on book-signing trips. When I earned degrees or was presented awards, he cheered louder than anyone else. My dreams became his dreams, because I showed confidence in myself, he had confidence in me. Confidence is another word for "faith." Have faith in yourself. I had to redevelop that same tenacity and self-confidence after his death.

Every achiever I ever met says, "My life turned around when I began to believe in myself."

Yesterday's experiences only have the power you give to them. You cannot change what happened to you in your past, but you can change where you end up in your future. I don't always know what will happen during my tomorrow, but I do know, if I have a tomorrow whatever does happen will be the result of my decision. Tomorrow is another day, make it a better day. Don't get stuck in yesterday, that's the path of a fool. The biggest obstacles that you face in your efforts to use more of your potential, is the limitations you place on yourself.

Don't dismiss your dreams as being unimportant. To be without dreams is to be without hope. To be without hope is to be without purpose. Don't run through life so fast that you forget not only where you've been, but also where you're going. Life is not a race, but a journey to be savored each step of the way.

Death is a natural part of life. We can't control it. We can't prevent it. We can't anticipate when it will come or how it will come. The only thing we can do is to ensure that we leave the world a better place because we lived. Don't spend time grieving over the loss of a loved one. Spend time celebrating the life you spent together. Don't spend the rest of your life mourning, spend it dancing!

I know God answers prayers and I know I am His child. I know He will never leave me. Therefore, when I am troubled, I ask Him for help and I leave my troubles at His feet. I know that God answers knee-mail, and when I am in need of His help, I go to my knees. If the world gives you the opportunity, the chance to sit life out or dance, I hope you dance. Life is too short and too precious to travel through it on a road to self destruction, while taking a guilt trip, participating in self-defeating and self-organized guilt parties along the way, filled with blame games, blaming everybody and everything, except yourself, for not realizing your dreams and pursuing and accomplishing your goals.

Life gives us alternatives. We can become a person we neither like nor respect, stay in a place in life filled with regrets and should-have-beens, or, we can grab life by the horns and ride it down the path we designed for ourselves. We have the ability and capability to turn obstacles into opportunities and challenges into conquered situations.

Giving someone all your love is never an assurance they will love you back. Don't expect love in return; just wait for it to grow in their heart; but if it doesn't be content that it grew in yours. When looking for a companion, don't go for looks alone, looks are deceiving and soon fade away. Don't go for wealth you can't take it with you. Money can't buy health or happiness. Go for someone who makes you smile; sometimes it only takes a smile to make a dark day seem bright. Find the one who makes your heart smile. Get rid of unnecessary numbers such as age, height, and weight and dance!

One winter day after Jerry died, I sat in the kitchen, looking through the double glass doors at our snow-covered backyard. Just a few months prior the yard was a green carpet-like grassy lawn, with stately oak trees, and squirrels running up and down them, while rabbits hopped in the bushes. Deer, fox and snakes made the bushes and trees their home and the birds claimed the sky.

But as I sat that day, the backyard was covered with snow. The pool company had come and put chemicals into the pool and covered it for the winter. I thought about the high costs to open the pool each summer and the monthly expenses of pool maintenance. But when I remembered the squeals of laughter from my grandchildren, the splashing of water, the shouts of pleasure, water glistening in the rays of the sun like diamonds, I said "yes" it's worth it. I will take that walk of faith into next spring and summer and find joy ahead.

IT TAKES A VILLAGE

Your job won't take care of you when you are sick or when you're too old to take care of yourself. Your family will. Stay in touch and put God first and family second.

Many people whose own children are now adults are suddenly finding themselves in positions of having to be parents to young children all over again. These individuals called "seniors" have established a lifestyle of their own during their retirement years. These are people who have retired from their jobs, and are looking forward to their golden years. They want to pursue their life's goals, or turn their hobbies into a business, or start traveling, or just relax and do nothing. They no longer want to get out of bed each day and go to a nine-to-five job, working with people they have come to dislike. Living as many years as they have, they now feel they have earned the right to live their life their way. However, some of them are now forced to change their lifestyles and assume the responsibility of caring for their grandchildren. These are responsibilities they neither asked for nor wanted.

These over-sixty people now have to cook dinner most days, wash and iron clothes, make sure their grandchildren go to school, schedule appointments with their grandchildren's teachers to ensure that their grandchildren are not "acting up" in school. They also have to help with homework that has changed since they were in school. There are doctor's appointments, PTA meetings, football games and practice, and other extra-curricular activities in which the children are involved. There are visits to barber shops for the boys and hair salons for the girls.

My daughter Jeanene, was a single parent in the Army Reserves. She was called to active duty in 2003 under President George W. Bush' administration and was deployed to Iraq. Her three children were still in school, when she received her orders to be shipped to Iraq within a matter of months. It did not matter that she had three small children — two boys, Joshua and Lybrant ages eleven and fourteen, and one daughter, Tyneisha, age nineteen. Jeanene was forced to put together a family plan indicating who would be responsible for her children while she was away defending her country.

Jeanene asked Jericka, Butch, Jeanese, her father and me, to care for her children while she was on active duty. Neither Jericka nor Jeanese had any children. Butch was a single parent who had custody of his own two children — son, Jay, age eight and daughter Bianca, age eleven.

Jeanese and Jericka could not assume full responsibility of caring for Jeanene's children. They both had demanding jobs and did not have time to devote to being parents to three children. Additionally, they resented the government seeming to force family members to be responsible for another family member's children. Because Jeanene re-enlisted in the Army Reserves, she was required to go to Iraq. According to her, she could not refuse to go. Her father and I questioned whether she volunteered to go or if she was actually forced. Either way, she went.

We asked Jeanene what would happen if she couldn't get family members to assume responsibility for her children while she was deployed. She said she would have to resign from the Army Reserves and lose the benefits she had accumulated over the years. My entire family resented the government's seemingly, "I don't care," attitude by making it "mandatory" that a single parent find surrogate parents for her children.

Jerry had retired from his job with W.R. Grace Company and was working in our family's business with me. He and I were both over sixty, had we not been the owners of the company where we both worked, we would have retired. We didn't want to alter our lifestyles and care for young children on a full-time basis. We certainly didn't want to be forced to come home each evening and prepare dinner. Jerry and I often ate out, or we'd stop on the way home, and get something for dinner, rather than cooking each day.

It apparently didn't matter to government officials that family members didn't have children by choice, or that grandparents felt they had already raised their own children, and didn't want the responsibility of raising another generation of young children. The government apparently didn't want to hear such complaints. Government officials seemed to have decided who would go into active duty and it was left to the individual to make provisions to carry out those decisions.

Although I resented someone dictating to me how my life should be lived, it remained that someone had to take care of my grandchildren. My family had to care enough to put aside complaints and resentment about the government's intrusion in our lives and realize that it was the children who would suffer if their needs were not addressed.

At first I resented being forced to assume the responsibility of taking care of younger grandchildren. Then I stopped complaining, and accepted the responsibility as a blessing rather than a burden. I changed my attitude about being forced into a lifestyle that I didn't want and realized that my daughter wasn't on drugs, in the streets, or in jail. She was doing a service to protect her country and her family. That was a blessing.

I also looked at the position in which God placed my husband and me. The fact that our family was financially able to care for the children was a blessing. Jerry and I were reasonably healthy and I realized that God was using us to bless his gift to mankind, our grandchildren. I reflected on the joy we got listening to our grandchildren's laughter each day. To watch them excel in school and know their success was directly related to our efforts, was a double blessing. My family decided that the welfare of the children was a family affair. That meant the entire family was involved in their care.

Butch brought his two children to our house each evening and all five of our grandchildren ate dinner together. Our family made a schedule where each day either Jericka, Jeanene or Butch took turns cooking for the children and helping them with their homework. Jericka assumed the responsibility of coming to our house three times a week to help with the laundry. She was also the contact person for the school where Lybrant and Joshua attended.

While Jeanene was in Iraq, Tyneisha lived with Jeanese and her husband Wendell. The boys didn't want to stay with them. Tyneisha wanted to stay with Jeanese and Wendell because they allowed her to go and come as she pleased. She didn't want the type of discipline and restrictions, she would have gotten living with her grandfather and me. However, Jericka kept as close a rein on her as possible.

The boys knew if they acted up in school they'd have to answer to their Aunt Jericka and they didn't want to face her wrath. Every Saturday and Sunday Jericka spent the night at our house. Sunday nights she laid out the boys clothes for the week — an outfit to wear each day. Their teachers called my home commenting about how nicely dressed the children were each day and how well behaved they were. The principal said there was a difference between the way Joshua and Lybrant behaved when their mother was home and when Jericka was the disciplinarian. The boys often wouldn't listen to Jeanene when she disciplined them, but they wouldn't dare disobey Jericka. Jerry and Jericka took turns driving the boys to games and other school activities. The boys understood that each school night they were required to do their homework before they were allowed to watch television. They had a structured routine where each night, if they had school the following day, they were in bed by nine.

When Jeanene returned home nineteen months later, Jerry and I were sadden to see the boys move back home with their mother. He and I had become accustomed to them being with us. They were company to us at night. We were blessed that our daughter survived the ordeal in Iraq and returned home safely. I would not have been able to care for the children without Jerry's help. It was a joint effort between the both of us.

My family and I have wonderful photographs and videos of Jerry in the backyard, him playing with the children, pictures of him and me celebrating our anniversaries, the Christmases and Thanksgiving holidays we spent together as a family. I thank God for the invention of video cameras. We can capture moments and keep them suspended in time. Jerry will live forever through the boxes and boxes of pictures we have stored in the attic, and memories stored in the library of our minds. I'm glad we had such fond memories. I feel blessed that we spent time together as a family and could generate such memories.

Don't get upset if you are forced into a role of being a parent. Look at it as God's way of using you to do His work. Remember the saying, "It takes a village to raise a child?" That's true. Make your family your village. Don't sing a "Woe is me" song. Be proud of your assignment and say, "Hallelujah, anyhow!" Our children are our future leaders, they just don't know it yet.

IT'S ABOUT ATTITUDE

*You may not be able to change your circumstances, but
you can change your attitude about your circumstances*

A young woman — we'll call her April — complained to her mother
— we'll call her mother Maggie— about how hard life was. April said
she didn't know how she was going to get through her troubles. She had
lost her job, her husband left her with three small children, she was being
evicted from her home, she received a letter from the Internal Revenue
Service saying she owed back taxes, her gas and electric were being turned
off, her car insurance had expired, she was pregnant with her fourth child.
She was depressed!

"I don't know what to do. I feel like committing suicide. Every time
I turn around it's another problem. I'm considering putting the baby I'm
carrying up for adoption when it's born. I can't take care of the three
children I already have. How am I going to feed and clothe another child?
I'm tired of fighting and struggling to make ends meet. It seems as soon
as one problem is solved, a new one comes up," she said in exasperation.

Maggie listened to her daughter's complaints. She then took April into
the kitchen. Maggie filled three pots with water, turned on the gas stove
and placed each pot on the fire. Soon the pots came to a boil. In the first
pot Maggie placed raw carrots. In the second pot she placed a raw egg and
in the last pot she placed ground coffee beans. Without saying a word,
Maggie let the three pots sit on the stove and boil for a few minutes.

April didn't know what to expect.

Maggie then turned off the burners and took three bowls from the cabinet. She took the carrots from the first pot and placed them in a bowl. She took the egg from the boiling water of the second pot and placed it in a bowl. She used a ladle to take the coffee beans out of the third pot and poured the coffee into a bowl. She then set all three bowls side by side on the table and turned to her daughter.

"What do we do now?" asked her daughter.

"Just be patient. Let them cool for a moment. I want to teach you something. What do you see?" asked Maggie.

"I see three bowls with carrots, an egg, and coffee," replied April.

Maggie brought April closer to the table and asked her to feel the carrots. April touched the carrots and they were soft. Maggie then asked April to take the egg and crack it. April took the hardboiled egg and hit it on the corner of the table to break the shell. She pulled off the shell, and saw the hardboiled egg.

"Okay! It's a boiled egg. Now what?" asked April, not understanding the message Maggie was trying to convey.

Maggie smiled and continued trying to teach her daughter by examples.

"Now take a sip of coffee," said Maggie.

April frowned as she tasted the unsweetened coffee. She smelled its rich aroma and smiled. She turned to Maggie.

"What does it mean, Mother? What are you trying to say with these experiments?"

Maggie smiled and placed her hands on April's shoulders.

"They are not experiments, they are examples.

"Each of these objects, the carrots, the egg and the coffee, all faced the same adversity, they were all placed in boiling water. However, each reacted differently. The carrot went into the boiling water strong, hard, and unrelenting. Yet after being subjected to the hot temperature, it softened and became weak.

"The egg was fragile. Its thin outer shell protected the liquid interior, but after sitting in the boiling water, the inside of the egg became hardened. The ground coffee beans were unique; while they were in the boiling water, they changed the water."

Maggie looked at her daughter and smiled.

"Which are you?" Maggie asked. "When adversity knocks on your door, how do you respond? Are you a carrot, an egg, or a coffee bean? The lesson I'm trying to teach you is that sometimes you have to be like all three. Sometimes you need to relent, not be weak, but also not be so rigid in your decision. Sometime you need to be strong inside, confident, protect your feelings and emotions. But there are times you must change the situation and alter your environment.

I challenge the readers to think on these things. Which are you? Are you the carrot that seems strong but with pain and adversity, do you wilt and become soft and lose your strength? Are you the egg that starts with a malleable heart, but changes with the heat of the situation? Did you have a fluid spirit, but after a death, a breakup, a financial hardship, or some other challenge, become hardened and stiff? Does your shell look the same but on the inside, are you bitter and tough with a stiff spirit and hardened heart?

Or, are you like the coffee bean? The bean actually changes the hot water, the very circumstances that bring the pain. When the water gets hot, the beans release their fragrance and flavor. If you are like the bean, when things are at their worst, you get better and change the situation around you. When the hour is the darkest and trials are their greatest, do you elevate yourself to another level? Think about how you are handling your grief. Did you become soft and weak like the carrot? Did you do like the egg and harden yourself, shut out things that made you happy, harden your heart against ever feeling happy again? Or did you do like the coffee bean and change the situation? Did you change yourself and learn to live alone? Did you learn to make the next half of your life as happy as God allows? Did you maximize your potential? The happiest of people don't necessarily have the best of everything. They just make the most of everything that comes their way. You can't go forward in life until you let go of your past heartaches. When you were born, you were crying and everyone around you were smiling. Live your life so at the end, you're the one who is smiling and everyone around you is crying. It's all about attitude.

IT TAKES TIME

You can't change the past but you can learn from it.
It's all up to you.

The longer you live, the wiser you become, the happier you should be, and the greater dreams you should have. Look back over your life and thank God for bringing you to the point where you now are in life. Don't give up your dreams because by society's definition you are old. God is still a dream maker and His blessings are bigger than man's vision. I may not have gotten everything I wanted in life but I did get everything I needed.

In February 2006, a Church in San Diego California sponsored a Sister's Summit. The featured speaker was Pastor Joann Browning, from Ebenezer AME Church in Fort Washington, Maryland. When she stepped to the podium to speak, she told the 900 women in the audience of the need to let go of their baggage, such as grown children still living at home, abusive spouses and boyfriends, disloyal friends, unrealistic goals and so on.

Her speech referenced Erykah Badu's song, "Bag Lady," and then she played the song in its entirety.

"It serves as a wake-up call for women," Pastor Joann said to the congregation.

She explained the meaning of each verse of the song and how the lyrics could be used as a source of healing for some of society's ills. I thought about what Pastor Joann said and I realized how right she was. I thought about the message in the song and realized how I could personalize the lyrics to fit my own life. I really did have baggage that I couldn't let go, especially after losing my husband.

I thought about the words, "Bag Lady, you gon' hurt your back draggin' all them bags like that."

Holding on to pain, hurt, anger and disappointments has a negative impact on our health. The results run the gamut from chronic illness to life threatening diseases. Sooner or later our baggage causes our bodies to give out. Before my husband died, I had pains in my arms and side. I went to the doctor several times about this condition, but the pain continued.

But the night he died, I don't know what happened. I cried, shouted, jumped up and down and fell to my knees. I didn't believe he was gone. The pain in my arm and side left me that night, and never returned. I guess my husband asked God to free me.

Jerry tried to get me to put the past behind us and make our future years together happy and enjoyable with each other, as we both wanted in the beginning of our marriage, when we were younger. But I wouldn't let go of the past. Every time he told me how much he loved me, I did not believe him, my thoughts would flash back to a time when he was unfaithful. I was so much in love with him, my heart broke each time I found evidence of his cheating, such as lipstick on his collar, makeup on his shirt, the telephone calls when the caller hung up if I answered, or the time I caught him talking on the telephone with another woman. He thought I had gone to work that morning, but I was listening on the extension in another room.

Instead of me playing the "He done me wrong," game, I should have also remembered that I wasn't sitting at home crying, wringing my hands, feeling sorry for myself and waiting for him to come home, I was also doing the same as he. I just didn't get caught.

Many relationships have come together on crutches. Women know they have no business getting involved in a new relationship when they still have unresolved issues from a past relationship. Still, due to fear of being alone or fear of missing out on a good man, we cover our wounds with tight hairdos, expensive clothes and a fake smile.

As time passes, the wounds get harder and harder to hide. When they're finally exposed, the relationship is over. We have no control over what others do or say about us, but we can control our reactions to what they say. Having baggage is nothing to be ashamed of. We all have issues. The shame is not in having baggage, it's keeping it.

Search yourself, be honest. Ask yourself what's in your bag that's interfering with your happiness and your success. Pray, cry, scream, go to church, go for therapy, do whatever it takes to free yourself of the baggage that keeps you from your goal, from realizing your dream from being happy. Just let it go.

PRAYER POWER

"And Jesus said unto them, Because of your unbelief;
for verily I say unto you, If ye have faith as a grain of
mustard seed, ye shall say unto this mountain, Remove
hence to yonder place; and it shall remove; and nothing
shall be impossible unto you," Matthew 17:20

During my earlier married life, I wanted freedom to do as I pleased, to come and go as I pleased without repercussions. However, I never wanted freedom at the expense of losing my husband. It takes a logical look at life to begin living it your way. After my husband's death, I was at a lost as to what I wanted to do with my new found "freedom." But was I really free? Sure I could come and go as I pleased but I was not free from the memories of what once was.

For years I have lived life as a mother, a wife, a grandmother, an adjunct college professor, a college student, a court official, and an entrepreneur. All those situations or roles, required a certain amount of restraints. I was expected to behave in a certain way in all of those scenarios. I have never lived totally free, of time restraints or constraints. I was always expected to come home at a certain time.

I left Columbus, Georgia where I was under the control of my parents' rules, where I was required to be home before sunset unless I was attending a special event. I have run home many times trying to beat the sun, by getting home before sundown, making sure I was on my front porch steps when it did.

When I got married, I was expected to be home at a "reasonable hour." I was to be home at least an hour after the bars closed at 2:00 a.m. Actually Jerry expected me to be home before the bars closed. He'd say:

"Any woman still in a bar when it closes is looking for something, waiting to be picked up by a man. A respectable woman leaves before the bar closes."

After Jerry's death and after moving into an apartment, free of memories, and a fresh coat of paint, I felt a new freedom. But that "freedom" was really loneliness. I missed coming home to our house where I knew if he wasn't there he soon would be. He had changed so much during our later years of marriage. He had become the man I wished he had been when we first married, a man who didn't stay out all night, someone I could trust and someone with whom I felt secure. He had become my best friend.

After his death, each time I saw someone wearing a hat cocked to the side, a cigar in his mouth and a gold tooth, I thought of Jerry. I miss him on dreary rainy days when the sky is grey. We sometimes spent time at home making love while listening to the rhythmical sounds of raindrops, falling against the window. I miss him on sun-filled days when we relaxed on the beach in some far away land, when he traveled with me on book signing tours or vacation trips.

I miss him each time it snows, when I remember how he enjoyed making ice cream for our children then for our grandchildren, mixing Pet milk, snow, sugar and vanilla flavor together in bowls. They enjoyed eating the milky snow-cream, while sitting on the warm stone floor in our den — family room — in front of the fire place. A roaring fire of logs filled the room with heat, and a warm orange glow.

I miss him when I hear BB King play his guitar, Lucille, and sings the blues. Jerry loved those down-home-somebody-done-me-wrong songs. I miss him every night I don't hear him snoring and breathing lying beside me in our king-sized bed. I only miss him on two occasions, day and night.

Jerry was there for me to lean on when the stress of our business became overwhelming. I thought of myself as a good business woman but sometimes, I just needed to be me, without having to make decisions that affected someone else. Jerry provided that space for me. He was aware of the problems I was having with one of the state operated health care agency's attempts to put SelfPride, Incorporated, out of business. In

Maryland during the 1990s, there were over two-hundred white-owned and operated agencies with lucrative state contracts in the health care industry. There were only four agencies that were operated by African Americans and that same agency attempted to coerce the four agencies operated by African Americans, to merge together to form one company. My company, SelfPride, was one of the four.

The four of us met and discussed this idea of merging. There were three black women and one black male. We each had fought hurdles and dealt with obstacles to become business owners. We didn't want to give up our dream and work for someone else. We all couldn't be the boss. We discussed the proposed idea at length, we then decided to remain as we were and develop our own businesses.

Since 1996 SelfPride had staved off government agencies that were trying to put us out of business. Some days I went home and cried on Jerry's shoulders about the way SelfPride was treated by agencies that our tax dollars helped to maintain. I sent letters to various people in an attempt to get help with the disparity treatment I felt businesses operated by people of color were receiving. I wanted someone to respond to my complaints, or at least care enough to verify if my complaints were valid.

I sent letters to political officials, to pastors of mega-churches in Baltimore, to the NAACP, to the Baltimore Urban League, to city officials, to the mayor of Baltimore, to President George W. Bush, and to the secretary of the Department of Labor, Elaine Chaoe. I also sent letters to the State's Attorney, to the Office of Health Care Quality, to the Department of Health and Mental Hygiene, to state delegates and senators. No one responded or even called me to say they had received my letters or even returned my telephone calls. One state senator to whom I sent a letter ignored me altogether. Since she was one of my sorority sisters, I was disappointed with her lack of response. I thought she would at least return my calls even if she couldn't help me. On several occasions I spoke directly with her secretary and sent her a registered letter to ensure she received my letters, and she still did not respond. Finally, Senator Larry Young heard of my problems, contacted me and offered to help.

My husband was buried in August 2004. In November, 2004, three months after his death, I was thrown into a trial that threatened to take my business, my home and any other assets I held, and leave me penniless and homeless. But strangely enough, I wasn't afraid. I knew God would take care of me. I hadn't done anything wrong but the Federal Department of Labor (DOL), an agency that seems to cater to employees and against employers, tried to paint a picture of me as a business owner who took advantage of people who were disadvantaged. This was following the three DOL investigators who visited me beginning in 1997. Had I paid the fifteen thousand dollars the last investigator, Sliwaka said I owed, we wouldn't have gone to court. But I refused to allow the government to beat me out of money I didn't owe. I wasn't afraid and I refused to be intimidated.

Felicia, a friend and my hair stylist for over ten years — she, her husband and two children moved to Atlanta, Georgia in 2006 just as my campaign began — called me the morning the trial began and told me to read *Psalm:35*. I read it that morning and every day before going to court. I also carried my Bible to court with me inside my brief case.

Now mind you, DOL was attempting to prove that I did not adequately pay former employees. It didn't matter that SelfPride had trained over two thousand people, who were once on welfare, had hired over eight-hundred and fifty people and over seventy-five of them were in top management positions with other agencies throughout Maryland. This means that SelfPride helped reduce the number of people on welfare in Maryland. SelfPride had also provided jobs for people who could not be hired by other companies because they had criminal records. SelfPride gave them a new start.

SelfPride had a system. When people applied for employment, we conducted a criminal background check. If their records returned showing they had been incarcerated or had a criminal charge within the past two years, based on what those charges were, the individuals would have a private meeting with me in my office. If they had a history of abuse or neglect in any form, I would not hire them. However, if they had drug related charges, or charges that did not cause physical harm to another person, I gave them a chance. I explained to them that I was giving them a hand-up and not a hand-out.

Some of the people we trained went on to change their life others wanted something for nothing, still playing games trying to beat the system. A lot of them committed fraud on their time sheets, indicating they were at work when they were not. Some entered overtime hours on their time sheets when they had not worked overtime. Some stole clothes from the consumers in our care and some stole food from SelfPride's houses where people with developmental disabilities lived.

One day after we had purchased groceries, Adolphus, SelfPride's program coordinator, went to one of SelfPride's homes and met a staff member leaving the house with a shopping bag filled with meats and toilet tissue she had stolen from the house where she worked. In another house we locked the supplies in a closet and the house manager kept the key in a place we thought was secure. When we checked the supplies some were missing. On a shelf inside the closet was a knife the thief had used to pick the lock to enter the closet. The staff person had forgotten the knife and left it behind inside the closet. It was used as evidence to catch the thief.

There were several occasions when staff people called in to say they were at work. When they failed to call every hour to ensure they were not asleep, Adolphus went to the house to check and sure enough the person was asleep. On an awake-overnight supervision shift, it was dangerous for a staff person to sleep on duty. In some of the houses, the consumers had acting out aggressive behavior and at times could be violent. Therefore, when staff falsely entered on their time sheets to be paid for that time, SelfPride said "no!"

However, DOL said they should be paid.

These are just some of the things with which we were confronted on a daily basis as we operated SelfPride. God allowed me to go through trials and tribulations to make SelfPride successful and profitable. It wasn't ours to keep. It was to build it so that many people could prosper and profit by its existence and its services. SelfPride was first assessed with a two- million dollars fine by the government it was reduced to one-mullion, then seven-hundred-fifty- thousand dollars. When it was lowered to five-hundred-sixty-four-thousand dollars, I decided to stop paying legal fees and fight politically. The penalty had gone from fifteen-thousand to more than half-million. I knew we had not done anything wrong and God knew it too. If He was allowing us to go through such problems, He had a reason.

My attorney, Neal Janey, was concerned about the amount of money the government was spending to fight SelfPride. Eight attorneys from

Pennsylvania came to Baltimore everyday for two weeks to appear at the trial against SelfPride.

After the trial was over Neal said that one of us — he or I — needed to be in Annapolis as an elected official to speak out about how the government treats small businesses. The government should not be allowed to go after a small business owner the way they went after SelfPride.

"Barbara, one or both of us need to be on the inside of the government. We need to be in a position to effect change. Something is going on. They're treating you as if you stole millions of dollars, or as if you're a drug lord. Have you ever gone out of the country and did anything illegally? I know you travel a lot because of your writing, but do you remember meeting anybody that could be the reason why the government is trying so hard to take your business?" asked Neal.

I looked at him in disbelief. I couldn't believe he was suggesting this trial was something I should be getting scared about.

"Are you serious?"

"I'm dead serious! Look at things the way they are happening. Why would the government spend thousands of dollars to send eight attorneys from Philadelphia, to come to Baltimore Maryland for several months, and one of the attorneys is a regional director in Pennsylvania, to 'investigate' a non-profit company operated by an African American woman?"

I thought about what he said and I realized he was right.

"I have done absolutely nothing wrong! I think this is the system trying to retaliate against me for refusing to let them push me around. Some state agencies can be vindictive when they're challenged. As a Black woman business owner, I think they're trying to put me in my place. I remember similar treatment when I worked in the court system in the early 1980s."

Neal considered running for mayor of Baltimore City. He certainly had the qualifications. He had been the chief city solicitor under Mayor Kurt Schmoke's administration. He had been a District Court judge and a Supreme Bench judge. He went back into private practice, and he can recall stories about how black attorneys had to fight for cases and justice during the early 1940s through the 1980s. I was working in the Maryland Court system during the 1960s through 1980s. I knew his background.

Neal asked me to consider running for mayor. I thought about it for a brief moment. It was really going to be an interesting race with two black women running for the same position."

Sheila Dixon was president of the Baltimore City Council, Martin O'Malley was mayor. Sheila, a long time acquaintance, was also a member of the church I attended. In 2006, after Mayor Martin O'Malley became governor of Maryland, Sheila automatically became the interim Mayor, until the next election a year later. Sheila would have to win the 2007 election. I didn't want to compete against Sheila, Joan, and Cathy. Four black women competing against each other, campaigning for the same position, would have split the black vote and possibly neither of us would have won. So I decided to run for state delegate instead.

Sheila and I had a long history of working on projects together. In 1984 she and I with other church members, prepared to go to Lusaka Zambia in Central Africa. I was going to Africa to teach business development classes to women. Sheila was going to teach women how to develop and operate a Food-Co-op program. During the planning stage, Sheila's car was stolen and she rode her bicycle to my house to attend a meeting with other people who planned to go to Africa with us. Sheila and I sat on my basement floor planning and strategizing about how to get to Africa. As it turned out, a city planner, a pediatrician, and I, were the only three who went to Africa that year.

THROUGH IT ALL

For with God, all things are possible -- Mark 10:27

The federal government put a lien on my home, and threatened to foreclose on the home that I paid for with my late husband's death benefits. The judge threatened to take the office building we purchased fifteen years prior. He also threatened to lock me up for five years if I didn't disclose my personal finances to him. He examined my bank statements, my insurance policies, had me place a value on my clothes, jewelry, home, furniture, and everything I owned. He then threatened not to "lighten up" on me. I felt he was hard on me because I was an African American woman. I felt as I did during my years working in the court system. It seemed that nothing had changed; it was still black and white races against each other.

"If you think the government will back off, you are sadly mistaken. You may be an Oprah Winfrey or a Martha Stewart, for all we know," the judge said.

I cried, I prayed, and asked God to step in, intervene and not leave me homeless, penniless, and destitute.

I was blessed to be in a financial position to fight the charges to keep from being forced out of business. Other small businesses, especially minority owned businesses, may not have been so fortunate. I wanted to assist women and minority businesses by using the experience I had obtained from twenty-five years of being a business owner.

Without my knowledge, Neal went to the board of elections and got a map of the 40th district. He also got a copy of the Baltimore Directory, Election Precincts, Wards, Streets, Zones, Codes, Congressional, Council, and Legislative Districts, and a book that listed address of various districts. He then brought that material to my house and left it in my door, rang my doorbell and left. When I answered the door and found the material, I realized that he was serious about me going in politics. However, I was reluctant to tell my family that I was going into politics. I felt they would feel that I was too old and too inexperienced.

Everyone with whom I discussed the idea of politics, encouraged me. Neal Janey said I should go into politics to represent the under-dog, people who are afraid to speak out about injustice. Therefore, I said I would run for a seat on the City Council. I knew I would have to be a city resident but I was considering moving into the city anyway to escape the memories our house held.

I called my friend Robert (Bob) Ambush as I usually did when I had a difficult business decision to make. Bob and I met when he sold me my first new car over thirty years ago and he became a friend of my family.

"Bob. I've been thinking about running for an elected position in politics. What do you think?"

"I think you'll be great! I say go for it! What do you have to lose?"

"Yeah, but the media will try to attack me and make my past public."

"So what? You don't have anything to hide and you certainly don't have anything to be ashamed of!"

"I know. But they'll probably talk about me being abused as a child, my mother being an alcoholic, welfare, projects, and all that negative stuff."

"Again, so what? You've already put that information out there for the public to read when you wrote your first book. Not only that, think about how many other people went through the same things you went through. At least they'll know they're not alone."

"You're right. I have already talked about my past when I wrote *And Still, I Cry*."

"Now you're talking. By the way, what position are you thinking about running for?"

"I was thinking about running for a seat on the City Council but I have to be a city resident to do that. Maybe I'll run for a seat on County Council, that way, I won't have to move, since my house is in the county."

Bob didn't like that idea.

"I totally disagree! Why? You don't need to be on the city or the county council. You need to be either in a state or federal government position. If you're gonna run, run big."

I knew he was right. I wasn't thinking high enough. I was about to make the same mistake I had made when I first went into business and was seeking 8(a) certification from the federal Small Business Administration (SBA). They asked me the question of how much money in contracts was I expecting to handle within the next five years?

"Fifty-thousand dollars the first year, seventy-five thousand dollars the second year, one-hundred thousand dollars the third year, one-hundred-fifty thousand dollars the fourth year, and maybe two-hundred thousand dollars by the fifth year," I said.

I made a big mistake; I should have been thinking in the millions, not thousands. When a contract in the amount of two-hundred thousand dollars was let within my first year of being certified, STAR wasn't included in the bidding process. I had entered on my certification that I could only handle contracts up to fifty-thousand. I had put limitations on myself. It was the fear of success that held me back. And now here I was again, twenty years later, still putting limitations on my capabilities. I decided I would not define my limitations to run for a seat in the House of Delegates.

The idea of politics was confusing and scary to me. It was a foreign area. I constantly thought about how Jerry would feel about me seeking an elected political position. But the truth is, if he were still alive, I wouldn't have thought about a career in politics. He and I would probably concentrate on traveling and writing another book. Or maybe we would just get away from Baltimore for a couple of weeks, to a place where he'd play golf every day, I'd sit on the balcony overlooking the ocean, listen to the waves beat against the shores, listen to the seagulls and work on my next manuscript.

I thought about the reasons Neal had suggested I seek a career in politics. Since the agencies whose practices I planned to challenge were state agencies, he thought I needed to be in a position that held more power than a city council position. Bob was right when he said I needed to be in a position at the state or federal level. I wanted to represent small businesses in Annapolis because I understand their needs. Neal said if I ran for a position as an elected official, he would be SelfPride's Lobbyist.

I was constantly redefining myself, forging a different road, a different career but each one was molding me into a new person, who liked herself and, who was learning to live differently in a world she had come to know.

From welfare to wealth, from the projects to prosperity, from Flag House Courts, to the District Courts, and from distress to success, I pursued my dream of becoming an author and an entrepreneur.

In 1972, Richard Nixon campaigned for his second term as president of the United States. Shirley Chisholm, a black woman from Maryland, was a presidential candidate. When asked about her decision to run for such a high profile office she said:

"I ran for the presidency despite hopeless odds, to demonstrate sheer will and refusal to accept the status quo. I am un-bought and un-bossed."

I found those words to be profound. I ran for a seat in the House of Delegates for the same reason. As my campaign slogan I used her "un-bought and un-bossed," and I added, "un-intimidated and unafraid."

I always said that if I ever went into politics I would have either Julius Henson, Arthur (Art) Murphy, or Mary Robinson — no relations — as my consultant to advise me how to campaign effectively. Mary's health was failing her. The last time I saw her at a sorority event — we both are members of the Alpha Kappa Alpha (AKA) sorority, she didn't recognize me. As long as she and I had known each other, her face was blank when she looked at me as if she was trying to remember who I was. For years we had attended the same church. Mary later died.

Arthur (Art) Murphy was my first political strategist and consultant. He had successfully helped a number of politicians win their elections. I knew him from over twenty-five years previously in the early 1980s, when I worked at the Supreme Bench. He represented the late Sandra Banks, who made a successful run for the position of Clerk of Court. Art was a skillful political strategist and one of the best in Baltimore. He was also a member of one of Baltimore's prominent families.

Art's father, William Murphy, Sr., was a judge at the District Court. In the late 1960s and early 1970s, when I was chief of the Traffic Division at the District Court of Maryland, Cheryl Andrews, who worked with me in the traffic division, Mary B. McCray (Bonnie), who was the first black woman to head the accounting department of the district court, Judge Robert M. Bell, who became Chief Judge of the State of Maryland, Judge

William Murphy, Sr., and I, all ate lunch together every day at the Horn and Horn Restaurant on the corner of Calvert Street and Madison Street.

William (Billy) Murphy, Jr., one of Baltimore's prominent criminal attorneys, was Art's older brother. I had known Art and Billy for years. Billy and the legendary Johnnie Cochran worked on several legal cases together.

I called Art and asked him to meet with me.

"Art, I want to talk to you about me going into politics."

"Are you serious?" he asked.

"As serious as a heart attack," I said and I laughed.

"Where did this idea come from?"

I explained to him about Neal, the trial and everything that led up to that decision.

"If you're serious, let's set a time to meet Tuesday."

Tuesday came, Art walked into my conference room slow and methodically. One of his partners, a white male — whom he introduced as "Jack" — appeared to be in his early to middle fifties, was with him. Art informed me that both he and Jack were members of an organization called the Demography Group, an Annapolis-based political consultancy where Art was known as an expert in direct-mail campaigns.

Art sat down slowly in one of the chairs as if it pained him to bend his knees. We discussed my wanting to run for a political position. I informed him that I didn't know which position, nor did I know how to organize and run a campaign.

Art asked me how badly I wanted to win the election. He said it would be a hard battle for me to win since no one in the political arena knew me. They knew Barbara Robinson within the small business community and in organizations that provided services for people defined as "disadvantaged" or "hard to serve," but I had never traveled in the political circle. People with political power couldn't help me. They didn't know me.

I also knew Art's wife Jacquelyn (Jackie) McClean. Jackie was the first woman and the first African American to be elected Comptroller of Baltimore City. Jackie and her first husband Jimmy were the owners of Four Winds and Seven Seas Travel Agency, one of the most successful travel agencies in Maryland with offices in four different states. In the early

1980s Jackie and Jimmy were featured in the local paper as earning over fifty-million dollars in the travel business.

My office building on Montgomery Street, the headquarters of STAR Associates, SelfPride, and BeuMar, LLC, was once the headquarters of Jackie's and Jimmy's travel agency. We purchased the building from them.

When I told Art of my political aspirations, he was surprised.

"I never knew you had political ambitions."

"I didn't. After my husband died, I went into a state of depression you wouldn't believe. I asked God what He wanted me to do the rest of my life, preach, teach, or politics. God said 'All three'.

"I wouldn't have any problems returning to the classroom as a teacher. I've taught credit and non-credit courses at three different colleges. I've taught inmates in prison for seven years, I've developed and facilitated seminars and workshops nationally and internationally. Although I don't have a desire to be a full time teacher, I could have easily adjusted to that profession.

"If God had said, 'Preach,' although I'm not a preacher, I wouldn't have problems with that. I don't have to be a preacher to spread God's Word. I have a testimony. I can talk about His goodness. I can say,

"'What God has done for me He will do for others.'

"I've been in pulpits across the country. With the way God has blessed me and brought me through a life of abuse, homelessness, racism, molestation and other obstacles, I would enjoy a life of ministering to others. Several years before my husband passed I had considered the ministry. I asked my pastor to write a letter of reference for me to enroll in graduate school to study theology. Over the years I've delivered the message from the pulpit in several churches both nationally and internationally, from Africa to Tennessee. I've also been the Women's Day Speaker several times at several churches.

"I've never in my life thought of politics. I often dreamed of being a doctor, a judge, an actor, an entertainer, a published author, but never a politician."

"The only way I'll represent you is if you run in the fortieth legislative district. That's where you're needed," said Art.

"But I live in the tenth legislative district."

"Yes but you can move to the fortieth."

"Move? Are you kidding? My house is paid for and I've been living in the tenth district for over thirty years. I don't want to move."

"But you aren't needed in the tenth district. I know all the legislators in that district and they are doing a fine job. You'll have a difficult time trying to unseat one of them. But the leadership is weak in the fortieth legislative district. There are three seats, one is filled by Juanita, the other two are filled with Cathy and Toby, who were appointed by the Democratic Central Committee to complete the positions left vacant by Pete Rawlings' and Tony Fulton's deaths. Juanita, the incumbent, is the only one who has campaigned for her seat. The other two have not. They'll have to run for election in 2006 just like you will. I think the fortieth district is where you need to be."

In the early 1980s, Sandra Banks asked me to be her speech writer for several political events. I declined. I didn't think I was good enough. When the late Tony Fulton was campaigning for a seat in the Maryland House of Delegates, he asked me to be his campaign manager. I declined, again I didn't think I was good enough, nor was I interested in politics. But it's ironic that after Tony's death, twenty years later I won the election to a seat in the Maryland House of Delegates, in the same legislative district he represented.

Now, God was saying to me, "It's time to dance to a new tune!"

I knew absolutely nothing about politics. But the idea of venturing into unknown territory was intriguing to me. It meant I didn't have time to wallow in self pity by constantly focusing on my husband's death. I didn't have time to reflect on my loss. I was too busy learning how to play the game of politics.

I surrounded myself with knowledgeable people from whom I could learn the ropes. Just as I had stood on the shoulders of giants in the business world when I first became an entrepreneur, I sought giants in the political world on whose shoulders I could stand. Ray Haysbert, one of the co-founders of Park Sausages in Baltimore and the owner of the Forum Caterers and Ballroom, was my mentor in business. Walter Dean, a former member of the Maryland House of Delegates and a professor at the Baltimore City Community College, and George Collins, a journalist, political activists and radio personality, were my mentors when I chose to get involved in politics.

In March 2006, I invited Juanita to have lunch with me at the Radisson Hotel in the Village of Cross Keys. At that time I explained to her my decision to run for a seat in the Maryland House of Delegates in the fortieth district.

She attempted to persuade me to run in another district.

"Why do you want to run in the fortieth? My fund-raiser person said you would be better off running in the eleventh legislative district."

I don't live in the eleventh district."

"Move there just like you're planning to move into Baltimore City in the fortieth district."

"But you don't seem to understand, the fortieth district is a part of my past. I met my husband in the fortieth district. I lived in the fortieth district with my husband before and after we were married. Before we had any children my husband and I moved from an apartment on Eutaw Place to an apartment on East Lafayette Avenue and both of those apartments were in the fortieth legislative district. When I first started my business my office was in the fortieth district for over ten years. The fortieth district is home to me.

"If I thought I'd hurt you by running for a seat in the fortieth district, I wouldn't run. You've been kind to me, and you've tried to help me each time I contacted you. I wouldn't do anything to hurt your career. But there are three seats in the fortieth district. I'm running for one of those seat. There's enough for both of us.

"I'm not upset. I just don't think we should have so many African American women running for the same seats," she said.

"We are not running for the same seats. There are three African American women running for one of three seats. We all can get elected," I said to her.

Regardless of what I said, I still couldn't convince her I was not her competition. I decided not to let it worry me and go on with my career plans.

When we left the restaurant, I said to her the same thing I had said to Cathy.

"I hope we both can have lunch this time next year as two Delegates."

"Yeah," she responded.

Apparently the special interest groups, unions, and my pastor, didn't think I was capable of winning either. Perhaps they thought I was too old or too inexperienced to win — I was sixty-seven years old. There were nine of us campaigning for three seats.

The first time I appeared with the other candidates to present my campaign platform, speaking to voters, telling them why I should be elected to the House of Delegates, I was scared and nervous. I walked to the front of the room and when I began to speak, my voice quivered, and I broke out in a sweat.

I wiped my forehead and looked at one of my competitors. I thought I saw a smirk on his face that I interpreted to mean, "I got you. You're out of your element."

It was as if he dared me to debate him, as if he was about to put me in my place. I thought about those same facial expressions from my Caucasian co-workers in the court system — especially the women — who tried to make me feel out of place, as if I didn't belong. I sure wasn't going to accept that treatment in my career, at my age without a fight.

I don't know where I got the strength from, but all of a sudden it appeared that I had new-found confidence.

I said to myself, "I don't know where that scared person came from but she won't show up any more."

I seemed to get adrenaline from nowhere. I wasn't about to let anyone see me fail. So when all the candidates had presented their campaign platform and the audience started asking questions, the old Barbara appeared. I didn't feel nervous anymore. I was inexperienced as a politician but I was not inexperienced in public service and helping others. I could speak from experience in ways some of the other candidates could not. I was the oldest candidate and the most politically-inexperienced. Therefore, I knew I had to make the voters understand that I was worthy of representing them and their interests. I could represent seniors and their needs. I was one of them. I knew what my needs were and my needs were their needs.

Being a black woman having been on welfare, I understood the needs of people classified as disadvantaged and under-served. I was one of them too. I grew up in a dysfunctional family but I didn't hear that term used until I became an adult. I was abused by my step father and my mother who was an alcoholic and eventually died from the disease of alcoholism and lung cancer. I was homeless at the age sixteen. I can tell you about the beatings from my step father and from my mother. He beat my mother as she lay on the ground in a fetal position. She tried to protect her face from the blows of his army boots as he kicked her. I went to her defense and he turned his rage on me. He held a wooden broom handle in his hands and swung it like you would swing a baseball bat, and hit me across my back so hard the handle broke. It knocked the wind out of me and I fell to the ground. He wasn't finished with me yet. He continued to hit me, all the while cursing me, telling me I was just like my so-and-so no good mama. Therefore, I could identify with child abuse and domestic violence.

I could also identify with people on welfare. It was necessary for my children and me to go on welfare when my husband was shot and in the hospital for over a year.

Jerry was at a gambling game at his uncle's house when Willie, a gambling buddy, was showing the other people in the gambling game a gun he had just purchased from someone on the street. They all were drinking and no one knew anything about guns. They didn't know the gun was loaded. When Willie and Jerry were handling the gun, it discharged and hit Jerry in his abdomen. The bullet circled his stomach six times before it exited his body. The doctor said his intestines looked as if a moth had eaten them. Jerry almost died from the accident. He stayed in the hospital for six months before he was released. He came home, the wound got infected and he was in Provident Hospital for another three months.

Because I had four babies, which included the two surviving triplets, and lived in the projects, I had to seek public assistance.

I can talk about standing in line on Greenmount Avenue, waiting for a monthly ration of powered eggs, powdered milk, jars of peanut butter, government cheese, flour, and yellow corn meal. A refrigerated truck was there to distribute butter. I can relate to the two-dollars per child given from Santa Claus Anonymous to families on welfare.

I understand the needs of small businesses, women-owned and operated businesses, non-profit businesses, minority businesses, and in-home care. I was an entrepreneur for over twenty-five years. I used an unemployment check to start a business that grew into a multi-million dollar enterprise and employed over one-hundred people.

Based on the experiences I encountered in life, my motto was, "Been there and done that is better than just getting there." When I finished speaking everyone applauded. I knew then that I could handle this "political thing."

During my campaign, people asked me whose ticket I was running on. I told them I was running on God's ticket. When other political savvy people identified special interest groups that had endorsed them and no one had endorsed me, I didn't let that concern me. I was endorsed by God and that was enough for me.

FINDING A NUETRAL PLACE

It is difficult to wring your hands in despair if you are busy rolling up your sleeves to change your circumstances

God obviously agreed with Art about me moving into the fortieth district. As long as I was out of the country traveling, everything was find. I didn't spend time thinking about my life the way it was when my husband was alive. I focused on sightseeing, experiencing a new culture, and shopping. After each trip, each time I returned to Baltimore, either Butch or Jericka met me at the airport and drove me home. During the drive, my mind focused on Jerry and how lonely our house, the city, and my life appeared to be without him. When we drove into our driveway on Essex Road, I didn't want to get out of the car. The feeling of being alone was overwhelming. I would sit in the car and stare out the window at the house and dread going inside.

I needed to pull myself out of my depression. I looked for an apartment in the city. I wasn't ready to sell my house, but I needed a place to stay where I could find mental peace. Bianca constantly reminded me that selling my house meant I would be selling our family home. My family wasn't ready to give up our traditional backyard barbecues and pool parties.

I knew I had to find a neutral environment so I could discover who I would become. Since God had put a period on the part of my life with Jerry, it was now time to discover who the new person was that God was designing, developing, and reinventing. I wasn't the same anymore. I started looking for a place to live where I could have mental peace. I didn't know what I was looking for, an apartment or a condominium. I just knew that I would know it when I found it. It was kind of like looking for a certain sofa. You don't know what color you want, what material it should be made of, or what shape it should be. You just know that when you see it, you'll know that's the one.

I looked at apartments all over Baltimore City but could find none I liked. Then one day while driving on Martin Luther King Boulevard, I saw a new brick building I hadn't noticed before.

"Where did that building come from? It must be new! Why haven't I seen it before?" I said aloud

Symphony Center Apartment Homes was a beautiful building, directly across the street from the Myerhoff Symphony Center, the premier center in Baltimore where concerts are held. The Myerhoff Symphony Center is the most elegant concert hall in Baltimore. I went inside the building and learned it had only been open three months. The manager showed me several apartments but the monthly rent was almost two-thousand dollars. I wasn't ready to spend that much money for rent but it was the most beautiful apartment of all the other apartment buildings I had seen during my search for a place to move. I put that apartment on my list of "maybes" and kept looking to ensure I was choosing the best. I saw others but they all paled in comparison to the Symphony Center Apartments.

Before I signed a lease for the apartment, I checked to see in which district the Symphony Center Apartment building was located. I checked the book Neal had gotten from the State Board of Election to see if it was in the fortieth legislative district. The building was so new the address wasn't listed in the book. I called the Board of Election to verify the location. It was in the fortieth district. It appeared that God was directing me.

The lease price was more than I wanted to pay, but I loved the building and wanted to stay there. Because the lease was expensive, I decided to think about it for a day before I signed the lease. I discussed it with Jericka and Butch. Jericka said paying two-thousand a month rent was crazy, especially since I would never own the property.

"If you were paying that much as a mortgage I would say go for it, but to pay that much for a place you'll never own, is crazy, especially since you don't have to. You own your house on Essex Road free and clear, but you're talking about spending twenty-four- thousand dollars a year for rent? I say, no!" said Jericka.

Butch on the other hand thought differently. He advised me to live my life as I wanted to. .

"Ma, life is too short not to enjoy it. Spend your money on yourself while you're still young enough and healthy enough to enjoy it. If you leave anything after you're gone, oh well. But I say, spend it like you want to and let them bury you face down so whoever don't like what you did with your money, the money you earned, let them pass by your grave and kiss your butt."

I thought about what he said and realized what he meant. I laughed and agreed with him.

I called the apartment management and told them to hold the apartment for me. It was a two bedroom apartment with a balcony overlooking the city. On a clear day from my balcony I could see the Chesapeake Bay.

When I met my husband, he lived in the fortieth district on Eutaw Place. When I first started in business, for ten years my office was located on East Chase Street in Downtown Baltimore, in the fortieth district. Jericka owns property in the fortieth district. I finally realized God was trying to tell me, to go back to my roots.

I took Butch's advice and my own decision and called the management of the apartment building and signed a one year lease.

I visited my house on Essex Road once a week but I couldn't stay there. It felt cold and unfriendly, as if I was visiting a stranger. Jericka lived in the house more than she stayed in her own house. She eventually sold her beautiful house in Davidsonville and moved into our house on Essex Road. I think she wanted to be close to the memories of her father. Each time I went to my house and prepared to leave to return to my apartment, if I said, "I'm going home." Jericka would get upset.

"That's not your home. This is your home. That is just an apartment where you stay temporarily!"

When I first moved into the Symphony Center apartment building, I constantly got homesick for my house and the memories it held. I slept in the apartment three nights a week, Tuesdays, Wednesdays, and Thursdays. Friday I packed my makeup and hair rollers and I went "home." I didn't have to take any clothes with me. I had plenty at each place. That continued until one day when the cleaning ladies, Nell and Angie, found a black snake in the basement of my Essex Road house.

I was in my bedroom when Nell, who was cleaning my club basement came running upstairs screaming my name.

"Mrs. Robinson! Mrs. Robinson!"

I was sitting at the computer in my home office when I heard her. Noticing the panic in her voice, I jumped up and ran to the door leading into the basement.

"What is it? What's the matter?"

"I don't want to scare you but there's a snake in your clubroom, lying right next to your bar."

"A snake? Are you serious? Is it a real snake? Is it alive?"

Nell was shaking with fear. Angie came running from cleaning the bathroom in the den.

What's wrong? What's all the shouting about?" asked Angie.

"I just saw a snake downstairs."

Nell pointed toward the stairs leading to the basement.

"You didn't answer my questions, Nell, is it alive?"

"Yes ma'am to all your questions! At first I thought it was trash laying on the floor cause it had paper on it. But when I went to pick it up, it moved. It's covered in some kind of white stuff."

"We had the attic insulated with foam. I bet the snake has been living up there for at least two months. I was on my way out my back door two months ago and I saw a black snake right outside the door. It crawled up the side of the house, onto the roof and out of sight. I bet it crawled into the attic. When my husband was alive, he found a snake trying to get into the basement and he killed it. The one down there must be its mate."

"What should I do?" Nell asked.

"I don't know! Call the police!"

"I already did. I called them on my cell phone," said Angie.

"Suppose it goes back into hiding before the police gets here, then what?" I asked.

"It's not going anywhere. It looks like it's sick. It barely moved when I touched it," said Nell.

"You ought to see it, Angie. It's about this long."

Nell opened her hands to give Angie an idea of how long the snake was.

"Uh, Uh! I'll take your word for it! I'm scared of snakes! I don't want to see it!"

"I'm with you, Angie. I don't want to see it either! I'll just have to pray that it doesn't go back onto hiding before the police gets here," I said.

I was terrified and confused. I didn't know what to do. In that split second. I thought about Jerry.

"I sure wish my husband was here to handle this."

Neither Nell nor Angie said anything. They both hugged me and we sat at the kitchen table to wait for the police to arrive.

Two police officers answered our call. They came into the house and Nell took them downstairs to show them the snake.

One of the officers shouted, "Wow! This is a big one!"

Then he came upstairs went outside and got a stick, returned and asked me for a pillow case. He went back down stairs picked up the snake with the stick, put the snake into the pillow case, and came back upstairs carrying the snake inside the pillow case.

"What should I do with it? Should we turn it loose?" asked one policeman.

"No!" I shouted. "If it came into the house once, it'll return. It knows its way back. Take it out back and kill it!"

"Okay! I just wanted to get your permission to kill it. Some people might think killing it is animal cruelty."

"'Animal cruelty' nothing! I don't want that thing crawling back into my house! Kill it!"

The officer laughed. They took it to the creek at the back of my yard and killed it.

"You won't have to worry about that one coming back into your house anymore," said one of the officers.

"Good! That makes me feel a little bit more relieved! At least that's one snake I don't have to worry about. I'm sure there are plenty more out there in those woods."

I pointed to the trees in the back of my house.

"If you ladies need us again, just call," said one officer.

Then they left.

Even after that episode with the snake, I still wasn't ready to sell my house. I wasn't ready to let go of the memories. The grandchildren had started referring to the house on Essex Road as "the family house." Bianca said to me one day when she overheard a conversation that I was having with someone about the possibility of selling the house.

"Ma Ma, you can't sell our house. That's the family house."

I listened to her anguish plea and decided against selling the house.

After seven years the apartment began to feel cold and empty, just as the house on Essex Road once felt. The house began to feel warm and friendly, and felt like "home," again. That is when I realized that I was on the road to healing. I could return home and sleep in the bedroom I once shared with my soul mate. Although I had given away our bedroom set, I kept the mattress

When I moved into my apartment, I didn't take with me any furniture from my house on Essex Road. I only took some of my clothes. I had the apartment repainted, and bought all new furniture. Although it was a new building, only three months old and no one had ever lived in the apartment before me, I didn't want white walls. I had them painted a neutral color, a warm beige. Suzanne, an interior decorator, helped me decorate. I had drapes custom-made for the windows and I immersed myself in decorating the place. By totally concentrating on the new apartment, my new home, I didn't have time to throw myself pity-parties.

When I moved out of the apartment seven years later I realized some of the mistakes I made when I was not thinking clearly. I guess I can say I was blindly trying to handle my grief and reinvent myself by building a new environment in which to feel comfortable.

My big mistake was having drapes custom made for an apartment I would never own. I had to find someone who could use them when I moved out of the apartment. I found someone who could use the drapes from my two bedrooms –– one of which I used as an office –– but I could not find anyone who could use the drapes I had made for my balcony sliding doors. I donated those to Goodwill Industries. I had to hire someone to repaint the apartment walls to the color they were when I first moved in. I gave away the furniture, dishes, pots and pans, wall paintings, tables and lamps, three televisions, computer, a copy machine, ceiling fan, and light fixtures. I spent money on items I only needed for a short time but I did need them at that time in my life. I felt that God used me to bless many people when I gave away three rooms of furniture.

LEARNING THE GAME

You don't have to be great to start, but you have to start to be great

Jericka and I were in Denver Colorado in 2008 watching history being made when Barack Obama officially announced his candidacy for president of the United States. The historic presidential election was a powerful reminder that regardless of where you come from, it's where you end up that makes the difference. That election sent the message that the only limitations we have are self-imposed. It says we can do whatever we want and become whomever we choose to become, if we work at achieving our dream. Many people tried to persuade Barack Obama not to run for president, but he ignored those naysayers and won. Therefore, the fact that naysayers tried to persuade me not to run for a seat in the House of Delegates, was immaterial to me.

I asked Barry to be my campaign chair. He traveled on business trips for STAR, and he sometimes traveled with his wife, Theresa, on her business trips. But I knew with him being my campaign chair I could trust him to have my best interest at heart. I asked my friend Gai to be my campaign manager. She and I were members of a professional women's group. I knew she would do as good a job as my campaign manager as Barry would do as my campaign chair. I asked several people to be my campaign treasurer; they all had excuses as to why they couldn't. Finally Leronia agreed to be my campaign treasurer. Leronia was the second person I had called the night my husband died.

I didn't know what to do to begin campaigning. Barry called his friend Ed who had been a lobbyist for over thirty-years and had since retired. Ed was eager to help. He missed interacting with politicians with whom he had worked for so long. Ed took Barry and me to Annapolis to see the General Assembly in session. I promised myself a year later I'd have a seat with my name on it in the Maryland General Assembly.

I observed the impressive meeting of the sessions in the House and the Senate, across the hall from each other and dreamed of being on the inside. I felt like an outsider, a kid with her face pressed against the window of a candy store, looking at the candy inside but having no money to buy any.

It was January the opening day of the 2006 General Assembly, election would be that coming September. After the session had ended for the day, some of the legislators attended the invitation-only reception at the Governor Calvert House, across the street from the State House. Barry, Ed and I went to the Governor Calvert House too, which was a historic hotel with banquet facilities. However, because we didn't have invitations and we weren't guests of any invited guests, we were not permitted to go in the back where the festivities were held. Instead, the three of us sat in the hotel lobby and watched the dignitaries, politicians and their guests going back, and forth to the celebration. Senators, delegates, lobbyists, the governor, Sheila who was a candidate for mayor, her aides — one who was a candidate for a seat in the House of Delegates in the fortieth district.

I sat and watched them all as they walked past, looked at me, smiled, and continued inside. I felt as if they were smirking because I couldn't join the festivities. They all knew I was running for election. But they, being elected officials, were prohibited by law from campaigning during the ninety days the Maryland General Assembly is in session — from the second week in January through the second week in April. Therefore, since I was not yet an elected official, I was not prohibited from campaigning, and campaign I did. Because of my campaign, people were beginning to recognize me. I heard some of them whispering my name as they walked past.

"Yeah, that's Barbara Robinson. I hear she's running a tough campaign."

"Yeah, but I'm not worried," said one delegate.

Cathy passed by with other politicians.

"Hello, Delegate," I said.

"Oh, hello, Honey. I'm sorry. My mind was on something else. How are you?"

She looked surprised to see me.

"I'm doing great."

She walked over to give me a hug.

"Next year, you and I can have lunch together as two delegates." I said.

She paused a moment, seemingly trying to understand the meaning of what I had just said. She then responded.

"That's a date. I'm looking forward to it."

She continued into the back where the festivities were taking place.

Being on the outside looking in was not fun for me. I was determined to return the following year and attend the celebration as an elected official. I made a vow to myself:

"Next year, I'll be walking into this reception by invitation."

I made good the vow!

One Sunday after the morning service at church I told Sheila, who later became the Mayor of Baltimore that I was running for a seat in the fortieth District.

She looked at me and adamantly said, "I'm supporting Juanita!"

"But there are three seats. I'm not running against Juanita. I'm running to win one of the three seats."

"Yeah, well I still say, I'm supporting Juanita!"

"That's fine, but why can't you support us both? I'm not competing against her!"

"Why do you have to run in the fortieth District? Why can't you find another district? Why the fortieth?"

"I met with Art Murphy and he told me to run in the fortieth district. He's the expert in elections, so I'm going to take his advice. I don't understand why people are trying to convince me not to run in the fortieth district. I've prayed about my decision and I think it's what God wants me to do."

"Well, if Art said so, I guess that's it! But for the record, I'm supporting Juanita!"

She then turned and walked away.

My campaign launching party was held at the Rowing Club, but we didn't raise much money. We had another fund raiser called "Hat's off to

Barbara Robinson." That event consisted of a fashion show, a comedian, and a poet, called Native Son, we still didn't raise any money. I gave most of the tickets away so that people would attend the event and fill up the room.

For three months my campaign volunteers met at my house to strategize. Barry, Ed and I went to the bowling alley on Security Boulevard where the league to which Ed belonged was bowling. There were several groups of older men and women in leagues that had been bowling together for over ten years. Ed seemed to know everyone in the bowling alley. The cook at the Snack Shop even knew how Ed liked his chicken. Ed introduced Barry and me to his bowling buddies and informed them that I was running for election and asked for their support.

During one of the campaign meetings at my house Leronia said she was concerned that although we were meeting and talking about what was going to happen or what was going to take place, nothing was actually happening.

"I don't mean to insult anybody, or step on anybody's toes, but I don't see anything happening. We keep meeting and talking about what needs to be done, but we haven't accomplished anything."

That angered Ed.

After I thought about what Leronia said and looked at the progress the campaign had made, I realized how accurate she was.

Two months after being my campaign treasurer, Leronia resigned to run for a judgeship position in Baltimore County. She didn't win but she came in close enough to let her know that she should try again in the 2010 election. She ran a great campaign in 2010 and although it was a close race, the incumbent won.

I then asked Victor Holliday another friend of the family, to be my campaign treasurer. Victor had been at my side when Jerry died.

He agreed.

I didn't know how to organize or manage a campaign and apparently no one else in my campaign knew either. They may have worked in campaigns and helped someone get elected by volunteering their services, but no one knew how to organize or manage a campaign. I realized that if I did not make some changes I would probably lose the election. Art was giving it all he had and he was doing the best he could but his health was fading fast. The Multiple Scloris had consumed his entire body. He started out walking slow, then he had to use a walking cane, then it was difficult for him to walk at all.

Art had great ideas as to what direction the campaign should take and he had a tremendous amount of experience. But he physically could not continue, especially in a campaign such as mine that needed grass roots hands-on management.

I called Julius Henson, another political analysts, who was well known in the Maryland political world and asked him to take over my campaign. Julius was disliked by some people because of his hard-nose tactics of winning at any cost as long as it was legal. Ed didn't like Julius and balked at the thought of me getting Julius to assist me.

I called Art.

"Hi sweetheart. How are you doing?" I asked.

"Well, I have good days and bad days and today is one of those bad days. I know I haven't been meeting with the campaign members but how is everything going? I want to send out several pieces of mail to the voters in the fortieth district. I sent you copies of what will be part of our mail campaign. How did you like it?"

"There were some grammatical errors in the text and I didn't like the pictures you chose but the idea was good. However, I think I need someone a bit more aggressive to handle my campaign. I know what you're trying to accomplish with the mail campaign but I think I need more than that. I understand that you know more about running campaigns than I do, but even my limited knowledge tells me I need more hands-on management. So, as much as I love and respect you as one of Maryland's greatest and most knowledgeable political strategist, I'm going to have to end our agreement. We never got around to signing a contract."

"I know what you're saying but you need someone. You're right about my health but I'm willing to keep going to try to help you win. You need someone who knows what they're doing. The race is yours to lose."

"You're right. That's why I called Julius Henson and asked him to help me. He said he would."

"Oh, okay! As long as you have someone to help you win. Julius is a good man. He's the only political strategist in Maryland who has had more candidates win than I did. He's the only one in Maryland who ever beat me and I swore that he would never beat me again."

We both laughed.

He continued.

"But my health won't allow me to fight like I need to, like you need me to. Good luck with your campaign and if you need me, call me. You'll do fine."

Julius was one of the best. He had represented Joan Pratt in her race for Comptroller of Baltimore city and she won. He represented Elijah Cummins, a U.S. Congressman when he campaigned against Pastor Reid for the congressional district and Elijah won.

While Julius was representing me, he was also representing twenty-one other people in various races throughout Maryland. Nineteen of the twenty-one candidates won.

When Julius agreed to represent me, he said I would need approximately sixty-thousand to one-hundred thousand dollars to win because no one knew me in the political arena. When I told Ed that I was going to use Julius instead of Art, Ed said I should not change horses in the middle of the stream. I told him if I didn't, I would drown.

"You already have a political strategist and it's not costing you anything." said Ed.

"What political strategist do I have?"

"Me!"

"Ed, I know you mean well and I respect your political experience but have you ever actually managed a campaign? I've got eight people to beat and they all are younger and more experienced than I am. Do you really think we can take them?"

"Yes I do. I haven't run any campaigns but I've worked in many of them. I'll listen to what Julius has to say but I'm not going to let him tell me what to do!"

I realized right then that I needed to make changes fast. Otherwise there would be dissension in my campaign. Julius came aboard and right away started making improvements. He didn't like the pictures or the makeup artist Art had used for the mail campaign. Julius changed everything, my hair, clothes, makeup poses, jewelry, campaign colors, and I must say, the changes were for the better.

Julius wrote the script and taught me how to ask for campaign donations over the telephone. I was not accustomed to asking for financial help. I prided myself on being a self-made person. I had pulled myself up by my own boot straps, from welfare to a successful business owner and radio personality. Another one of my campaign slogans was: "From the outhouse to the State House," referring to the outhouse in our backyard in Alabama where I was born and where I spent my summers growing up in the South. I never had indoor plumbing until I came to college in Baltimore. Sometimes I used the slogan, "From welfare to faring well." Therefore, it was extremely difficult for me to ask my friends, family or colleagues for money to fund my campaign.

Yet, I must admit, I was pleasantly surprised at the extent of the help I received. Friends donated thousands of dollars to my campaign. I raised over twenty-thousand in contributions and I wrote a check to myself for Eighty-thousand, as a personal loan to the campaign. The fact that I was financially able to do that, to me it was an indication that I was following God's plan.

I didn't know what to say to people when I went through neighborhoods, going door-to-door, knocking on doors, and asking people to vote for me. Julius taught me what to say to those potential voters. He sent a woman with me to coach me on what to say and how to say it. He taught me how to keep accurate records of campaign funds, voters, volunteers, people who allowed us to put signs in their yards, on their property or cars.

He implemented several marketing strategies to get my name recognized in the political arena. For example, the Black Heritage Festival was held in Druid Hill Park. The park is located in the fortieth district. The apartment building at 2347 Eutaw Place, where Jerry was living when we first met, was up the street from the park. Many nights, he and I went strolling in the park when we were dating. When we lived in the projects after our children were born, I carried our young children to the zoo in the park. I held fond memories of Druid Hill Park, which made me hold fond memories of the fortieth district.

My campaign volunteers attached posters to bamboo sticks, marched in a straight line throughout the park chanting my name, while holding the bamboo sticks high above their heads, and handing out campaign literature. The parade of fifteen volunteers, wearing red campaign tee-shirts, matching caps and chanting like they were raping, commanded quite an impressive commotion throughout the crowd of over ten-thousand people.

One of my opponents had a booth at the event and handed out his campaign literature to people who stopped and listened to what he had to say. My campaign carried the message to the people. We didn't wait for people to come to where we were, we went to them, and distributed free gifts such as ball point pens, key chains, and fans.

Whenever there was a large gathering anywhere in Baltimore, my campaign volunteers attended and distributed campaign gifts and literature. The fans were a hit in the over one-hundred degree heat. The colors of the fans were bright red with yellow, and white writing. My name, campaign headquarters telephone number, email address and my favorite Bible verses — *Psalm 35 and Romans 8:28*— were printed on them. Those fans stood out in the crowd like a sore thumb.

At one event, when my campaign workers and I first arrived in the afternoon and offered fans to people in attendance, they waved us off, indicating they didn't want the fans. However, as the evening progressed and the weather got hotter, more humid, and the hungry mosquitoes starting biting, people came looking for us to get fans. The fans had become a great hit. The event was being aired live on the radio, and the commentator over the microphone, talked about the, "sea of red fans that had just about taken over the event."

Everyone applauded and laughed.

As part of our campaign strategy, one day we formed a fifteen car motorcade and went throughout the fortieth district neighborhoods with a bullhorn shouting my name while I rode in my convertible Mercedes waving to people. We had huge campaign signs posted all over the fortieth district. The signs were bigger than any of the other candidates' signs.

By then, Ed had decided that if I used Julius, he was going to stop working in my campaign. Barry and I called Ed almost every day for three weeks, he wouldn't answer his telephone and wouldn't respond to the many messages we left. After two months passed and he still wouldn't respond, I stopped trying to reach him. Barry wasn't ready to give up reaching him. They were buddies and had once worked together at Sparrows Point.

Wednesday, August 16, 2006, Julius engaged a media group to film a television commercial for my campaign. That commercial really helped me win. According to several political sources, no one had used television commercials to be elected for either a State Delegate of a State Senator. That type of campaign strategy was reserved for the mayor, governor, or president. But I was determined to win. So many people didn't think I had a chance of winning. I had to prove that I could campaign with the best of them.

My campaign paid for radio and television commercials. We also had a telephone campaign where we called thousands of people asking for their vote. Art had mentioned using a billboard as advertisement.

Julius disagreed. He said our money would be better spent communicating with people in their homes through radio and television commercials, rather than posting messages on billboards. "Billboards can only be seen if a person happens to drive in that neighborhood on that street," he said.

He was right.

Senator Hughes, who was the senator in the fortieth district at the time I began my campaign, decided to retire and not run again after twenty-four years of service. That left his seat vacant. Some of my friends and Julius tried to convince me to run for that seat. I thought about it. The sound of, "Senator Barbara Robinson" had a nice ring to it. Since I had already invested forty-thousand dollars in my campaign for a seat in the House of Delegates, I put my campaign on hold for three days, to decide whether or not I wanted to change and run for the Senator position.

Changing plans meant that I would have to change all my campaign signs and other campaign marketing material. Running for the position of senator would have cost more money to win. Plus, there was only one seat for senator, there were three seats for delegate. That meant for delegate I had three chances of winning, for senator I had only one chance. Julius was convinced that I could win and so were my colleagues. However, because I was new to politics, and there was only one chance to win against eight opponents, I was apprehensive.

Juanita and Cathy gave up their delegate seats to run for senator. That left Toby as the only incumbent. Technically, he was not an incumbent he had not been elected to that position. He was appointed by the fortieth district State Central Committee to fill a vacancy until an election occurred.

Cathy said Senator Hughes told her that when she goes door-to-door campaigning, she should take at least two or three people with her.

"That way, voters will think there are a lot of people who support you and are willing to work to get you elected," he said.

But the problem was, I didn't always have two or three people available to go door-to-door with me. Going door-to-door required walking in different neighborhoods, sometimes running from dogs and going up and down steep concrete steps that led to yards sitting on high hills. Often during the day it was only Gai and I. In the evenings it was always one other person and me.

I threw myself into a totally unfamiliar new career change, and learned the rules along the way. No one thought I could win the election. No special interest groups, no lobbyist, no union, no news paper, no one but God, family, friends, and some colleagues, supported my efforts and believed in me. Each time I got confused about what decision to make, I went to my knees and asked God for directions.

At night I planned the strategies for the next day. My family was glad I had found another project interesting enough to bring me out of my depression over my husband's death. One day I overheard Butch talking to a colleague in the office.

"Man, you don't know how glad I am to have my mama back. My mama is a trooper, she's a fighter, but after my father died, she just didn't seem to have that drive anymore. It seemed that all the fight left her and she just gave up. I was worried there for a while. But with people counting her out, not having faith in her ability to win the election, not believing her when she said she was doing what God wanted her to do, especially being disrespected by the pastor of her church, she still won. Man, that was messed up! My Mom just worked hard and prayed hard. That's a praying woman!"

"How could I get so lucky? How could I be propelled into a completely new career and not only enjoy it, but also be good at it?" I asked myself.

I discovered that I knew more about politics than I thought I knew. It appeared that all of my life's work had been in preparation for my new career in politics.

FOOTPRINTS

My precious child ... I would never leave you. During your times of trial and suffering, when you see only one set of footprints, it was then that I carried you –– Mary Stevenson, 1936

It was during the summer of 2006 when the temperature reached one-hundred-five degrees. It was hot! Gai, my campaign manager, and I would meet at seven every morning at the Seven-Eleven store on Liberty Heights Avenue. We filled our ice chest with ice and bottled water, strategized what neighborhood we would concentrate on that morning and headed out to those places. When it became too hot at eleven o'clock in the morning, we went back home, waited until it got cooler in the afternoon, and at approximately four or five o'clock, we went back out again and started knocking on doors, campaigning throughout neighborhoods, asking for votes.

The two months prior to the primary election in September, I went out knocking on doors in the district every day, rain or shine. If it rained I waited until the rain stopped or slacked off then I used my umbrella and went back out into the neighborhoods. That's how I fractured my elbow.

One Thursday evening at about four o'clock, Gai and I were walking through neighborhoods on Bentalou Street, a moderately well traveled street off of busy North Avenue. As the candidate, it was my job to knock on doors, meet people, ask them to vote for me and ask if we could put a campaign sign in their yard. If they didn't have a yard, we asked to put a sign in their window or on the rail on their porch or steps. We carried with us note books to write the names and addresses of the people who gave us permission to put up signs. It was the job of another group of people from my campaign to take the addresses from the notebooks, return to the houses with the signs and put them in the appropriate yards.

When I fracture my elbow it reminded me of the time I had surgery on my shoulder, except Jerry was there to help me get dressed, shower, and do all those things that were too difficult for a one armed person to do. This time, I did not have Jerry to help me. I was on my own. Living in the apartment alone I could only depend on myself. Yet I still had to campaign if I wanted to win the election. I did not have time to feel sorry for myself. I had to stay in the race and fight.

After we visited three houses that day, it started to rain a steady flow, just enough to make the grass slippery. Gai and I put signs in several yards as we went along knocking on doors. The fourth house we visited sat high on a grassy hill. We obtained permission from the home owner to put a sign in their yard. I pushed the stick that held the sign deep into the ground so the wind wouldn't topple it. When it was secured, I turned to walk back down the hill when my feet slipped on the wet grass, and I started sliding down the hill and couldn't stop.

Gai was standing at the bottom of the hill holding an umbrella over her head and holding another sign I was planning to put in the next yard. When she saw me falling, she jumped back so I wouldn't fall on her.

"Oh, Barbara! watch yourself! Watch yourself!" she shouted.

My body lunged forward and I fell down the hill and landed on the concrete sidewalk below. I used my left hand to try to brace myself. I cushioned my head with my arms. I landed on my hands and knees which injured my wrists and fractured my right elbow. I was wearing white deck pants, walking shoes, a campaign red tee-shirt, and a red campaign cap. The bruise on my knee bled onto my white pants. My elbow also started to bleed. My hand and wrist started to swell and throb. It was five days later before I learned the extent of my injuries.

When I managed to stand, so as not to alarm people at the houses by the sight of my blood on my white pants, I took the sign Gai was holding and held it in front of me. Drivers in cars passing by had witnessed me fall and stopped to see if I was alright.

When Gai saw the blood, on my pants, she looked scared.

"Oh, you really hurt yourself. Look! You're bleeding. Barbara you should go to the hospital. You might have really hurt yourself!"

"I don't have time to stop and go to the hospital. I'm all right. We still have two signs left, let's put them up before we leave. You are going to have to put up the last two. I can't climb the embankments anymore. My leg hurts too badly," I said.

Gai reluctantly agreed and put the last two signs in the next two yards.

"Move it over a little off the hill!" I shouted.

Gai didn't pay any attention to my instructions. I didn't blame her. I had taken a hard fall. She was apprehensive about walking in the wet grass. She didn't want to fall as I had.

"Let's go. I'm in pain. I need to go home!" I said.

"You need to go to the hospital! That was a nasty fall! I'll call you later to see how you're doing."

We got into our cars and left.

I had planned to attend a candidates' forum that evening at seven o'clock where the candidates for the House of Delegates and Senators were to appear in front of voters of various organizations and present our platform. But I was hurting so badly, I went home and got into bed.

The following morning was Friday, when Nell and Angie, came to clean my apartment. For more than ten years, they cleaned various properties my family and I owned: my house on Essex Road, my office building, other homes SelfPride owned, Jericka's, and Jeanene's houses. Therefore, they were like family. This day they saw me struggling, trying to get dressed, and they helped me. My body was in so much pain, I couldn't tie my shoes.

"Ms. Robinson, you seem to be in a lot of pain. You should go to the hospital," Nell said.

"Yeah, and if you don't go, we're going to call Jericka," said Angie.

Everyone teased me about Jericka acting as if she is my mama, always trying to boss me around. But I don't mind. I know it's always out of love and concern for me.

"I'm going to the doctor but not today. I have too many candidate forums to go to today. I have a campaign to run."

"It's not going to do you any good to win if you can't walk," said Angie.

I knew they were right, but I didn't have time to go to the doctor right then. Plus the following day Saturday I had another candidates forum to attend. Sunday I had to visit churches in my district asking for votes. Monday was another forum where I had to present my campaign platform.

After each painful event was over I went back to my apartment and got into bed. I was in so much pain, it was getting increasingly harder for me to dress myself. My arms and legs hurt so badly I could hardly get out of bed. At night I couldn't sleep because of the pain. If I did manage to fall asleep, the pain woke me up and I'd spend the rest of the night sitting up in bed rocking from side to side, holding my elbow and crying.

Tuesday morning I got up to get dressed and meet Gai to go door-to-door. I couldn't lift my leg high enough to step into the shower. I could not use my right arm at all. I was hurting so badly, I started praying.

"God, should I go to the doctor or should I go out and campaign today?"

When I couldn't tie my shoes, put on my brassiere, or even brush my teeth, I knew God was telling me to go to the doctor.

I had fallen the previous Thursday, August 10, it was now Tuesday, August 15, the pain was getting worse and I had not seen a doctor. I could no longer stand the pain so I finally called Dr. Lotlikar, made an appointment. I couldn't drive so Jericka came to get me; she helped me to get dressed and scolded me all the way to the doctor's office for waiting so long to go. Dr. Lotlikar also chastised me for waiting so long to see him. He gave me medicine for the pain and sent me to the hospital to get an x-ray of my shoulder, elbow, wrist and legs.

The x-ray showed that my elbow was fractured, my shoulder dislocated and my wrist sprang. I was blessed. It could have been worse. I didn't have any broken bones and that was a blessing. Dr. Lotlikar sent me to an occupational therapist, but on my second visit to the therapist, my whole arm hurt more than it did before I went to the therapist. Their treatment was too rough and they had prescribed the wrong types of exercises for me.

I went to see another doctor, Dr. Murthi, an orthopedic surgeon who had operated on my son's knee years prior when he played football in college. Dr. Murthi sent me to have a MRI. That test showed, I had ruptured the rotator cuff in my right shoulder. He said I would need surgery to repair the injury. I didn't want to hear that word, "surgery," so I went to see another doctor, Dr. Freidman, seeking a second opinion. Dr. Freidman concurred with Dr. Murthi's diagnosis that I needed surgery.

Therefore, I resigned myself to accept his diagnosis and my surgery was scheduled for November 1, 2006.

I continued to campaign with my right arm in a sling, a shot of cortisone in my shoulder, my right wrist bandaged, and limping on my right leg. There were many forums where I had to appear with the other candidates — some for the House of Delegates and some for the Senate — to present my platform and convince voters to vote for me. I also still had to continue knocking on doors. I took pain medicine and kept going. When I appeared at places where I had to step up on stage or climb onto a platform to reach the podium to speak to the waiting crowd, Jericka was always at my side to help me. She was my driver. When the pain became too intense, she gave me her shoulder to lean on. She never said a word, when I stood to walk to the podium to speak, she came and stood by my side so that I could use her shoulder for support. Sometimes as I sat and listened to the other candidates, I tried not to cry because of the pain. If Jericka knew how much pain I was really in, she would insist that I leave and go home.

Finally, Election Day came for the primary election. It was a cold day in September 2006. My buddies Regina, Alice, Frances, and Regina's friend Ella were working at the poll that in the past elections had the largest voter turn-out. Regina and I lived in Flag House Courts Projects in the 1960s and early 1970s. We were best friends, our children were friends, we were like family.

At the polls on Election Day, other candidates purchased food for their volunteers. They had fried chicken, sodas, cake, donuts, and hot coffee in the cold brisk morning air. I, on the other hand had purchased box lunches for my volunteers. Those lunches consisted of either cold turkey or roast beef sandwiches, potato chips, cookies, sodas and bottled water. I could not afford elaborate lunches. I didn't have a large budget. Because I was not known in the political community, I didn't have many people making donations to my campaign. I was the primary contributor.

After eating their elaborate lunches, the other candidates' campaign workers sat under a tree, listened to music on their radio, and rested. They attempted to entice my volunteers to do the same. However, my volunteers refused to stop working, and continued to pass out campaign literature. My volunteers said they had a job to do and didn't have time to rest. It wasn't necessary for them to read the campaign material they were distributing to know what it said. If a voter asked one of my volunteers why should he or she vote for me, without hesitation, my volunteers told them what I stood for and what my issues were. They knew enough about me to speak for me. That was a blessing.

One of the volunteers of another candidate asked Alice when was she going to stop and rest.

She replied, "We'll rest when we know our candidate has won."

I was apprehensive about having surgery on my shoulder. I had won the primary election on September 12, 2006, and I needed to also win the General Election on November 11, 2006. I wouldn't have to campaign as hard to win the General Election in November as I did to win the Primary. I was already in second place and the only competitor was a woman who was running on the Green Ticket, no republican was opposing the three Democratic winners of the Primary election. Therefore, I decided to postpone my surgery until after the general election. The day before I was to be admitted to the hospital for surgery, I called the doctor and canceled. He wasn't too pleased and neither was my family.

After winning the election, the swearing in ceremony for the new elected officials was scheduled for January 10, 2007 at the State House in Annapolis, the Capital of Maryland. The new date for surgery on my shoulder was December 6, 2006. When I first considered having surgery on my shoulder on the December date, I thought I would be healed enough to handle the responsibilities of my new elected position in Annapolis. I thought if I had the surgery in November 2006, I'd be healed enough by January, 2007, to participate in the swearing in ceremony. Rather than drive the forty plus miles back and forth from Baltimore to Annapolis every day for ninety days while the Maryland General Assembly was in session, I chose to live in a hotel in Annapolis and return home to Baltimore on the weekend. I decided to return to Baltimore either on Friday evening or Saturday morning and return to Annapolis Monday afternoon. On Mondays the session didn't convene until eight o'clock in the evening. Tuesday, Wednesday and Thursday, it convened at ten o'clock every morning, and eleven o'clock Friday morning. I thought I'd be able to take care of myself if I lived in a hotel.

Several events scheduled in November, December and January were important for me to attend. Therefore, I didn't have time for the December scheduled surgery. After such a win, with being the underdog in the race, winning first place in several polls, and second place in others, I couldn't begin my new career limping. I had to hit the ground running. I postponed the surgery again and this time my doctor and family were more upset with me than ever.

I needed constant physical therapy to get strength back into my right arm. I couldn't lift my arm any higher than my waist. I hoped with exercise, I could at least raise it high enough to take the oath on January 10, 2007, when administered by Delegate Michael Busch, the Speaker of the Maryland House of Delegates.

Friday, December 8, 2006. I went to Kernan Hospital for physical therapy. But I was in so much pain I had to leave. I couldn't raise my arm high enough to participate in the scheduled exercises.

The following Sunday, December 10, 2006, I was at Bethel AME Church when I had a conversation with the First Lady Marlaa' Reid, the wife of Pastor Frank M. Reid, III, the senior pastor of Bethel A.M.E. Church.

"How are you doing, Sister Barbara?" she asked.

"Not very well. I'm in a lot of pain."

"What happened?"

I shared with her my shoulder injury and the fact that I couldn't lift my arm shoulder high, and against the orders of my doctor, I have postponed surgery twice.

She smiled.

"Which shoulder did you injure?"

"My right shoulder."

"Let's pray!" she said.

She put her hand on my shoulder and prayed that it would heal.

"You'll be alright. God has work for you to do!" she said after she finished praying.

I hugged her and thanked her for her prayers.

I went home and as much as I could began taking care of my household duties. That evening, Jericka and I went to Morgan State University to hear the Morgan Choir in concert. The following day I was in my kitchen,

171

washing and drying dishes, putting them away into the cabinets without any effort. I wasn't thinking about my injuries; my mind was on the upcoming swearing in ceremony and my late husband.

I was thinking how proud he would be of me and how at the swearing in ceremony, he would be standing beside me with his head held high and his chest out, grinning. I was excited about winning and having to live in a hotel in Annapolis for three months at the state's expense. I was thinking how Jerry would have enjoyed that too, especially since he had retired. Then as I put a plate away, I noticed my arm was up above my head, putting dishes on the top shelf of the cabinet. I was reaching up high with my right arm. The previous day, I couldn't comb my hair nor use my right arm to take a shower. But there I was, using my arm as if it had healed and the pain was no longer there.

I started crying, shouting, and thanking Jesus.

I went to physical therapy the next day, and before the therapist began my routine, I was excited and happy, anxious to show off what I considered an answer to my prayer, a miracle.

"Wait a minute! I want to show you something!" I said to the therapist.

I lifted my arm over my head, touched my back and performed exercises without the aid of the therapist.

The therapist was amazed.

"What happened to you?" he exclaimed, almost in disbelief.

"Sunday after the morning services at my church, the First Lady of my church prayed over my shoulder. I just wanted to show you the power of prayer!"

"Wow!" the therapist said, "Tell your First Lady that she can pray over you and lay hands on you anytime she wants to. If she could bottle that powerful prayer, she'd make millions."

We both laughed.

"It'll work for anybody. All they have to do is pray and believe. It's already bottled," I said.

We laughed again.

That was the power of prayer yet again. Prayer had helped me through the rough times of grief. Prayer was now taking me successfully through another journey of physical pain.

Following my fall, I suffered another physical upset but God intervened again and saved me. Saturday, December 29, 2007, on my way to a community meeting, I was in an automobile accident while driving my Jeep Cherokee, which I had purchased three months prior. A driver ran a red light on the corner of Charles Street and Mount Royal Avenue and hit my car on the driver's side. Both cars were totaled, and we were blessed that we weren't seriously hurt. I was also blessed that I was driving my jeep, had I been driving my convertible Mercedes-Benz I might not have survived the crash.

The police arrived on the scene and pulled me from the wreckage. I wasn't bleeding from any wounds and I felt blessed. However, as the weeks progressed, my body ached all over. That year, I lived at the Sheraton Hotel in Annapolis during the ninety days the General Assembly was in session. I went to a doctor at the Anne Arundel General Hospital. I also visited a physical therapist around the corner from the hotel. I received therapy until the session was over.

People say that Satan is always on his job, and they are right. When I survived the two accidents, Satan tried again to stop me. I was sitting in committee meeting one morning during session and I felt sick. I couldn't identify what was wrong. I just felt sick. I had only drunk orange juice that morning, yet I began the day feeling as if I had indigestion. I drank more orange juice, thinking it would make me feel better; however, the more juice I drank, the worse I felt. I left the committee meeting and sat in the committee lunch room. Adrienne Jones, the Speaker Pro Temp, came into the lounge and asked if I was okay?

"No, I'm not! I feel so bad."

She was concerned about me and put her hand on my forehead to see if I had a fever.

"What's wrong?"

"I don't know. I just feel sick. That's the only way I can describe how I feel."

"Are you in pain?"

"No, that's the strange part. I don't hurt. I just feel sick. I feel as if I have to vomit but I went to the restroom to try and I couldn't. Maybe if I go the hotel and rest, I'll feel better."

I stood up to leave.

"No! You're not leaving! You don't know what's wrong. I'm calling the nurse."

She picked up the telephone and dialed the nurse's office.

"I don't need a nurse. I just need to go to my hotel and lie down," I protested.

She insisted that I wait for the nurse.

The nurse arrived in a matter of minutes; I told her I just wanted to go to my hotel room and lay down. The nurse was adamant that I not go to the hotel.

"There is no way you are going to the hotel and someone can say I let a delegate walk out of here sick. You have one of two choices, either we call the paramedics to come and take you to the hospital, or we will have a state trooper drive you in a trooper's car, but one way or the other you are going to the hospital!"

Because of my symptoms, the nurse thought I was having a heart attack.

A state trooper was called he drove me to the hospital and stayed with me until Jericka arrived. Adrienne had called her and informed her that I had been taken to the hospital.

I stayed in the hospital two days and thank God I had only acid reflux, gerd. God continued to bless me by not allowing me to have a heart attack or stroke. God protecting me from the two accidents and the illness are reasons why I believe that God has an assignment for me. I know the power of prayer is always at work in my life.

I was excited about winning the election to a seat in the House of Delegates. At the inauguration of the new delegates, Jericka asked every person with a camera who appeared to be a reporter, to take a picture of me and to interview me. John Rydell, a reporter from channel forty-five, was one of the reporters who interviewed me. Jericka met him in Annapolis at the State House on January 10, 2007, the beginning of the 423rd session of the Maryland General Assembly, when I was sworn in as one of the new delegates. I was one of thirty-four newly elected state delegates and one of three from the fortieth legislative district in Baltimore City.

As John and I talked that day, he asked me why I ran for public office. I told him I had never run for a political office in my life, and it was amazing to me that I won. During the interview, I explained to him that I wanted to make a difference in the way seniors and people on welfare were treated or were represented in Annapolis.

"How old are you? He asked. "You don't appear to be old enough to have lived through the troubles you are talking about."

I smiled.

"I'll tell you my age but it's not for publication. I don't want you to say on air how old I am. People tell me that I don't look my age. Besides, I was the oldest candidate in the race, so I don't want to focus on my age."

"I won't mention your age. That'll just be between you and me. I want to know for my own personal knowledge."

He lied! When the interview aired that night on television, John Rydell began the report by saying, "Sixty-eight-year-old Delegate Barbara Robinson has experienced the life of homelessness and being on welfare."

The very first thing he said was my age; therefore, I was apprehensive when he asked to interview me again after the session started. He called my office, talked with my assistant, and told her to ask me if he could do a feature story about me. I figured since he had already put my age out there for the public to know, he couldn't do anymore damage. I'm glad I agreed to the interview. He and a camera man spent three hours following me around the State Capitol, during the General Assembly, filming me in my office, in the assembly room, walking to the State House, and standing in front of the State House. He sent a cameraman to photograph me that following Saturday as I gave a speech at a local church.

During the interview in Annapolis, while we were standing in front of the State Capitol John asked me what was the one thing I was the proudest of by being elected. I looked at the steps of the State Capitol that led to the General Assembly rooms, and I smiled.

"I'm most proud of being here as an elected official in a place where my ancestors were brought in on slave ships. I'm a black woman from Alabama, who went to high school in Georgia. I grew up at a time and in a place, where I couldn't sit at the counter with white folks in public places and eat lunch. I had to sit at the back of the bus on public transportation. I couldn't drink from the same water fountain as white folks. Our schools were separate but were anything but equal. Restrooms had signs that read, 'Ladies, Gentlemen,' and 'Colored.' We weren't respected enough to be thought of as men and women, we were lumped together as, 'Colored.' But for me to have been elected by white and black voters to represent them in the State's Capitol, and to walk up those steps," I pointed to the steps of the State House, "and go into an assembly room where my past generations were not permitted to go, and I get to have a say about laws that affect people in a state that once held slaves, I am most proud of the opportunity to stand on the shoulders of past generations and perhaps be able to share my shoulders with future generations of my people."

GOD'S PUZZLE OR PLAN

While I was trying to figure it out, God had already worked it out. Life is not so much a puzzle as it is a plan, God's plan.

Today is my birthday, Sunday, June 8, 2008. I'm 70 years old today. My grandmother, Beulah Beatrice Dark, my mother's mother, my biological father, Houston Robinson, Reverend Nunn, the late pastor of Bethel Baptist Church in Alexander City, Alabama, my home town, Bishop John R. Bryant, the former pastor of Bethel AME Church in Baltimore, and I, were all born on June 8.

Jericka and I have just returned home from Sunday morning 8:00 a.m. services at Bethel A.M.E. in Baltimore where the pastor preached about champions.

"Start thinking like a champion and stop thinking like a loser," he said.

Joan Pratt, sat beside me on my right and Jericka sat next to me on my left. Behind us sat Irene Reid, Pastor Reid's step mother. Irene's maiden name is Schmoke. Her only son was once Mayor of Baltimore City. I am sad to say that Irene was buried Saturday, January 15, 2011, after a battle with cancer.

Sheila sat across from us on the second row.

In May 2008 Bethel honored women leaders in Maryland. Joan, Sheila, Irene Reid, and I were among those being honored.

I whispered in Sheila's ear.

"You ever think during the time we sat on my basement floor planning a trip to Africa that we both would end up in politics, you mayor and me delegate? Who'd a thunk it?"

She laughed.

"We both have come a long way," she said.

Today is a milestone in my life. To reach the age of seventy and be in good health is a blessing. When I went to get a physical examination, my doctor asked me how was I feeling?

"Ms. Robinson, how are you feeling?"

"I'm feeling great, Doctor!"

"Are you taking any type of medication?"

"No, I'm not taking any medication at all."

"You're in pretty good shape."

"I know if it wasn't for my knees hurting every time I try to stand from a sitting position, and my legs giving out on me every now and then, I have sleep apnea and I snore so loudly when I sleep that sometimes my snoring wakes me up, my hair is grey and regardless of how it's styled, even with the weave or new wigs, I don't like my hair. My eyesight isn't so good anymore and neither is my hearing, but aside from that, I'm as good as I ever was. One of my late husband's buddies used to say:

'I may not be as good as I once was, but I am as good once as I ever was.' So, that's how I feel!"

We laughed.

Before I confronted the puzzle of entering politics, God gave me another puzzle to solve. When I worked with non-profits, my office building at 12 West Montgomery Street, was connected to another brick building: the Ebenezer AME Church. Reverend Bald was the senior pastor of the church. One day in May 2002, I was sitting in my office and Pastor Bald called me on the telephone.

"Hello, Mrs. Robinson, this is Pastor Bald. How are you this fine morning?"

"Good morning Pastor! I am doing very well, thank you. What a pleasant surprise!"

"I was walking past your building and the Lord lay on my heart to call you to tell you that you should deliver the Mother's Day Sermon at my church this year."

I was flattered and honored but I hadn't ever done that before and the thought of trying to deliver a sermon to church folks scared me.

"Thank you so much Reverend Bald for thinking about me. I am truly honored. But I'm afraid I will have to decline. I am not a preacher and I wouldn't know what to say."

"Mrs. Robinson. I have been a preacher for over twenty years. I have delivered hundreds of sermons and many, Mother's Day sermons. I can deliver the one this year. But God said He wanted you to do it. Now you can call it a speech, a presentation, a sermon, or whatever you want to call it. I just know that God said He wanted you to deliver the message at Ebenezer AME Church this Mother's Day. So please let me know what your topic will be and we'll talk later. I will not take 'no' for an answer."

What could I say after that obvious directive?

"Yes, Pastor! We'll talk later."

We hung up the telephone. And I started talking to God.

"Father, what am I supposed to say? I have never done this before. You have to help me. You know I am out of my element!"

I thought about the sermon I had delivered in Lusaka, Zambia, in Africa. All of a sudden I started getting excited at the prospect of me delivering a sermon in church. I called Jericka and told her. She was excited. I called Butch and my husband. They were excited. I then called Jeanese and Jeanene. They both promised they would be in church that Mother's Day. I called my sister Sandy and learned that she was to deliver her trial sermon at a church in Boston that Mother's Day. I spoke with my brother Al whom I had not heard from in almost a year. Sandy called him and told him I was going to preach the sermon on Mother's Day. Al was excited and promised to come.

I then understood God's reasoning about telling Reverend Bald to contact me to deliver the sermon. It wasn't about me. It was about pulling my family together. Pastor Bald was the vehicle that God used to pull all of us together. In church that Mother's Day, my husband, my children, my grandchildren, my son's fiancée, my brother and his wife, Wendell, Jeanese's husband, were all present. Jeanese and Wendell had started to church that morning and their car broke down on Interstate Highway eighty-three. They left their car and walked three miles to get to the church to hear my sermon. I know that my mother was looking down from heaven that Sunday. I know she was proud to see her family in church and her two daughters standing in the pulpit, one in Boston Massachusetts and the other in Baltimore, Maryland. During the 1950s we lived on Coolidge Avenue in the East Wynnton section of Columbus, Georgia. Folks in the neighborhood called my mother "Old Drunk Louise." But look at her family now. That was God's way of making a monument out of ashes.

In June, 1988, I was in Lusaka Zambia in Central Africa attending services at Ebenezer AME Church with Reverend Simfukwa, the pastor of Bethel AME Church in Lusaka. That Sunday, Reverend Simfukwa was the guest preacher at Ebenezer. As he neared the end of his message, he looked at me, smiled and said something to the congregation in Bimba, one of their languages. I didn't understand what he said to the congregation, so when they looked at me and smiled, I smiled back.

Reverend Simfukwa continued to communicate to the congregation in their Bimba Language. The more he spoke the louder they applauded and the wider their smiles were. As they smiled and looked at me, they nodded their heads and whispered to each other. They appeared to be in agreement with whatever Reverend Simfukwa was saying.

I pretended I understood what Reverend Simfukwa had said. I also began to applaud. Then I realized they were applauding for me. I stopped applauding, stopped smiling, and started feeling uneasy.

I turned to the young man sitting beside me who was chosen by the church to be my interpreter.

"What is he saying?"

"He's telling us that he is going to Ndola next weekend and will not be at Bethel to preach the sermon next Sunday. He says, 'The American Lady,' meaning you, will preach the sermon next Sunday at Bethel and he is inviting everyone to come to church to hear your sermon."

I was shocked!

"What?" I whispered

"I'm not a preacher! I can't do that! What will I say? Plus I don't speak their language."

I started pulling on Reverend Simfukwa's pants leg, trying to get his attention. I wanted to let him know that he and I needed to talk before he continued to make promises.

He brushed my hand away from his pants leg, stepped out of my reach, continued to address the congregation and ignored my frantic attempts to get his attention.

"Reverend Simfukwa! Reverend Simfukwa!" I anxiously whispered.

He continued to ignore me. When he finished talking and the services were over, I pulled him aside.

"Why did you do that? I don't know what to say in church. Why did you do that?"

In his heavy British accent he looked at me, smiled, and took both my hands in his.

"Don't fret daughter. Ask God to help you. He will tell you what to say."

We left the church and had dinner without further discussion of what he had said to the congregation.

That night, I prayed about it.

I was living with the Chintu family who were all members of Bethel AME Church. Mrs. Elizabeth Chintu was a nurse and her husband an engineer. They were not the typical African family that is often portrayed by the media, where fifteen or more live in a small round one-room hut made of either mud or branches. They had a beautiful home, with an in-ground swimming pool, a tennis court, and servants quarters where their house servant lived. Elizabeth Chintu gave me a Bible written in English and contained the most basic stories that I had ever read. I wanted to bring the Bible back to Baltimore with me but she wanted to keep it. It was her only one.

I worked on a sermon for the following Sunday. I used the love chapter, I Corinthians 13, to write my sermon. That following Sunday, in Lusaka, I delivered the message. Ten people joined the church that day and gave their life to Christ. I then understood that it wasn't about me. It was about the message. There was an interpreter in church that Sunday interpreting my words for the congregation. Everyone understood my message.

I've presented workshops for women at the Mt. Pleasant Baptist Church in Maryland. The following year they brought me back as the guest speaker for the Women's Day Service that was held at Martins, Crosswinds, a large ballroom in Maryland.

I was the guest speaker and delivered the sermon from the pulpit at the Ray of Hope Baptist Church. The following year they contacted me to return for a second time.

I delivered a message from the pulpit of several other churches in Ohio and Tennessee.

Therefore, if God had said "preach" when I was contemplating what to do after Jerry died, I would have understood His reasoning.

I would also have understood God saying teach. I have taught credit and none credit courses at three colleges in Maryland. I developed the curriculum for a court reporter's class that was taught at the Baltimore City Community College. I used my own material to teach business courses at Anne Arundel Community College. I taught inmates in prison for seven years. I applied to Johns Hopkins University and the University of Maryland to get a doctorate degree in education. I did not complete the application process but took courses toward the doctorate.

I taught first-line supervision and business management at Baltimore City Community College. I was a member of the Criminal Justice Advisory Committee overseeing the Community College of Baltimore's partnership with the Supreme Bench of Baltimore City which is now the District Court of Baltimore City. The college provided the material, I recruited the judges to teach the courses. The college paid their salary as part time instructors. That meant the judges were making extra money.

The college provided the text books and the marketing material to recruit students for the Supreme Bench's classes. Participants were students not just from the court system, they were employees from the police department, the fire department, from State and city agencies, and from the private sector. I handled the advertising, the registration, the applications, the supplies, training material records, and all other administrative functions. I worked with the college's finance department to maintain financial records of expenses for the classes that were taught in various rooms in the court house. I formed a committee from the college to assist me in developing the course content to ensure the subjects taught met the requirements of the college and the needs of the court.

I was not compensated by the college or the court system for my work developing and monitoring the program. It was often necessary for me to stay late to ensure the classrooms were available, and that the instructors had adequate supplies. All of that was on my own time. I just wanted to see the court reporter's training program succeed. The judges — mostly white — constantly said they couldn't attract qualified minority employees to work as court reporters, which paid a lucrative salary. Therefore, I figured if I provided a training program at a time and location where the training was affordable and accessible, we could generate a larger pool of minorities from which to recruit employees.

A month into the development of the program, Debi, a young woman who had worked with me from the inception of the program, committed suicide. I almost decided not to finish working with the program, until I started thinking about how much it was needed by people of color. Debi's suicide reminded me of another suicide that impacted my life.

Prior to my family and I moving into the house on Essex Road, a young man, Walter, (Not his real name) was doing minor repair work and repainting the inside of the house. Jerry and I had gone to the house several days to see how soon he would be finished with the work, and Walter wasn't there. He had only been married a few months and since it was a few days before Christmas, we thought he was out Christmas shopping with his new wife. When we went to the house the third day and still didn't find him there, I called the company where he worked. They hadn't seen him at the office for several days and assumed he was out working on our house. When they learned we hadn't seen him either, the office manager went to Walter's house and found his body hanging from the ceiling in his basement. He left a note addressed to me and my family apologizing for letting us down by not completing the job. We learned that he and his new wife had an argument and she walked out.

I guess Debi's death upset me so much because she too committed suicide during the Christmas holiday season and her suicide was attributed to depression. Years later, after my husband's death, I was also depressed but I never considered suicide. I just wanted to go to sleep and not wake up.

When I started working in the court system, there were even fewer options for people of color, especially women of color. In 1966 when Butch was three years old, I got a job as clerk in the traffic division of the then Municipal Court, stamping "W" in warrant books, indicating that a traffic warrant had been issued for that particular citation number. That was before computers were used in the court system. Two years later the Municipal Court which was under the jurisdiction of the city, became a state operated agency and the name was changed to District Court.

From the Municipal Court we could walk around the corner to Baltimore Street, right in the middle of the white night life of strip clubs, burlesque bars, prostitutes and crime. What Baltimore street was to the predominantly white community, Pennsylvania Avenue was to the Black community. Many famous people came to the Royal Theater on Pennsylvania Avenue. The first time I saw Tina Turner dance in high heel shoes and a short skirt was at the Royal Theater. The first time I saw James Brown was at the Royal Theater. I remember thinking how handsome Cab Calloway was when he performed there.

The Jewel Box Review was one of my favorite shows that annually came to the Royal Theater. It was a show where female impersonators and some gay men came together and traveled around the country performing shows of musical selections, fashion shows and comedy.

DOTS BETWEEN THE DASHES

It doesn't matter where you started, it's where you end up that makes the difference

I look back on the time after Jerry died and marvel at where life has taken me. I could not have guessed what the future would hold for me at that depressing time. In addition to my career in politics, I have also learned things about lifelong relationships. Don't try to find fault with your mate. You can always find something you don't like about him or her. Examine yourself and ask yourself, how perfect are you? You say he doesn't satisfy you sexually anymore, he's impotent. Does having sex with you still feel the same to him? Think about it.

There's a reason why God left you here on earth. It has no connection with how much money you earned, how much you donated to the church or, how good looking you are. God has a plan for you and for your life. He may want you to minister to "Mrs. Johnson" who lives next door. She may be helping her grandson stay out of jail. God may be planning to use her grandson thirty years from now to mentor to another young man who will discover a cure for cancer, or that grandson may father a child who will father a child who will build homes to help thousands of disabled people. You may not live to see God's plan but that's not your assignment. Your assignment is to continue God's plan. It began years ago before you were born. God had a plan for you before you came out of your mother's womb. Life is hard and it's often not fair but it's the one God gave you.

Don't question God as to why did he take your spouse.

The death of your spouse is more intimate, more personal, more devastating and more profound than any other death you may experience. That person shared your secrets, habits, likes and dislikes, more than any other person in the world. You have shared precious moments, sexual preferences, intimate needs, and so much more from the depths of your soul. That was your soul mate. That was the person who God meant for you to spend your life with.

Something else happens when you are confronted with the loss of a loved one. When that person dies, you come to grips with mortality, you realize that life is short and you are only here on this earth for a little while. You wonder where do you go from here? What do you do with your life until your dying day comes. What do you do each day? How do you fill the emptiness of losing the person with whom you shared your life?

There are two important points in our lives called "dots." Those points are birth and death. The first dot is life and the second dot is death. Life between those dots are called "dashes." We live phases of our life as dashes between those dots. It's what we do with those dashes that determines how we are remembered when we get to the second dot. If we travel through life so fast we don't enjoy the journey we will have wasted a trip many people don't get the chance to take. Stop and smell the roses of life and make memories along the way. Memories are dashes.

It's how we live between those dots that determine the quality of our life. The dashes between those dots are different stops in your life. They are our dances. You decide what your dance should be. You decide that when it's your time to be the host of your going home celebration, what will be said about your life, about the memories you leave behind, about the dance steps you chose.

Memories are flowers in the garden of life that God plants in our minds to allow us to continue to enjoy moments long after they have passed. It's not that life is short, it's that we wait too long to start living. When you travel with the word of God you're traveling first class.

One regret that I have is that I fail to have the memory of my husband and me watching the sunset over the ocean in Myrtle Beach South Carolina. While vacationing one year, he wanted me to get up with him early in the morning as he prepared to go and play golf.

"The sun rising over the ocean in the morning is beautiful. Watch it with me tomorrow morning and let's have a cup of coffee on the balcony and watch the sun rise," he said.

We were staying in a hotel suite on the beach that had a balcony overlooking the ocean.

I didn't want to get up early. I chose to sleep late. Now that he has gone, we can never share that memory. You can always sleep, enjoy life while you have someone with whom you can share those memories.

You are hosting from your casket. You cannot make a speech to those in attendance. You cannot welcome your guests. You cannot thank them for putting aside their busy schedule that day to attend your celebration. You cannot thank them for the beautiful flowers and wonderful cards they sent at their own expense. You cannot thank them for the food they brought to your home to feed the friends who had come to console your family and to pay their respects. You cannot apologize for the hurt feelings you left behind. You cannot finish that project you promised to complete "one day." You have no more chances to get it right.

Don't let your past live rent free in your head. Don't let your fear of trying something new, something different, prevent you from living a quality life. To wake up each day waiting for time to go back to bed is a waste of the gift God gave you called, "life".

You owe it to your family, to the world, and to yourself, to utilize the skills and knowledge you have acquired during your time on this planet call "earth."

I attended a funeral where the deceased, Mr. Levy, was the father of a close friend. While sitting in church, reading his obituary, I learned where he and my late husband's paths had crossed. They both belonged to the same social club, but the most memorable thing about Mr. Levy was what was said about his life at his funeral. People talked about him being a car salesman. But he didn't only sell cars, he taught the young people in the neighborhood how to care for cars, how to check the tires, change the oil and perform other maintenance services. But more importantly, he taught them that they should always keep themselves clean to match the cleanliness of their automobile.

One young man went into the pulpit and spoke about how Mr. Levy had touched his life. He said keeping his car clean meant that he had to keep his records in order to know about making car payments, maintenance checks and what products to use on his car. Those same organizational skills manifested themselves in the successful operation of his own business.

Live your life between the dots so that when the dots come together at life's end, there will be no regrets. Your family will be at peace that you lived a good life. You are not in this world alone. You will leave behind memories for your family to endure for generations yet unborn. Don't be selfish and think you are the only one on this trip called "life," have great dashes!

LEARNING FROM EXPERIENCE

"Wisdom is the principal thing, therefore, get wisdom, but with all thy getting, get understanding."--Proverbs 4:7

I've learned lessons from many people. In some instances I don't remember whose words I'm quoting, but I do remember the message. I believe that people were put in my life for specific purposes. Some were meant to stay and some were sent only for a season, some were sent to deliver a message and to get me to where God needs me to be mentally.

The most important message is to live each day as if it were your last and never leave your talents undeveloped or under-developed. Live each day to the fullest. Tomorrow is not promised to us and neither is the rest of today.

Every now and then it's necessary to revisit affirmations to motivate ourselves, to stimulate our thinking power, and to give us a "jump-start" for success. The information in this section contains lessons I have found helpful over the years. I'm sharing them with the readers with hopes they are found to be workable in someone's life.

When we lose a loved one, Thanksgiving, Christmas, the New Year's holidays, and Valentine's Day, are the most traumatic. At least they are for me. It's the time of year when I feel most alone. I miss my husband sitting at the table during Thanksgiving and leading the family in saying the grace. I miss him during Christmas when it's time to go shopping for presents for the family, especially our grandchildren. He and Jericka were the two who went to get our Christmas tree. They were also the two who took charge of decorating the house for Christmas.

Every New Years Eve we always had a party at our house. If not, Jerry and I went out together and visited nightclubs. During our later years, we went to church on New Year's Eve, then came home and had friends over.

One year Jerry and I decided we weren't going to stay at home and host a party. We wanted to get dressed and go out on the town. First we were going to visit friends whom we thought may have a party at their house, then we were going to visit various night clubs that were having special New Year's Eve celebrations. I put on a fancy party dress and Jerry wore the new suit I had given him for Christmas. I wore my new mink coat that Jericka had put on lay-away and paid on for a year before she could afford to get it out for my Christmas present. Jerry and I went out in the cold January night, "Steppin' high!" as he said.

We visited night clubs but didn't see any of the old crowd. We saw people we knew but none with whom we socialized on a regular basis. We visited the homes of personal friends and they were not at home. We thought they had gone to a holiday event and had not invited us. We went back to several night clubs but didn't enjoy being there. The drinks were watered down to accommodate the large crowd and the music was too loud. When the bewitching hour of twelve midnight came, we kissed and wished each other, "Happy New Year."

Disappointed that we hadn't enjoyed New Year's Eve with our friends when the crowd started to thin out at the night club, Jerry and I decided to go home. When we drove onto our street, there were a lot of cars parked on the side of the street in the block where we lived. Some cars were parked in our driveway.

"I guess one of our neighbors is having a party," said Jerry.

"Yeah, but we weren't invited," I said.

"You're right. We weren't. But why would they not invite us yet think it's okay for their guests to park their cars in our driveway? Man! That's what I call nerve!"

I was aggravated!

Jerry sounded disappointed and so was I. We searched for a parking space and we found one several houses from our house. We parked and started walking home; all the while complaining about the inconvenience of having to park several houses down the street and walk back to our house. As we got closer to our house, we could hear music and laughter that appeared to be coming from our house. When we walked into our front yard, we learned indeed the music and laughter were coming from our house. We went inside and as soon as we walked into the living room, we heard music and voices coming from downstairs in our basement clubroom. Our bedroom door was open and we saw a pile of coats lying across our bed. We didn't take off our coats, we just rushed downstairs to the basement. As soon as we got to the top steps leading into our basement, we saw a crowd of people — our friends.

"Happy New Year!" they shouted as Jerry and I walked down the steps.

There were all our friends, having a grand party without us. Eddie was behind the bar acting as bartender. Food was on a table in the laundry room.

"Where have ya'll been? You're missing a great party," said Jeanie.

"We went out to party. How did ya'll get in?" asked Jerry.

"Your children let us in. When we got here and we saw ya'll weren't at home, we said, 'Oh well!, we'll see them when they get home. So we all chipped in and sent Eddie to buy liquor, fried chicken, pizza, potato salad, cole-slaw, chips, dip, sandwiches and cookies. Some of us bought a bottle with us and ya'll already have plenty behind the bar. Fix yourself a plate and have a drink, we have plenty," said Beverly

They all laughed.

"You two can go out all you want to but on New Year's Eve, we're gonna be right here partying. Ain't no sense in changing something we've gotten accustomed to all these years," said Johnny.

We all laughed.

The party lasted all night. Those who wanted to go home left about five in the morning. Those who were too drunk to drive found space on the carpeted floor anywhere they could and went to sleep. They woke up the next morning, New Year's Day, cooked breakfast and started all over again. That was a "Robinson New Year's Eve Party."

After my husband's death, I had one New Year's Eve party and it was the most miserable time I have ever experienced at a party at our house. I missed him so much, I couldn't wait until everyone went home so I could go to bed and be alone with my memories.

Every New Year's Eve, we make resolutions and promises to ourselves, but most are broken before the month of January is gone. Just like we make resolutions for the New Year, make them for your new life. Decide what you want to do now that you have the time to do it. Try something new and begin your new life. I know it will not be easy. There is a hole in your life that cannot be filled but since you cannot change the situation, you cannot bring back your loved one, make the most of your life. Come up with some principles of your own to make each year the best year, yet!

There is an Indian Proverb that says, "Walk a mile in my moccasins before you tell me how they feel." This means no one can tell you how to grieve if they are not and have not experienced your pain. There is a time to talk and a time to listen. Someone once said the reason we have two ears and one mouth is so we can listen twice as much as we speak.

I tried to find a meaning from the experiences of my life. But when I was trying to cope with the loss of my husband the pain was so great I could not deal with meanings. I only focused on how I was hurting. I didn't think anyone could understand my pain. I was hurting because my husband never had the chance to see his great-grandson. I was hurting because he never got the chance to see Jericka's new house finished. I was hurting because I was alone. I was hurting because I didn't have a companion to escort me to social events. I was hurting because when he was alive, he was the one with the friends. I was hurting because death is final.

Regardless of the storms of life Jerry and I encountered, we weathered them together. I have dealt with the storms of the outhouse in Alabama, racism in Alabama, Georgia, and Maryland, homelessness, abuse, the stereotyping of being, "Old Drunk Louise's daughter," the projects, the streets, unfaithfulness, welfare, drugs, alcoholism, domestic violence, and many other storms. But I can also talk about the blessings and I thank God for my troubles. They are not as bad as some. I discuss my blessings in my book, *Someday Is Now.*

This book is intended to be a celebration of my life with my husband and a testimony of how I am constantly reinventing myself and to show readers when God closes one door He opens many more and helps you to walk through them all. When your heart breaks, God comes in through the cracks. This book is an attempt to see the rainbow after the rain and to send the message the storm is over, enjoy the rainbow.

This is my story and a "Thank You" message to God for allowing me to have shared my life with Jerome Robinson, Senior, because from that relationship came my beautiful family.

You don't get over the loss of a loved one, or recover from it, or forget them — instead you learn to live with memories and to make a new life for yourself. There is no time lines on grief; you're never finished grieving. It won't hurt less, it will just hurt less often. These are the lessons I've learned:

First: A grieving person needs to laugh. Often friends, wanting to protect the feelings of the grieving person, don't think that person is in a laughing mood and may try to keep the atmosphere somber. When the grieving person enters a room filled with laughter, the laughter stops or tapers off out of a show of sympathy for the grieving person. But if you are one of the people laughing, please don't silence yourselves. The person who is grieving may need to laugh at a good joke. That person will thank you for making them laugh. Laughing helps release tension and anxiety brought on by the death of their loved one. I know it did for me. I went to comedy shows and laughed as often as I could. While laughing, I forgot about crying.

Second: If you are one of the lucky ones who have not experienced the death of your spouse, you may not understand what people are going through during their period of grief. If you don't understand, it's okay to tell them that. They would rather you tell them that you don't understand what they are feeling than to pretend you do. Feelings of grief and despair don't last forever. I can't say how long they will last, each person handles grief differently. I can't tell you how long I will grieve. But I do know that God does not put anymore on us than we can bear. I knew that I could handle the pain, when I put my trust in Him.

There were times when I was talking to a friend and by the end of the conversation I was crying. That person didn't make me hurt, I was already hurting. That person didn't upset me, I was already upset. That person didn't make me sad. I was already sad. That person didn't make me cry, losing my soul mate made me cry.

If you meet a grieving friend and begin a conversation about the lost of your friend's loved one and your friend begins to cry, don't feel bad. The tears may make your friend feel better. They made me feel better. This too shall pass.

Third: Stop trying to change traditions. It won't make you feel better. That's why it's called "tradition," because it has always been done that way. It's to make you remember and celebrate the past by practicing what made you happy. Welcome new challenges and appreciate new beginnings but also respect traditions," was the lesson I learned Memorial Day, 2005.

Fourth: Friends and family members have homes, family responsibilities, and their own personal lives to live. It's you who must find your own style. You are the one who decide how you will spend the next half of your life. I never really gave a thought as to how and where I would spend the balance of my earthly life. I just lived each day in the moment and the "now" of life. But without having my husband to fall back on, to pick up the slack, and to be there to say, "I got your back," the future looked frightening. When reality sets in and you realize you really are alone except for the Lord, it's scary. He'll never leave or forsake you. My faith that God would make a way, somehow, was all that kept me going.

The difference between being buried and being planted is that when you are planted, you return, something different grows from the planted seed. During planting season, what is planted gives new life if nourished with God's water and God's sunshine. But when you are buried, you don't come back, there is no new life, it is a final act.

Sometimes we don't want to be planted. If we are buried we don't have to do anything. We can feel sorry for ourselves. The dirt is heavy, the dirt of lies, bills and the burdens of the world. The seed of God is inside of you.

You have a new beginning. Instead of a little seed buried in the ground you punch dirt out of your way, dirt such as welfare, unemployment, unpaid bills, sickness and so on. When you lean on God, give Him your burdens and leave them, you are not buried you are planted. Shake off the dirt, shake off the self pity. I am blessed to be where I am in life and at my age to have a second career that I truly love.

Fifth: Heal yourself by providing service to others. Serving is taking cues from followers, providing what others can't get on their own. A reporter was interviewing me one day and he asked me if I felt important that my company employed one-hundred people that meant I had one-hundred families, one-hundred households depending on me for support. I told him I didn't feel important. I felt blessed.

If God provides enough for you to be able to give to others, He has already blessed you abundantly. The fact that you have enough to share is a blessing. The more you give the more you receive. If you are in a position to serve, it means you have been abundantly blessed.

Your purpose in life is your assignment. It's what you were sent on earth to do. No one else can fulfill your assignment but you. Sometimes people knowingly and unknowingly keep you from fulfilling your assignment. They may not know it and at first, may protest. But what's meant to be will be.

Sixth: Don't dwell on regrets and the "if only" in life such as, "If only I had done something different" or "If only I had not said what I said, or "If only I could take that back," and so on. When you do that, you are only feeling sorry for yourself. Look inside yourself for your motivation. Don't let your past and the baggage it brings prevent you from reaching the stage in your life that you call "peacefulness." I dwelt on "if only" after my husband's death. In fact, in this book I speak of "if only" and that's okay for a while. This is expected when dealing with a "sudden" death or an "unexpected" death such as an accident or a heart attack or a stroke but don't keep beating up on yourself with the "If only "syndrome. Let go and let God.

Seventh: Learn ways to defeat challenges and overcome obstacles. It takes courage to go through life alone after the loss of your spouse, especially if your time together was a span of years. You feel as if a part of you is missing. The hurt will always be there, but you must ask God for courage to handle the pain and look for a better day.

Eighth: We often put off for tomorrow what can and should be accomplished today. It doesn't matter how old you are or how young you are. What matters is what you do with the gift you have called, "life." You are never too old to live your dream if you turn your dreams into goals and develop plans to achieve them and make them a reality.

Ninth: Stand on God's promises and step out on His word. Prayer changes things. *Matthew 6: 9-13and Luke 11:2* teaches us how to pray and what to say when we pray. *Matthew 17:20* says if we have faith the size of a mustard seed we can move mountains. Some of us have mountains in our lives, mountains called grief, guilt, depression, aloneness, emotional pain, spiritual brokenness, lack of finances.

Matthew 6:6 says if you pray in secret you will be rewarded openly. Pray anywhere, while you're driving in your car, in your bathroom, in your bedroom when you're all alone at night. Pray while you're ironing clothes humming an old gospel tune like my grandmother used to do. Pray when the world pushes you into a hole and you don't know how you'll survive. Pray when the world, and people whom you considered to be your friends throw dirt on you. God promised if you take one step He will take two.

In the Bible the word "Exodus," means "a way out" or "a going out." Weakness, sickness, old age and heartache, all these attack our body. The body in which we live is not as important as the person who lives in the body. We are merely "strangers and pilgrims" here on earth *(1Peter 2:11)*. One day we too are going to move out of this old tent, called a "body." It is easy to become wrapped up in the things of this brief life and in this passing world that we forget our coming "exodus." We can look forward to the end of life without fear. Death for each believer will be the sweet release of being "absent from the body" and "at home with the Lord," *(2 Corinthians 5:8)*.

Death and the grave are not a blind alley, but a thoroughfare into Heaven. According to Lehman Strauss in the book, *When Loved Ones Are Taken in Death*, Death for the Christian is an "exodus" a way out and a way in. It's the way out of life's trials and uncertainties and the way into the presence of our blessed Lord and those loved ones who have gone on before,"

God never acts without reason. When He permits death to take our loved ones, He has a purpose for doing so and that purpose is always for our good as well as for His glory. *Romans 8:28* says: "And we know that all things work together for good to them that love God to them who are the called according to His purpose." Remember the operative word is according to "His" purpose not "our" or "your" purpose.

Tenth: Create effective systems to meet your needs. Your human resources are your systems. Create resources in your family, in your school, in the business world, with your peers. Networking is an excellent means of getting emotional needs met. Your family is the best system you have for meeting your emotional and mental needs. However, if the family structure is not there, a counselor, or a friend sometimes can fill that void. Remember God plus one is an army. If you don't get the support you need from your own chosen human support system, God is always the answer.

Eleventh: Cherish your spouse. You know that your spouse's back hurts once in a while. He sometimes falls asleep when you want to be cuddled or you want to make love. Once in a while he comes home from work and doesn't smell so good and falls asleep without taking a shower. Sometimes he passes gas and you find that habit disgusting and you wonder why you stay with him. Sometimes he belches loudly and you find that embarrassing. Sometimes when in public, he uses incorrect grammar, he is not as educated as you are. But then there is that "once in a while" when he feels like making love and his touch, his caresses, the sound of his voice, the warmth of his body and his smile, make you feel as if you are the most desirable woman in the world. Take advantage of that, "once in a while."

Twelfth: : "FROGGIE" means to faithfully rely on God's grace, in everything you do, His goodness, His mercy, and His blessings. Rely on the concept of FROGGIE in everything you do, in every prayer, in every challenge, to overcome every obstacle, to deal with all hurts and tribulations and in every situation. It's a blessing to know that I can take my problems to God and leave them. I can take my hands off my problems knowing that He can do anything but fail. So when I say, "I feel FROGGIE" I am saying I feel like relying on God, taking him at His word, relying on His promises to never leave me alone.

Growing up in the South as a child, my childhood friends and I made up many games to amuse ourselves. Although we were sometimes scared, especially if the other person was bigger or tougher than we were, we tried to be brave when we engaged in fights with other children. Sometimes we put an item on one shoulder, such as a rock, a stick, a pebble, a piece of broken glass, anything we could find that would stay on our shoulder, and we would dare the other person to knock it off our shoulder. Or sometimes we would draw a line on the ground and dare the other person to step over it. Stepping over the line was an indication of a dare. Either act would trigger a fight. We would blame the person who knocked off the item or stepped over the line as the instigator or the person who started the fight.

Sometimes we would dare one another by saying "If you feel froggie, jump!" provoking a fight. As I grew older, I was less prone to engage in fights or a physical violent confrontation. I was more incline to engage in communication and discuss controversial issues. I now realize that God will fight my battles. I still say, "If you feel froggie jump!" but rather than jumping into a physical altercation with another person, I jump for God, shouting a Hallelujah Anyhow dance to celebrate the many blessings He has given me.

Grace and mercy shall follow me all the days of my life. It's a blessing to know I can rely on God for everything in every situation. I found in my own grief that work is the best medicine. That was one of my dances. Therefore, as you travel down the road of life, never stop doing the FROGGIE dance.

Thirteenth: Identify who you are in life, who you perceive yourself to be. Don't judge yourself by who others say you are, or who other people think you are. Judge yourself by who you know yourself to be. Be determined to live your life without worrying about someone judging you. Who you are or who you think you are may be totally different than how others see you. Image is important; therefore, identify what image you want to project to the world and strive to perfect that role. Don't try to be someone you're not just to please someone else. You are valuable as you are. Be thankful for your place in the world. Change what you can change, do not accept what you cannot, change what you cannot accept.

Fourteenth: God made us all according to His plan. When you lose your spouse, especially if you are a woman, self-confidence is extremely important. You have to go on with your life without your partner and you have to learn to believe in yourself, your abilities, and your capabilities. Self-confidence means being self-disciplined, having the ability to self-start, and having confidence to go the distance if it means going it alone. Some people may try to break your confidence by telling you that you can't accomplish a certain deed. But if you pray and have confidence that prayer changes things, you can succeed. You owe it to yourself to be all you are capable of being and live your best life according to God's plan for you and according to your own goals. Therefore, live your life with confidence.

My mother told me to, "walk like you know where you're going even if you don't. It looks as if you have confidence."

Fifteenth: Don't wait for someone to motivate or encourage you. Motivate yourself. Be too proud to give up. The road to success is filled with roadblocks, and so-called friends who may say that you never will succeed. It may be necessary to read affirmations on a daily basis. It may mean you listen to motivational tapes. Whatever is necessary to keep you motivated and excited about life, do that. You are the only person who has complete control of your life and your destiny.

Had I listened to the naysayers, I would never have run for public office. They attempted to convince me that I was too old and too inexperienced. For a brief moment, they succeeded. That lack of confidence in myself is what led to the reluctance of confiding in my family about my decision to pursue a career in politics. But after I won, the naysayers changed their attitude. My perseverance made believers of them.

"I always knew you would make it. You have that kind of spirit of never giving up," they said.

Don't waste time with people who have negative thoughts about your capabilities. Some people feel good when they're tearing someone else apart. As long as they are looking down on you, they feel important. If you listen to their negative comments and allow their vision of you to be accurate and to determine who you are and who you become, they will be able to say, "I told you so."

Sixteenth: Look inside yourself for your healing. Look to God for your comfort. Without the help of God, you can do nothing about your situation but complain. Meet the Lord individually and don't make prayer so complicated, be simple like a child.

Have control over your own actions, be able to discipline yourself. Self-discipline means to determine how long you should grieve and in what manner you reflect your grief. Do you spend the rest of your life in a state of depression, opting to bow out of life? Or do you face it head-on staring the world in the face and saying, "I will survive?"

There is no right way to grieve. Screaming, wailing, crying, yelling, jumping up and down, or silence, these are all normal reactions. I did them all during my grieving. Grief is unique. Find the reactions or the behavior that allows you to release the silent pain that death brings.

Grief has five main stages deal with each stage in your own way: Elizabeth Kubler Ross describes the stages as: denial, anger, bargaining, depression, and finally, acceptance.

Denial is masked as shock and numbness. These are nature's ways of allowing us to cope with our pain. Anger is sometimes directed at friends, family, doctors, God and even may be directed at the deceased for leaving you alone. Bargaining is characterized by, "If only," "what if" and giving yourself guilt for things you feel you should have done or should have said while your loved one was alive. Depression comes as sadness, involving a temporary withdrawal from life. Acceptance is learning to go through life without your loved one.

Often we can't identify the stages as, "This is the stage I am in now." Stages are the responses to our feelings. People grieving may experience these stages at different times and completely unique from another person who is grieving.

If you are experiencing thoughts of suicide, if you feel helpless, hopeless, and are chronically unhappy, having trouble sleeping, withdrawing from the real world, refusing to eat, have lost interest in what normally made you happy, seek professional help. Crying every day the first six months or even the first year is understandable. But if you're crying all the time four or five years after the death of a loved one, seek professional help. You may cry when you hear a certain song, remember a certain moment, look at videos or photographs of your life together, that is understandable but crying continuously is not normal. Put the idea of suicide out of your mind. It doesn't take courage to drop out of life's battles. It takes courage to live and fight the daily battles of life.

Cherish the memories but don't dwell on them. Don't dwell on the final moments of his or her life when death was claiming the body. Remember the good times, the happy moments, the laughter and the love.

Do something symbolic in memory of your loved one. As long as he or she is remembered they will never die. Start an organization in your loved one's name designed to help others. Organize a not for profit organization and have fund-raising events. Raise funds to finance the organization. Have programs in his or her name, give scholarships in their memory.

Talk about your loved one. Don't avoid mentioning his or her name.

Don't take guilt trips. If you are still hurting filled with guilt for some unresolved differences that happened before your loved one died or you are feeling guilty for something you did or did not do, let the baggage go. If you don't let it go and stop punishing yourself for things that throwing a pity party won't change, you never will realize your full potential. Yes the past sometimes hurts. But tell yourself to move on, then follow your own advice and move on.

Find a safe haven, if living in the house or apartment that you and your deceased loved one shared holds too many painful memories of your life together, get away until you can deal with the memories without feeling overwhelmed and depressed. Don't sell your home right away if you don't have to. Don't give away any of his or her belongings until you have had a chance to think about it. Days or even weeks after the funeral may be too soon. The wound is still open from your loss. The wound is too fresh and too deep. So soon after your loss you may not be thinking rationally. Wait a few months or a few years until you can think with your head and not your heart. You may find that it's not necessary to sell the family home.

When Jerry's aunt Julia died, immediately following the funeral Julia's best friend Mary, asked Jerry's uncle Jackie, — Julia's husband — for Julia's jewelry. Mary had admired the jewelry when Julia was alive.

"I was her best friend and she would want me to have them," said Mary.

Jackie was consumed with grief and sitting in his living room crying.

"Take them. I don't care. Since my baby won't be coming back and wearing them anymore, I don't care what happens to them," said Jackie.

I was furious. I felt that Mary was taking advantage of the situation and of Jackie's grief.

"No you won't give them away!" I said adamantly. "Julia is gone and Jackie, you need to take some time to grieve. You are not going to give away anything yet! If, after you have had some time to get accustomed to being without Julia and you decide you want to give her things away, that's your decision. But right now you are not thinking clearly and I won't let you make a mistake and give away something that you'll regret later."

Needless to say, Mary was furious with me. However, months later Jackie thanked me for intervening on his behalf. He wanted to keep the items Mary had asked for. They were precious family jewels he wanted to remain in his family.

Find something you like to do and go for it. When you get involved in activities, you don't have time to think about your loss. Maybe go back to school and earn that degree you kept putting off until "someday" or "later-on." Take a writing course and write that book you said you would write "someday." Change careers, do something to prevent you from having time to throw yourself pity parties. Form a support group if necessary to help yourself and others.

Find your niche and discover what you like to do. When I was in Africa a woman had the idea of going to construction sites and selling food to the workers. It became a lucrative business for her. The workers, — all men — waited for her to bring them hot, home cooked food each day at lunch time. That was an example of looking at her environment to determine a need that was not met.

What were you doing before you met your spouse? Did you complete your past passion? Build your hobby into a business. If you don't have a hobby, start one. Travel and see the world. Volunteer at churches or at senior centers or schools. Dare to dream and do what's necessary to make that dream come true. Don't worry about age, dress size, height, or weight. Worry about the way to add years to your life in the way of dancing to your own tune.

Let your life make a difference. When you leave this world, leave your footprints in the sand of time. You can accomplish this by reflecting on what you need to do to make a lasting impression in the world. Everybody is not good at everything but you are good at something. What has your life been like all your years? Where can you get involved and love what you're doing? What will people say about you when you're gone?

Often we don't look into what we did prior to our loved one's death to see if it fits in with what we are called to do after our loved one dies. It may not be a profession with which we are familiar. Ask God to guide you and to show you what His plans are for you. His answer may be terrifying but rewarding. He'll never leave you alone. He'll either catch you if you fall or teach you how to fly. Try something new.

When one reads my first book, *And Still, I Cry,* it shows the tumultuous life my late husband and I shared in the beginning of our marriage. But we overcame those hard times. We evolved into totally different people. God has a way of turning ashes into gold.

I know that you, the reader, may get the idea that my husband and I were unfaithful to each other that we did not respect our marriage and we spent time drinking, going to nightclubs, having parties, and doing whatever we were big and bad enough to do. And you know what? You are right! But one thing you cannot say is that we were unfit parents. The only harm we did was to ourselves. We did all those things that one use as excuses for breaking up a marriage. We did not get married because we were ready for marriage, but because I was pregnant. Jerry had already been married once and it didn't work. I was his second wife. He and his first wife were married less than a year.

I was pursuing a college degree in medicine but I eventually earned several degrees in business. Jerry, on the other hand, never graduated from high school nor did he earn a GED. However, that did not matter to us. He had a brilliant mind. He could work numbers in his head better than most mathematicians and he always kept a job. But God makes the decisions about your life. Obviously Jerry and I were meant to be together. We were together for forty-seven years. Had I left him in the early years of our marriage when we both were acting like children, I would have left a man who was becoming my soul mate, the man he eventually became. I would have prepared him for another woman to enjoy while I continued searching for what I already had.

We grew old together. We matured together. We changed together. We found God together. We realized the inner person we both came to love and respect was actually the people we were all the time. It just took years for those persons to mature. We both loved our children. I used to say he was a great father but a lousy husband. I decided it was best to accept that part of him that was a great farther. I remember my turbulent past with my step father and I did not want my girls to suffer the same fate. I also wanted my son to have his father in his life.

After my husband's death I realized how blessed I was to have him in my life for as long as I did, I remember the good times. I remember his smile, the sound of his laughter, the way he tried to protect me from finding out about his wrong-doings and accepting mine. My children and I have never gone to bed hungry, never been evicted. Although there were times the sheriff put eviction notices on our door when we lived in the projects, we always managed to pay our rent before we were evicted. Those were the lean years my husband and I went through together.

I have always had my space to be me. I had to fight for it and accepted nothing less. I eventually convinced Jerry that regardless of the price I had to pay, I would pursue my life my way. That's why it took eighteen years to earn my bachelor's degree. But I did it, my way.

God knew that Jerry was a good man. He took him from nightclubs, cleaned him up and put him in church. The road of life has many bends, many turns, many hills, many valleys, many curves, and many mountains, all called obstacles and challenges. You will walk those curves, travel around those bends and realize around the next bend will be another obstacle but if we look at our troubles through God rather than looking at God through our troubles, we will allow Him to lead us around every bend. Regardless of what's around the next corner of life, with God as our co-pilot any bend in the road is conquerable.

THE PATH OF WISDOM

I could not have reached this age in my life and this stage in my career without having learned something along the way. I share with the readers the results of the seventy plus years of my life's journey. The following are 101 tips I offer to help the reader live a quality life.

1. Growing old beats the alternative — dying young.

2. Get rid of anything in your life that isn't useful, beautiful or joyful. Life's too short to waste time being depressed. No matter how you feel, get up, dress up, and show up. Don't let depression claim your joy.

3. You don't have to win every argument. Agree to disagree without being disagreeable. Take a deep breath before lashing out to others and saying harsh words that you can't take back. Taking a deep breath calms the mind. Keep an open mind. Discuss but don't argue there is always another point of view.

4. Cry with someone. It's more healing than crying alone.

5. Make peace with your past so it won't screw up your present.

6. It's okay to let your children see you cry. They'll understand how human you are.

7. Don't compare your life to others. You have no idea what their life's journey is all about.

8. If a relationship has to be a secret, you shouldn't be in it.

9. Everything can change in the flash of an eye but don't worry, God never blinks.

10. When it comes to going after what you love in life, don't take "no" for an answer, be persistent. Success comes to those who do not give up.

11. Believe in magic. It's called self-confidence.

12. Don't put off for tomorrow what you can enjoy today. Today is tomorrow. Use your nice sheets, wear your fancy lingerie. Don't save things for a "special occasion." today is special. Each day you are alive is special. You may not get another chance to enjoy what you can enjoy today.

13. Enjoy your loved one while you can. You never know when the last day will come.

14. Don't complain or criticize things that complaints or criticism can't and will not change. Over prepare, then go with the flow.

15. Make yourself a bucket list, things you want to accomplish before you "kick the bucket," then accomplish as many of the things on the list as you can. Remember that no one is in charge of your happiness but you.

16. Frame every so-called disaster with these words, "In five years, will this matter?" Time heals almost everything. Give time, time. However good or bad a situation is, it will change, nothing stays the same.

17. What other people think of you is none of your business. You can only control your own thoughts. Pay no attention to ill-natured remarks about you. Remember in order to be talked about you have to be thought about. The fact that you are on someone's mind speaks

volumes about you. Simply live so that false things spoken about you will not be believed.

18. God loves you because of who God is, not because of anything you did or didn't do.

19. Don't audit life. Show up and make the most of it now. Life isn't fair, but it's the one God gave you. It's up to you to make of it what you will.

20. Your children get only one childhood let them remember it fondly. If you have painful memories of your childhood try not to expose your child to the same. Make theirs better than yours.

21. All that really matters in the end is that you loved and someone loved you — that's a blessing many people never experience.

22. If we each threw our problems in a pile and saw everyone else's, we'd grab ours back. Regardless of how bad you think your problems are, there is always someone who wishes they were in your shoes. Remember the old saying, "I cried because I had no shoes until I met the man with no feet."

23. Envy is a waste of time. You already have all you need. The best is yet to come

24. Life isn't tied with a bow, but it's still a gift. Enjoy it!

25. Friends are the family that we choose for ourselves.

26. Be mindful of not only what you say, but how you say it. The tone of your voice can say more than the words you speak.

27. Make your word your bond. If you give it, stand by it. Make promises sparingly and keep them faithfully, regardless of the costs.

28. Never let an opportunity pass to say a kind and encouraging word to or about somebody. Praise good work regardless of who did it. If

criticism is needed give constructive criticism. Criticize only that which can be changed.

29. Show genuine interest in others. Be happy with those who rejoice, mourn with those who weep, listen non-judgmentally to those who need to talk. Let everyone you meet, however humble, feel that you regard him or her as a person of importance.

30. Don't burden or depress others with your troubles, remember everyone is carrying some kind of load.

31. Let your virtues speak for themselves. Refuse to talk of another's vices. Discourage gossip. It is a waste of valuable time and can be destructive.

32. Respect another person's feelings. Wit and humor at the expense of another person's expense are rarely worth it.

33. Don't be too anxious about being acknowledged for your achievements or accomplishments. Be proud of yourself. Let the person who looks back at you from the mirror be the person you most admire and respect. Like yourself and the person you have become. Don't be too anxious about the credit due you. Do your best and be patient. Forget about yourself and let others "remember." Success is much sweeter that way.

34. Make your own decisions about how you live your life. You are the only person who can die for you, you should be the only person living for you. Don't set your goals by what other people deem important. Only you know what's best for you.

35. Never love anything or anyone better than you love yourself. Always remember, you are special.

36. Remove the word "failure" from your vocabulary. Change the word "mistakes" to "trial runs."

37. When in doubt about what action to take remember to PUSH (Pray Until Something Happens).

38. When you need healing remember ASAP (Always Say a Prayer)

39. Adopt an, "I'm not perfect, but I am forgiven," attitude.

40. Live with the 3-E's — Energy, Enthusiasm, and Empathy

41. Make time to pray and when you pray spend time thanking God for what He has already done in your life.

42. Don't have negative thoughts or things you cannot control. Instead, invest your energy in the positive, present moment.

43. Surround yourself with positive-thinking people. Negative-thinking and negative-talking people can drain you of your positive energy to succeed.

44. Find a niche in life. Determine what you want to do or who you want to become, then devise a plan to reach your goal.

45. Dream more while you are awake. Then put foundations under those dreams and turn the dreams into goals.

46. Forget issues of the past. If you are in a new relationship, don't remind your new partner about your former mate. That will ruin your present happiness.

47. Realize that life is a school and you are here to learn. Problems are simply part of the curriculum that appear and fade away, but the lessons you learn will last a lifetime. Always keep your eye on GOALS (Go on and Learn Something)

48. Start each day with a "Why not?" attitude and end each day with a "Hallelujah, Anyhow!" praise.

49. Let your mind think on virtuous things as stated in *Philippians 3:8* — Finally, brethren, whatsoever things are true, whatsoever things are honest, whatsoever things are just, whatsoever things are pure, whatsoever things are lovely, whatsoever things are of good report; if there be any virtue, and if there be any praise, think on these things.

50. Please God in all you do as directed in *I Thessalonians 4:1* — "Furthermore then we beseech you, brethren, and exhort you by the Lord Jesus, that as ye have received of us how ye ought to walk and to please God, so ye would abound more and more."

51. Do not give up on your dreams. To quit is to lose courage and to declare the devil the winner. "Wait on the Lord; be of good courage and He shall strengthen thine heart; wait, I say, on the Lord," *Psalm 27:14*

52. Ask yourself this question: "Is what I'm doing getting me what I want?" If your answer is "No," it's time to change what you are doing. Only a fool keeps doing the same thing expecting different results.

53. A friend is someone who knows all about you and loves you just the same.

54. It's true that we don't know what we have until we lose it, but it is also true that we don't know what we have been missing until it arrives. Don't sweat the small stuff.

55. The happiest of people don't necessarily have the best of everything, they just make the most of everything that comes their way.

56. Don't hold a grudge. If you walk around not speaking to someone and they are not aware of your feelings, you are the only one miserable. Let it go.

57. Don't let life slip through your fingers by living in the past or the future. Live in the NOW of life. The brightest future is sometimes based on a forgotten past.

58. You can't go on successfully in life until you let go of your past mistakes, and heartaches. Don't be ashamed of who you are and from where you've come, overcoming your past mistakes gives you a testimony of victory.

59. You should dream what you want to dream; go where you want to go, be who and what you want to be. You have only one life and one chance to do all the things you dream of.

60. Don't take for granted those things closest to your heart. Cling to them as you would your life. For without them, life is meaningless.

61. Don't put off for tomorrow what can be done today. Tomorrow is not promised to us.

62. Don't give up when you still have something to give. Nothing is really over until the moment you stop trying.

63. Don't be afraid to encounter risks. It is by taking chances that we learn how to be brave.

64. Don't shut love out of your life by saying it's impossible to find again. The quickest way to receive love is to give love. The fastest way to lose love is to hold it too tightly.

65. Stand aside and watch yourself go by. Think of yourself as "you", instead of "I."

66. Don't think that you are too old to enjoy life according to your own dreams.

67. The best kind of friend is the kind you can sit on a porch and swing with, never say a word, and walk away feeling like it was the best conversation you've ever had.

68. You should always try to put yourself in others' shoes. If you feel that something could hurt you, it probably will hurt the other person too.

69. Do something nice for someone as often as you can, even if it is to leave them alone.

70. There are three things you cannot get back, a spoken word, time past, and a missed opportunity. Therefore, watch what you say, don't waste time, and seize every opportunity to dance.

71. Don't sit back and wait for life to come to you. Go out and make things happen. God gives every bird its food but He does not throw it into its nest.

72. Be the source of change you wish to see in the world. Keep only cheerful friends. You don't need people who always see the negative side of things. Stay away from people who always talk of doom. You'll never take risks in life listening to such people. They will always find fault in everything and never have a kind word to say about anybody.

73. Live your life as an example for others to follow. If your actions inspire others to do more, dream more, and achieve more, you are a leader.

74. Sometimes it's your own ego that gets you in trouble. Be proud of who you are and what you have achieved but don't allow self-pride to turn into self-egotism.

75. Have faith in God and stand on His promises. When you are DOWN to nothing, God is UP to something! Faith sees the invisible, believes the incredible and receives the impossible.

76. When Satan is knocking at your door, simply say, "Jesus, could you get that for me, please?"

77. In the search for me, I discovered truth. In the search for truth, I discovered love. In the search for love I discovered God. And in God, I have found everything.

78. Don't be afraid to believe that you can have what you want and deserve. The minute you settle for less than you deserve, you get even less than you settle for.

79. Watch your thoughts, they become words
   Watch your words, they become actions
   Watch your actions, they become habits
   Watch your habits, they become character
   Watch your character, for it becomes your destiny

80. Don't worry about things that worrying will not change. Worrying does not empty tomorrow of its troubles, it empties today of its strength.

81. Be grateful for your blessings, for friends, for family and for life.

82. If you lose a loved one, your life has to go on. Don't close your eyes to the great person hidden inside of you. None are so blind as those who will not see their potential.

83. Being successful does not mean everything is perfect, it means you have chosen to see beyond the imperfections and expectations of life.

84. Make Christ your backbone. He will straighten you up.

85. If someone offers assistance to you to help you achieve your goal, don't be too proud that you dismiss the importance of accepting help. He who accepts nothing, has nothing to return.

86. Nothing happens by coincidence. God has a plan for you. Coincidence is God's way of staying anonymous.

87. When you get out of a bad relationship and you are still resentful and angry, you are letting the devil leave his baggage.

88. Deception is when you think you can do everything by yourself. Honesty is when you accept that you need help. Don't let pride get in the way of logic.

89. What we do for ourselves dies with us, what we do for others is immortal. When you help someone else, you heal your own wound.

Sometimes helping others takes your mind from your own grief and allows you to bring happiness to others.

90. Do not limit how you define your potential. Don't minimize the definition of your abilities and capabilities. Let your imagination be so big, it can be called an industry.

91. In your home, surround yourself with things you love: whether it's family pets, keepsakes, music, plants, or hobbies. Your home is your refuge, enjoy it!

92. Enjoy life. Always find an opportunity to laugh, then laugh often, long, and loud. Go to comedy shows, enjoy your favorite comedian. You don't stop moving because you get old, you get old because you stop moving.

93. Cherish your health: If it is good, preserve it. If it is unstable, improve it. If it is beyond what you can improve, get help.

94. There are millions of people in the world but only one soul mate, only one person who loves you like none other. If you are blessed enough to find another love after the death of your spouse, don't compare him or her to your first love. Appreciate your second blessing.

95. Make the comfort of your memories be greater than the sorrow of your lost. Enjoy the simple things in life. Enjoy the sunset, the sound of the ocean, the smile of a baby, children at play. Enjoy a good cup of coffee or tea in the morning air. Go walking in the Sun. Let your hair blow in the wind. Every day this side of Glory is a good day. Be grateful for everything. Be alive while you are alive.

96. Let the life you live speak for you. Put enthusiasm in your life: Get excited about living, excited about life, excited about who you are, and the possibilities and opportunities for you to challenge. You may still be hurting, feeling alone, and lonely, now that your loved one has gone. But there is so much for you to accomplish in today's world.

Life should be lived with passion and excitement. Every day you get out of bed should be filled with exhilaration.

97. My favorite number is "3;"
Three things in life that once gone never come back: *time, *words, *opportunity.
Three things in life that are most valuable: *family, *self-confidence, *friends.
Three things in life that are never certain: "dreams, *success, *fortune.
Three things in life that define a man or a woman: *hard work, *sincerity, *commitment.
Three things in life that can destroy an individual: *jealousy, *pride, *anger.
Three things in life once lost are hard to rebuild: *respect, *trust, *friendship.

98. Face your pain head on. Problems are challenges turned upside down. Look at the big picture, look beyond what is to see and focus on what can be. Your pain won't go away because you refuse to acknowledge that it exists. Don't try to disguise your pain by seeking relief in a bottle, or by using drugs, you are only exchanging one problem for another.

99. Disregard non-essential numbers: Age is only a number, a dress size does not determine beauty or sexy, and height is relative.

100. Keep learning. Learn about the computer, learn crafts, gardening, whatever you always wanted to learn but never took the time. Never let your brain go idle. An idle mind is the devil's workshop. We should never let our fears or the expectation of others, decide the fulfillment of our lives.

101. Finally and most importantly, keep dancing, keep loving, keep laughing, and keep living. Don't just exist, waiting for death to pay you a visit. Enjoy the time you have left so that when it is your time to leave this world, you will have exhausted every minute you had on earth and enjoyed each moment. Yes, your loved is gone, and yes

you wish time would stand still so you can recapture some of those moments that you wish you could change. But time does not stand still and you can't go back into the past and change things. Enjoy your memories, enjoy your dreams, but realize this is reality. You will see your loved one someday but until then the music of life plays on. Dance to life's music so that when the dance is over there will be no regrets. If you must leave with regrets, don't regret the things you have done, regret the things you never took the time to do.

ABOUT THE AUTHOR

Barbara and her husband, Jerry, were together forty-seven years until his untimely death in 2004. Barbara was always thought of as a woman of strength and endurance. She is a trailblazer in many areas and the "go-to" person in many situations concerning women issues and issues affecting vulnerable populations of people, such as seniors, women, troubled youths and individuals considered disadvantaged and hard-to-serve. Having confronted racism, sexism, sexual abuse, physical abuse, welfare, homelessness, infidelity, ageism, gender-biasness, and drug abuse Barbara adopted a "yes I can" philosophy and a "why not" attitude.

It was eighteen years before Barbara earned her first college degree. Barbara did not allow her past to determine her future. From a childhood with a mother who abused alcohol and a step father who abused Barbara and her mother, Barbara continued her climb to success and earned degrees from three universities. She was inducted into the Maryland Women Hall of Fame, honored at the White House by President Clinton, recipient of more than one-hundred awards, a national and international motivational speaker, author of six published books, member of the Maryland House of Delegates, board member of twenty organizations, chair of the Legislative Black Caucus of Maryland, the first woman and first African American to hold positions of Deputy administrator of the Maryland District Court, the Supreme Bench and the Circuit Court. She was presented the Key to the City in three states. She is a mother, grandmother and great-grandmother.

With all her strength and perseverance, the death of Barbara's soul mate sent her into a state of depression and anxiety. Barbara bounces back and takes the reader on a journey from meeting her soul mate, building a family, his death, her self-reinvention into a new life and turns her life's experiences into a blue print for endurance

Printed in the United States
By Bookmasters